191 St
1

HIGHBRIDGE
PARK

81 St

AMSTERDAM AV

WASHINGTON HEIGHTS

168 St
A·C·1

163 St-Amsterdam Av
C

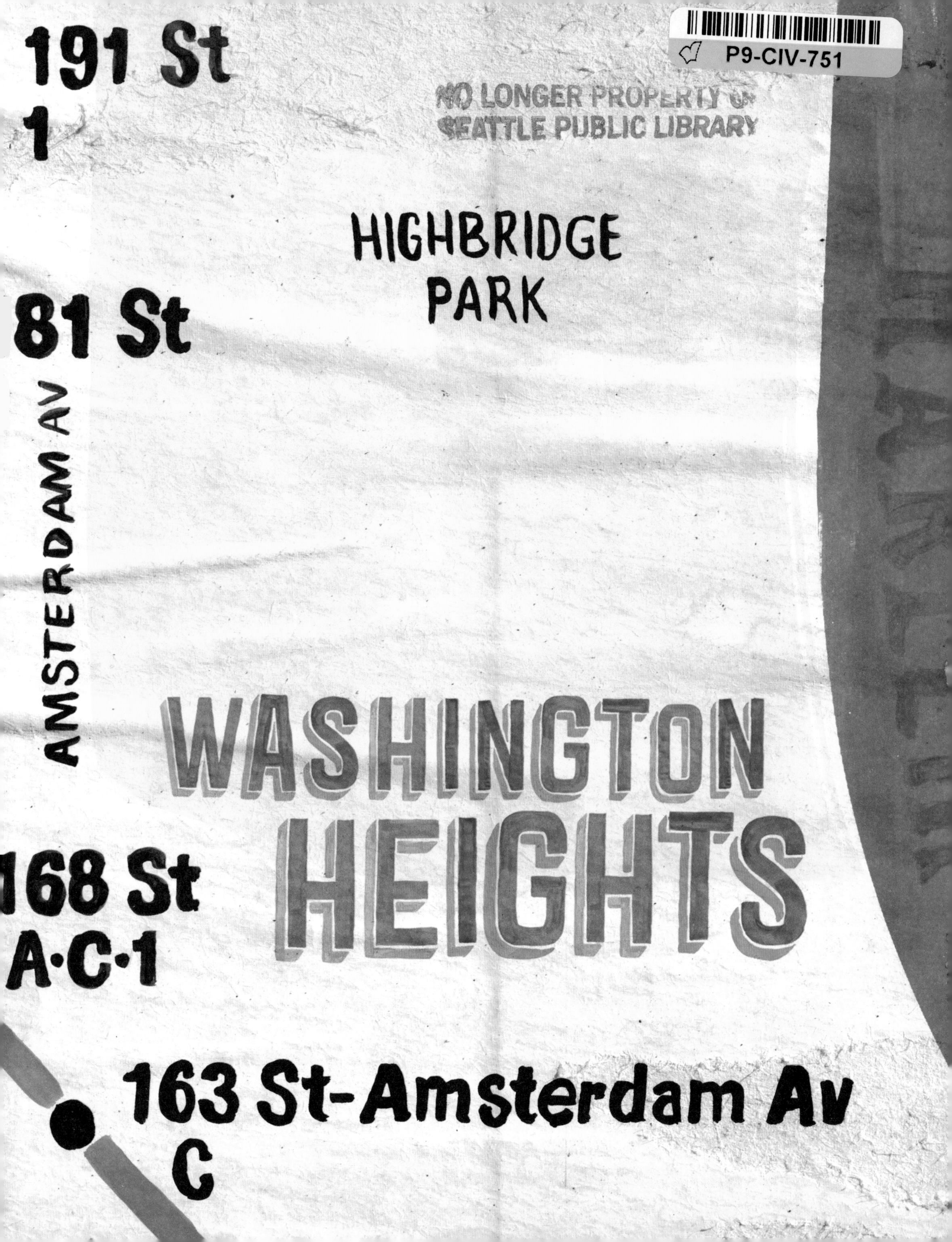

IN THE HEIGHTS

Finding Home

LIN-MANUEL MIRANDA, QUIARA ALEGRÍA HUDES, AND JEREMY McCARTER

RANDOM HOUSE
NEW YORK

Published in the United States by Random House, an imprint and
division of Penguin Random House LLC, New York.

RANDOM HOUSE and the HOUSE colophon are registered
trademarks of Penguin Random House LLC.

"In the Heights" and related characters and elements are trademarks of 5001 Broadway
Productions, LLC and Barrio Grrrl! Productions, Inc.

Additional photo credits and permissions appear on page 267.

Hardback ISBN 9780593229590
Ebook ISBN 9780593339695

Printed in the United States of America on acid-free paper

randomhousebooks.com

246897531

First Edition

Illustrations on pages ii, 25–26, 91, 96, 107, 118–119, 149, 153, 169,
190, 197, 213, 228 and 235 © 2021 by Krystal Quiles

Art direction, design, and lettering by Laura Palese

THIS BOOK IS DEDICATED TO

DOREEN MONTALVO

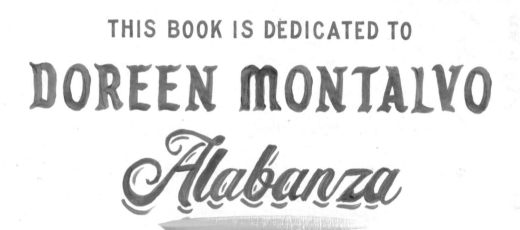

Alabanza

CONTENTS

★ Act One ★

INTERMISSION: TONY NIGHT

ESSAYS BY QUIARA ALEGRÍA HUDES

THE SALON LADIES 58 · THE DINNER SCENE 110 · THE BEACH 160 · SONNY 216

Heights
ONSCREEN

This book presents Lin-Manuel Miranda's songs in the order of their appearance in the stage version of *In the Heights*.

To follow along with the songs as they appear in the movie—and to see some key changes that Lin made to his lyrics—read them in this order:

INTRODUCTI

THE ACTORS TOOK THEIR BOWS, the crowd finished cheering, and everybody headed for the doors. Spotting a friend, I cut across the lobby. I asked, *Did you just see what I just saw?*

Or words to that effect. It's been fourteen years, so I can't remember exactly what I said that night. But I do remember exactly how *In the Heights* made me feel.

I had gone to the show from a certain sense of obligation. Back then, I was reviewing plays for *New York* magazine. Since I had argued repeatedly that musical theater needed to embrace a wider range of sounds and styles, duty compelled me to see a show that (according to the press release) was trying to supply them. The track record of such evenings was not stellar, to put it gently. But that night at 37 Arts, the Off-Broadway complex where *Heights* had its world premiere, I found what you always dream of finding.

Here was something vibrant and original. Two new writers, the composer/lyricist Lin-Manuel Miranda and librettist Quiara Alegría Hudes, had used their hearts, brains, and imagination to evoke life in Washington Heights, a predominantly Latino neighborhood near the northern tip of Manhattan. They and their collaborators had created a show that was smart, moving, and skillfully staged.

In the next issue of the magazine, I heralded the show's arrival, particularly the work of its implausibly gifted composer/lyricist. *Heights* had made more expansive, more sophisticated use of hip-hop than any musical that had gotten near Broadway. That would have been reason enough for a rave. But Lin also tapped into salsa and merengue—*and* he demonstrated an uncanny gift for writing evocative Broadway ballads. It didn't make sense that a first-time songwriter could do so many disparate things so well. Plus he had enough charisma to play Usnavi, the bodega owner at the heart of the show.

Who *was* this guy?

I didn't know. But I was happy to see his show transfer to Broadway, where it won four Tony Awards, including Best Musical. And I was glad, and not at all shocked, to see Lin's star rise and rise (and rise and rise). After I left the magazine, Lin and I became friends, so I got to watch the ascent up close. (I saw the parabolic part, when he wrote and starred in *Hamilton,* from *very* close. We co-authored a book about the show: *Hamilton: The Revolution.*)

So imagine my surprise to discover, years after that night in 2007, that I hadn't grasped the most extraordinary thing about the show after all.

BY JEREMY McCARTER

xi

ONE DAY IN 2019, Lin called with an idea: Let's write a book about *In the Heights*.

The show had closed on Broadway eight years earlier, but the timing was right. Warner Bros. was turning it into a major motion picture, directed by Jon M. Chu. I liked the notion of tracing the musical's many lives. Lin had gotten the idea for the show in college, when the prospect of it one day going to Broadway was the longest of long shots. But somehow *Heights* got there—and now, after many false starts and setbacks, it was making another leap to the big screen. I also liked the idea of revisiting themes and people we'd written about in our earlier book. It would be a kind of sequel, even though a lot of the action takes place before *Hamilton*. Like *The Godfather Part II,* but in a bodega.

It was only when I started doing interviews—more than fifty, by the end—that I came to see the extraordinary thing I hadn't discerned in 2007. Again and again, people said that working on *Heights* felt different from other jobs. They described growing closer to colleagues on this show than on other projects—and keeping those bonds for years. It came to feel, they said, like a family.

Now, let's be clear. I, like you, have read a celebrity profile. I have watched a morning talk show. I find people talking about "family" in show business to be just as corny and clichéd as you do. That's why I didn't take full account of what I heard about family in the first few interviews. But once I heard it a dozen times, then two dozen—once I heard it from people who had no connection to the original production, from actors and directors who staged the show all around the world; once I heard people who were making the movie say that the tight bond they'd forged with their colleagues was absolutely the most valuable part of the experience, even though the experience hadn't yet ended—I started to think, *Maybe there's something here.*

What's the source of this strange adhesive power? People first felt it, and tried to explain it, twenty-two years ago. They are still trying. As this book traces the unlikely journey of *In the Heights* from Lin's undergraduate brain to Broadway to Hollywood, it considers some of the ways that this musical has made people feel differently about themselves and the folks around them—how the depiction of a community can give rise to a community.

Lin-Manuel Miranda and Jeremy McCarter at the book party for *Hamilton: The Revolution*

Like the *Hamilton* book, the story proceeds along parallel tracks. My chapters trace episodes in the development of *In the Heights:* first the stage version, then the film. (Though as you'll see, the development of the stage version is a huge part of the development of the film. In order for Leslie Grace to sing "Breathe" onscreen, Mandy Gonzalez had to sing it onstage—and *that* could only happen after Lin had composed and rejected countless other songs that might have introduced Nina Rosario, a character that he and Quiara spent years fashioning out of their lives, dreams, and writerly imaginations. The pot is always bubbling.) Lin's annotations to his lyrics reveal where his songs came from and what they mean to him. In many cases he is reflecting on work he did many years ago. So are his collaborators, when they're quoted in the chapters. That long reach back through time is one of the reasons we wanted to do the book. It's a chance to hear artists at the highest ranks of their professions contemplate what they did, and who they were, when they were still learning to fly.

One big difference between this book and the *Hamilton* book reflects a difference between the shows. *Hamilton* is sung through, so the song lyrics capture virtually every word of the script. But *Heights* has dialogue scenes, which Quiara wrote for the stage version, then rewrote significantly for the movie. Since it wasn't possible to include two full scripts in the book, she wrote essays about a handful of key moments in the story. Each one traces her creative process from inspiration to stage version to screen. Think of these essays as the stitches that bind the lives of *Heights* together.

(The order of the songs, like the dialogue, changed between Broadway and the film version. We've kept the

IT CAME TO FEEL, THEY SAID, LIKE A ★★★ FAMILY.

order from the stage version; the lyrics printed here follow the original Broadway cast album. But if you want to read Lin's annotations as you watch the movie, look at the second table of contents, on page viii. It lists the songs in their movie order and will tell you where to turn next.)

One last feature of the book takes its inspiration from the show. In "Everything I Know," Nina, the neighborhood's wayward Stanford student, looks through a scrapbook created by Abuela Claudia, the community matriarch. By revisiting images from her past, Nina gains a new understanding of who she is and what she ought to do. Scattered throughout this book, you'll find recuerdos, reproductions of images and objects preserved by artists involved in *Heights*. The word "recuerdo" captures their character more fully than any word in English. It means "memento," but it also means "I remember." It implies not just recollection, but tribute. The recuerdos weren't chosen on the basis of intrinsic historical significance. They're here because they meant something special to a member of the *Heights* community. In the text that accompanies the images, the artists share that meaning in their own words.

IN EARLY 2020, Lin, Quiara, and I had nearly finished our book. All that remained was a final chapter about the movie's world premiere, which was set for June. But people began to fall ill: first far away, then painfully close to home. COVID-19, sweeping around the world, put American life on hold. It led Warner Bros. to delay the movie's release until after our intended publication date that fall.

The fact that a virus could spread around the planet so rapidly underscores the final reason to tell this story. Our world is in motion. Social scientists say that in the twenty-first century, people will pick up their lives and—out of choice or necessity—start over in greater numbers than ever before. In this Age of Migration, they will need to learn how to live in new places and assert their dignity among new neighbors, far from the habits and customs they've known. All of them will try to turn unfamiliar places into home.

A vast capacity for helping people to feel that they belong—that's the quality that most distinguishes *In the Heights*. This book is an account of gifted artists telling a story about home—and making one.

THE WORDS
★★ I NEED ★★

"OKAY," SAYS LIN-MANUEL MIRANDA. "I'm going to tell you the very painful origin story of *In the Heights*."

He smiles as he says it. He's not joking; it's just that he's telling a story that happened a long time ago and a long way away. His college, Wesleyan University, is a hundred miles from where he sits, in his dressing room at a Broadway theater. It seems a lot farther than that, when you consider what's happened in the meantime.

The Lin who is telling the story, a few weeks shy of his fortieth birthday, is the winner of almost every award that an American artist can win, a movie star, and a MacArthur-certified genius. (In a few hours, he'll step onstage in *Freestyle Love Supreme* to Beatlemania squeals.) The Lin who was living the story, a few weeks shy of his twentieth birthday, was a sophomore dreaming distantly of becoming a writer (or maybe an actor—or a director?) and nursing a serious talent crush.

The crush is what makes the story painful.

M. Graham Smith—who went by his legal first name, Matt, at the time—was one of Wesleyan's star directors. "*The* senior god," according to Lin. His work was more sophisticated than anything else on campus. When

Lin learned that Matt had started a program called Playwrights Attic to develop new works by student writers, Lin asked if he could take part.

"Sure," Matt said. Which was all the encouragement Lin needed.

Lin had written short musicals in high school, but now he wanted to do something more ambitious: a full-length show that would reflect his world. His head hadn't stopped spinning from seeing *Rent* two years earlier. Jonathan Larson's musical gave him permission to write a story about young people, in the present day, using popular music. Only Lin's show wouldn't lean on rock music the way *Rent* had. If he was going to capture the sound of Washington Heights, the world of his youth, he would need salsa and hip-hop.

No one had ever done a show like that before. Which was one of the reasons to do it.

As Lin generated material, he shared it with Matt. In 1999, that meant singing it into Matt's answering machine.

"What do you think?" Lin would say.

Matt was unfailingly encouraging. "You make an audience feel so taken care of," he told Lin.

"And I'll never forget the compliment," Lin says twenty years later, "because it's something I still aspire to."

A few weeks later, Matt assembled a trio of actors, led them through some rehearsals, and made arrangements for a late-night reading at the 92 Theater. In that converted library, a few dozen students gathered for the world's first taste of what Lin had titled *In the Heights*.

Or a bit of it, anyway: It had only two songs—it ran only twenty minutes. But it excited the people who saw it.

Encouraged by the response, Lin went on writing and sharing with Matt. One night, they met up at the Wesleyan student center (which is like every student center—the microwave, the mail room). Lin said he wanted to apply to do the show in the spring semester—not a staged reading this time but *a full-fledged musical,* with sets and lights and choreography, and naturally with Matt directing.

Even now, twenty years later, Matt can see the expression on Lin's face—the look of disappointment—when Matt said *no*.

It was the only answer he could give. He was about to graduate, he had to finish his thesis, he couldn't direct a new musical, especially one about a world as foreign to him as Washington Heights.

"That's awful," Lin said. He asked if they could shift things around, find some wiggle room. But they couldn't. It was "just the worst timing it could have been," Matt says.

Lin hadn't seen that coming. He was crushed, he says, "but understanding."

Many things might have happened next. Lin could have given up. He could have waited. He could have looked for someone else to tell the story. Instead, he made what seems, in light of everything that has happened since then, like one of the most consequential decisions of his life.

Two hours later, by his recollection, he called his friend, the stage manager Anne Macri. He told her he still wanted to do the show.

And not only that: "I think I'm directing it."

LIN MUST HAVE TAKEN CLASSES that spring, but he doesn't remember them. What he remembers is writing a show and figuring out how to stage it.

"It was a stressful thing," says Owen Panettieri, a friend who took part in the first short reading. "It was his creation and he was directing."

Lin-Manuel Miranda and M. Graham Smith

THE CRUSH IS WHAT MAKES THE STORY PAINFUL.

He did even more than that. Because the musicians on campus were all tied up doing another event, the actors had to sing to prerecorded music. So a band needed to pre-cut all those demos. Lin joined the musicians in a Middletown, Connecticut, recording studio to play the piano. He also hand-wrote the sheet music.

He had enough time for this tedious task because he wasn't spending it with his girlfriend. After four years together, she had left to spend a semester abroad. The separation and his general uncertainty about the relationship put him "in as dark a place as I'd ever been," he says. That early-twenties anguish went a long way toward shaping the show.

In that first incarnation, *In the Heights* was a story of fraught, crisscrossing love affairs. Benny is in love with Nina, a Yale student who has returned to her old neighborhood, Washington Heights, for the summer. But Benny is the best friend of Nina's brother, Lincoln, who disapproves of their relationship. He disapproves because—the big twist!—Lincoln is secretly gay and in love with Benny.

Their love triangle unfolds through nights at the club with their friend Usnavi, the bodega owner, and his unattainable dream girl, Vanessa. Even now, the score doesn't sound like anything else. Benny, Lincoln, and Usnavi's raps are dense, rhyme-packed, self-consciously lyrical—the offspring of '90s hip-hop acts like the Pharcyde, Black Sheep, Big Pun, and Fat Joe. The salsa sounds like the theatrical extension of what the whole world (except for Broadway, anyway) seemed to be listening to at the time: the Latin boom of Marc Anthony, Jennifer Lopez, and Ricky Martin. Mixed in with the rest were lovely ballads that wouldn't be out of place in a much more conventional show, such as "Never Give Your Heart Away"—the dubious advice that Benny gets from his mother, Alma.

To find a cast capable of playing these characters and delivering these songs, Lin needed to look far beyond the theater department regulars. He reached out to his fellow residents at La Casa, the Latino house on campus. But the show also acted as what Lin calls a "Bat signal" to people like him all across Wesleyan.

Matt had done all he could to help Lin secure one of the precious spots in the spring season. The playbill would list Matt as the show's "consigliere." But even he wondered if a mere sophomore would be able to draw enough of an audience for a full weekend of shows in a 150-seat theater. He didn't need to worry. All of Lin's outreach contributed to the place being packed.

"It just felt like—*how did he do that?*" Matt recalls.

YOU CAN SEE IN EMBRYO FORM a lot of what would come later for Lin: trying to put new sounds onstage, casting a wide net for actors, changing who's in the room, treating a yellow light as an imperative to go faster. Some of his most important relationships date to those days. Sara Elisa Miller, who manages his philanthropy, choreographed the show.

By all accounts, the crowd liked what they saw. "I knew my audience," Lin says. "My audience was college kids. So it played great." But two decades later, he doesn't get much joy from revisiting what he created. Pressed for an explanation, he laughs and says, "It's just—the writing is *bad!*"

The show at Wesleyan might have been called *In the Heights,* but it wasn't yet *In the Heights.* It would take time, change, and growth—also trial and error, false starts, wrong turns, inspired leaps forward. It would take collaborators, lots of them. In fact, it would take the loving effort of a whole community.

The problem is, Lin had never felt that he was at the center of one of those.

"IT'S JUST—THE WRITING IS *BAD!*"

¡WEPA! AUDITIONS for...

In The Heights
A new musical by Lin-Manuel Miranda

On SUNDAY, FEBRUARY 6th, in the
Theater Studios
Performance Dates: April 27-29, in the '92
Theater

Auditioners are asked to prepare 2 out of the
3 options below for their audition:
1. A dance piece, to whatever music you want, 1-2 minutes.
2. A song that you love to sing, 1-2 minutes.
3. A 1-2 minute monologue
*Also, all boys auditioning **must** prepare to rap a 1-2 minute
section of your favorite hip-hop song, in addition to the above
options.*

Wanna know more about the show? Read on, brave ones!

In the Heights is an original musical tragicomedy that takes
place in Washington Heights, New York. Musical Styles
range from pop to Salsa to Hip-Hop and back. We are
looking for as diverse a cast as humanly possible. That
means not just culturally diverse (Although this is VITAL),
but those of you excelling in different disciplines, such as
dance, spoken word, drama, comedy, music, all that shtuff.
It'll be a blast. Questions? Call Lin-Manuel at x7098. And
don't be nervous about auditioning. I love you guys already,
just for reading this. Ah love.

A COPY OF THE LIBRETTO IS NOW
AVAILABLE IN THE THEATER OFFICE!

in the heights

written & composed
by lin-manuel miranda

the original wesleyan cast recording · april 2000

second stage and encore musical theater present

in the heights
a new musical
by lin-manuel miranda

april
27, 28, 29
7:00 pm
29
2:00 pm

'92 theater

free admission

IN THE HEIGHTS
by
Lin-Manuel Miranda

In the Heights

1. Right from the top, we're teaching the audience how to listen to our show, a hybrid of hip-hop and musical theater lyric traditions. We have the pure rhymes of lights/heights, break/wake, and day/away. But the very next lines have hip-hop slant rhymes, by which I mean they only rhyme with the correct pronunciation: awning/morning. (See the Notorious B.I.G.'s immortal opening lines to "Warning": "Who the f—k is this, pagin' me at five forty-six in the morning?/Crack of dawn and now I'm yawning.") I'm telling the story, but I'm also trying to get musical theater purists *and* hip-hop heads on board.

2. Re: Spanglish. In our neighborhood, people go back and forth between English and Spanish all the time. Our goal was always to have the amount of Spanish ring true to any New Yorker. Almost anytime you hear Spanish in the show, a translation is around the corner (more on this in "Breathe"), but sometimes the context is enough to make the gist clear, as in this greeting.

USNAVI: Lights up on Washington
  Heights, up at the break of day
I wake up and I got this little punk I
  gotta chase away. ①
Pop the grate at the crack of dawn,
  sing
While I wipe down the awning, hey
  y'all, good morning.

(USNAVI opens the bodega.)

PIRAGUA GUY (SCRAPING FROM HIS ICE BLOCK): *Ice-cold piragua! Parcha. China. Cherry. Strawberry. Just for today, I got mamey!*

USNAVI: *¿Oye, piragüero, cómo estás?* ②

PIRAGUA GUY: *Como siempre, Señor Usnavi.*

USNAVI: I am Usnavi and you prob'ly
  never heard my name.
Reports of my fame are greatly
  exaggerated
Exacerbated by the fact
That my syntax

Is highly complicated, cuz I
  immigrated from the single
  greatest
Little place in the Caribbean ③
Dominican Republic.
I love it.
Jesus, I'm jealous of it.
And beyond that
Ever since my folks passed on, ④
I haven't gone back.
Goddamn, I gotta get on that.

(He sniffs the milk carton.)

Fo!

The milk has gone bad, hold up just a
  second
Why is everything in this fridge warm
  and tepid?
I better step it up and fight the heat
Cuz I'm not makin' any profit
If the coffee isn't light and sweet! ⑤

(ABUELA CLAUDIA enters.)

ABUELA CLAUDIA: *Ooo-oo!*

USNAVI: *Abuela, my fridge broke. I got café but no "con leche."*

ABUELA CLAUDIA: *Try my mother's old recipe: one can of condensed milk.* ⑥

USNAVI: *Nice.*

(ABUELA CLAUDIA kisses a pair of lottery tickets and holds them up to the sky.)

ABUELA CLAUDIA: *Paciencia y fe . . .*

(She exits.)

USNAVI: That was Abuela, she's not
    really my "abuela," ⑦
But she practically raised me, this
    corner is her escuela!
Now you're prob'ly thinkin', "I'm up
    shit's creek
I never been north of Ninety-sixth
    Street."
Well, you must take the A train
Even farther than Harlem to northern
    Manhattan and maintain. ⑧
Get off at 181st and take the escalator.
I hope you're writing this down, I'm
    gonna test ya later. ⑨
I'm getting tested, times are tough on
    this bodega.
Two months ago somebody bought
    Ortega's.

(USNAVI points to the salon.)

Our neighbors started packin' up and
    pickin' up
And ever since the rents went up
It's gotten mad expensive
But we live with just enough.

COMPANY (EXCEPT NINA): In the Heights

3. When I was growing up, my neighborhood was largely Dominican, thanks to a surge of Dominican immigration in the 1970s. But you could see the earlier waves of Latino immigrants as well—Cubans in the '40s, Puerto Ricans in the '50s. So we stratified the generations accordingly: Usnavi and Sonny, our youngest characters, are from D.R.; Kevin and Camila Rosario came from P.R.; and Abuela Claudia is from Cuba.

4. Usnavi's parents used to be alive and living in D.R. I suppose I orphaned him when I realized he was a little too young to come here and start a store all by himself. By having his parents start the bodega and leave it to him, he'd come to both idealize the homeland he'd never really lived in and have more complex feelings about the store that has been his inheritance.
    But, yeah, I'm aware I'm two for two when it comes to playing orphans onstage. Annie, here I come. . . .

5. We go to the New York haunts that make coffee the way we like it. The test is if you can say "light and sweet" and the person behind the counter knows instantly what that means.

6. My dad's mom used to do this.

7. This line is probably the most autobiographical in the opening number. My father's nanny when he was growing up in Puerto Rico was an incredible woman named Edmunda Claudio. When I was born, she moved from Puerto Rico to live with us in New York and help raise my sister and me. To me, she was always "Abuela," more present in my life than my flesh-and-blood grandparents. So I said this sentence all the time as a child. So much of Abuela Claudia (beginning with the name, changed from Claudio) is my love letter to her: her gambling habits; her songs; above all, her unconditional love. She's not really my "abuela," but her legacy forms a huge part of who I am.

8. When I wrote this line, it was to give New Yorkers a frame of reference: I've spent my life annoyed at tourist maps that stop after 125th Street.
    Now, as I reread it, I can't help but think of my son Sebastian. Ella Fitzgerald's recording of "Take the A Train" is his bedtime tune every night.

9. Always a fun moment to break the fourth wall for the actor playing Usnavi. Once, when an audience member pulled out an *enormous* camera to illegally film, I modified this lyric on the fly to "You better put that away, they might eject ya later."

CARLA, DANIELA, CAMILA, WOMAN, KEVIN, BENNY, SONNY, PIRAGUA GUY, MEN: I flip the lights and start my day.

COMPANY: There are fights

CARLA, DANIELA, WOMEN: And endless debts

KEVIN, BENNY, PIRAGUA GUY, MEN: And bills to pay.

COMPANY: In the Heights

WOMEN, BENNY, KEVIN, PIRAGUA GUY, GRAFFITI PETE, MEN: I can't survive without café—

USNAVI: I serve café.

COMPANY: Cuz tonight seems like a million years away!
En Washington—

USNAVI: Next up to bat, the Rosarios. ⑩
They run the cab company, they struggle in the barrio.
See, their daughter Nina's off at college, tuition is mad steep
So they can't sleep, and everything they get is mad cheap!

(KEVIN and CAMILA enter.)

KEVIN: Good morning, Usnavi!

USNAVI: ¡Pan caliente, café con leche!

KEVIN: Put twenty dollars on today's lottery. ⑪

CAMILA: One ticket, that's it!

KEVIN: Hey! A man's gotta dream.

CAMILA: Don't mind him, he's all excited
Cuz Nina flew in at three A.M. last night!

KEVIN: Don't look at me, this one's been cooking all week!

CAMILA: Usnavi, come over for dinner

KEVIN, CAMILA: There's plenty to eat!

(They exit. DANIELA and CARLA enter.)

DANIELA: So then Yessenia walks in the room— ⑫

CARLA: *Aha . . .*

DANIELA: She smells sex and cheap perfume!

CARLA: *Uh oh . . .*

DANIELA: It smells like one of those trees that you hang from the rearview!

CARLA: *Ah, no!*

DANIELA: It's true! She screams, "Who's in there with you, Julio?"
Grabs a bat and kicks in the door!
He's in bed with José from the liquor store!

CARLA, USNAVI: ¡No me diga!

USNAVI: *Daniela and Carla, from the salon.*

(They grab their purchases and go.)

DANIELA, CARLA: Thanks, Usnavi!

(They exit. SONNY runs in.)

USNAVI: *Sonny, you're late.*

SONNY: *Chillax, you know you love me.*

(SONNY exits.)

USNAVI: Me and my cousin runnin' just another dime-a-dozen
Mom-and-pop stop and shop. ⑬
And oh my God, it's gotten
Too darn hot like my man Cole Porter said.
People come through for a few cold waters and
A lottery ticket, just a part of the routine.
Everybody's got a job, everybody's got a dream.
They gossip as I sip my coffee and smirk
The first stop as people hop to work.
Bust it—I'm like—

(People come through his store.)

USNAVI: One dollar, two dollars, one fifty, one sixty-nine,
I got it. You want a box of condoms, what kind? ⑭
That's two quarters.
Two quarter waters. *The New York Times.*

10. They've always been named Rosario . . . because it rhymes with "barrio." And here I will remind you that the main character of Sondheim's *Company* is Bobby because of the variations (Bobby/Robby/Robert/etc.), so I am not alone in naming characters for lyrical expediency!

11. My abuela played the numbers every day. My mom would play only when the Mega Millions got newsworthy-level big. I liked the idea of Kevin going big on tickets because he's feeling happy and expansive.

12. Eagle-eared listeners will notice that this is the chord progression to "No Me Diga," which comes a little later in the act. After I wrote that song, we came back to the opening number and used it as the salon ladies' intro. We call it a "pre-prise"— a theme we hit you with before the actual tune lands—but I don't know if we made that up or not.

13. Bodegas are the lifeblood of New York. Smaller than a supermarket, often family-run, they're where you go not for your weekly groceries but your daily ones. As a child, you buy the cap guns and plastic toys. As a teenager, you buy the most caffeine-filled new sodas they stock (or if you're a more adventurous teen than I was, the age-restricted items behind the counter). As an adult, you're there for the morning coffee and conversation. You can see your whole life in every section of the bodega.

14. Flash forward to our first performance at the Macy's Thanksgiving Day Parade, and we are informed that we cannot say the word "condoms" in this family hour on TV. I change it to "You want a box of candy, what kind?" The performance is on YouTube: It never fails to make me laugh how embarrassed Javier Muñoz is to buy a simple box of candy!

15. The first appearance of Usnavi in the Wesleyan *Heights* was a hip-hop freestyle with Benny, wherein they trash-talked each other. I'll never forget the audience sitting bolt-upright at that brash energy in a musical: It's informed everything since, and its spirit survives into Benny's introduction.

16. The right-hand piano tinkles are *very* Dr. Dre circa his album *2001*.

17. I love introducing Vanessa mid-struggle. She's a fighter. Also, the "Nooooooo . . ." section is every three-year-old's favorite part of the show.

18. The thing about opening numbers is that everything you write forces you to rewrite your opening number. A great example: "Champagne" was one of the last songs written for the show, between Off-Broadway and Broadway. Which necessitated setting up this lyric. We make it Vanessa's first line to Usnavi in the show, so it pays off in Act Two.

You need a bag for that? The tax is added.
Once you get some practice at it
You do rapid mathematics automatically
Sellin' maxi pads and fuzzy dice for taxicabs
    and practically
Everybody's stressed, yes, but they press
    through the mess
Bounce checks and wonder what's next.

COMPANY: In the Heights

GROUP 1 (CAMILA, CARLA, DANIELA, ABUELA CLAUDIA, WOMAN, SONNY, USNAVI, MEN, KEVIN, BENNY, GRAFFITI PETE): I buy my coffee and I go.

GROUP 2 (WOMEN, PIRAGUA GUY, MEN): I buy my coffee and—

COMPANY: Set my sights

GROUP 1: On only what I need to know.

GROUP 2: What I need to know

COMPANY: In the Heights
Money is tight

GROUP 1: But even so

GROUP 2: But even so

COMPANY: When the lights go down I blast my radio!

(BENNY enters, dressed in a shirt and tie like KEVIN.)

BENNY: You ain't got no skills! ⑮

USNAVI: Benny!

BENNY: Lemme get a— ⑯

USNAVI: Milky Way.

BENNY: Yeah, lemme also get a—

USNAVI: *Daily News*—

BENNY: And a—

USNAVI: *Post*—

BENNY: And most important, my—

USNAVI: Boss's second coffee, one cream—

USNAVI, BENNY: Five sugars—

BENNY: I'm the number one earner—

USNAVI: What!

BENNY: The fastest learner—

USNAVI: Yup!

BENNY: My boss can't keep me on the damn back burner!

USNAVI: Yes he can.

BENNY: I'm makin' moves, I'm makin' deals, but guess what?

USNAVI: What?

BENNY, SONNY: You still ain't got no skills!

USNAVI: Hardee-har.

BENNY: Vanessa show up yet?

USNAVI: Shut up!

BENNY: Hey little homie, don't get so upset.

USNAVI: *Maaaaaan.*

BENNY: Tell Vanessa how you feel, buy the girl a meal,
On the real, or you ain't got no skills.

(VANESSA walks by on the phone.)

VANESSA: Nooo!
No no nooo!
No no nooo, no no no!
Nooo, no no no!
No no no no no no no no no no no no no!
Mr. Johnson, I got the security deposit ⑰
It's locked in a box in the bottom of my closet.
It's not reflected in my bank statement
But I've been savin' to make a down payment and pay rent.
No no, I won't let you down.

BENNY: Yo, here's your chance, ask her out right now!

VANESSA: I'll see you later, we can look at that lease!

(She hangs up.)

BENNY: Do somethin', make your move, don't freeze—

USNAVI: Hey!

(VANESSA approaches USNAVI.)

VANESSA: You owe me a bottle of cold champagne. ⑱

USNAVI: Are you moving?

VANESSA: Just a little credit check and I'm on that downtown train!

USNAVI: Well, your coffee's on the house.

VANESSA: Okay!

BENNY (UNDER HIS BREATH, TO SONNY): Usnavi, ask her out.

SONNY: No way!

VANESSA: I'll see you later, so . . .

(VANESSA waits a moment before exiting. USNAVI misses the moment.)

BENNY: Smooth operator, aw damn, there she goes!
Yo, bro, take five, take a walk outside!
You look exhausted, lost, don't let life slide!
The whole hood is struggling, times are tight,
And you're stuck to the corner like a streetlight!

USNAVI: Yeah, I'm a streetlight, ⑲
Choking on the heat.
The world spins around
While I'm frozen to my seat.
The people that I know
All keep on rolling down the street
But every day is different
So I'm switchin' up the beat.
Cuz my parents came with nothing
They got a little more
And sure, we're poor, but yo,
At least we got the store.
And it's all about the legacy
They left with me, it's destiny,
And one day I'll be on a beach
With Sonny writing checks
To me.

19. The introduction of Usnavi's central metaphor: when he first self-identifies as a streetlight, affixed to the block, firmly rooted. It'll take the whole show for that metaphor to blossom.

20. The joy and challenge of these choruses is in finding group vocals, group sentiments that unite all these residents, no matter where they hail from.

21. Again, this speaks to one of the themes we stumbled upon in writing this show: there are a million stories to be told from the specifics and differences among *any* of the Latino cultures in our show. *This* one focuses on our common ground and what we share. Keep reading.

22. The line "En Washington Heights" is literally the only five notes and lyrics that survive from the Wesleyan version to the present.

MEN): In the Heights
I hang my flag up on display. [20]

USNAVI: We came to work and to live, and we got
a lot in common. [21]

ENSEMBLE +CAMILA, VANESSA, SONNY, KEVIN: It
reminds me that I came from miles away.

USNAVI: D.R., P.R., we are not stoppin'.

COMPANY:	**ABUELA CLAUDIA:**
In the Heights	Every day,
	paciencia y fe.
Ooh	
Ooh	
	USNAVI:
Ooh	Until the day we go
	from
	Poverty to stock
	options.

COMPANY: In the Heights
I've got today.

USNAVI: And today's all we got, so we
cannot stop,
This is our block.

COMPANY: In the Heights
I hang my flag up on display.

PIRAGUA GUY: Lo le lo le lo lai lai lo le!

COMPANY: It reminds me that I came
from miles away.

USNAVI, PIRAGUA GUY, WOMAN, MAN:
My family came from miles away—

ENSEMBLE: In the Heights
It gets more expensive every day.

WOMAN, USNAVI, MAN, PIRAGUA GUY:
Every day

COMPANY: And tonight is so far away—

USNAVI: As for mañana, mi pana ya
Gotta just keep watchin',

USNAVI:
You'll see the
Late nights,
You'll taste
Beans and rice,
The syrups and
Shaved ice,
I ain't gonna
Say it twice.

BENNY,
GRAFFITI PETE,
MEN:

Late nights

Beans and rice,

Shaved ice

Say it twice

ALL OTHERS:
In the Heights

In the Heights

In the Heights

USNAVI:
So turn
Up the
Stage lights,
We're takin' a flight
To a couple of days
In the life of what it's like

COMPANY:

Ah
Ah
Ah

COMPANY: En Washington Heights! 22

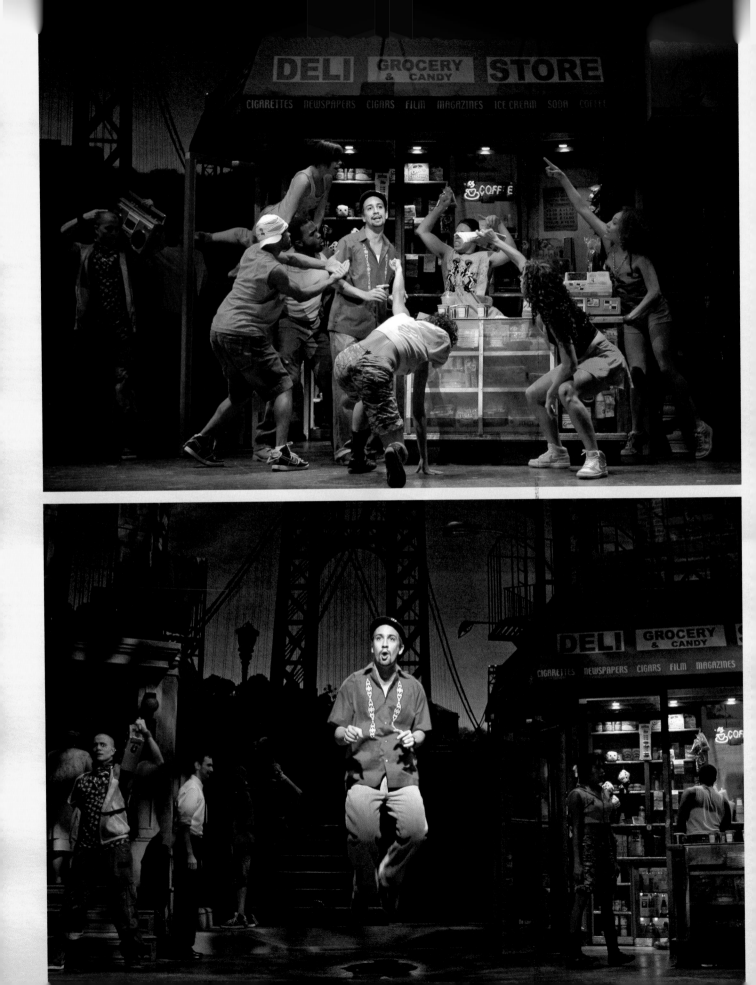

WELCOME HOME ★ ★

ALL NEW YORK STORIES are real estate stories. Life here is governed by a pair of ineluctable facts: There isn't enough room for all the people, and new people show up all the time. Even the simplest aspects of life are shaped by negotiations over space. Who controls a place? Who belongs? Very frequently, those questions lead to conflict. But now and then, when people find creative ways to share these tight quarters, astonishing things can happen.

Here is a New York story.

In 1866, a theater burned down, leaving a company of European dancers without a space to perform. Some innovation born of desperation gave the dancers a chance to go onstage at a different theater, as part of a spectacular melodrama. The resulting fusion of acting, singing, and dancing was messy, unlikely, and scandalous. It was also a huge hit. Aspects of that history have been disputed over the years. (All New York stories aren't *true* real estate stories.) Still, *The Black Crook* is generally regarded as the birth of the Broadway musical.

For the next hundred years, the musical was disproportionately an art form by and for New Yorkers. (There's a reason why we call them *Broadway* musicals.) It was also disproportionately shaped by immigrants and their children. Irving Berlin, Dorothy Fields, George Gershwin, Ira Gershwin, Lorenz Hart, Moss Hart, Jerome Kern, Frank Loesser: Their formative years in and around New York gave them crucial training for their peculiar trade. After all, the musical is actually five or six art forms in one. To make a musical that works, you need to reconcile old traditions and new forms, arranging unlike parts to fit together on one crowded stage, coaxing dozens of artists to dance in rhythm, to sing on key.

And since we all bear the marks of where we're raised, is it any wonder that the musical shows traces of its hometown? The influence pops up even where you don't expect it. Consider *West Side Story,* a masterpiece of the form. It's a quintessential New York story, not just because of how it starts, with two gangs fighting over turf—a very serious kind of real estate dispute—but because of how it ends. When Tony and Maria let their imaginations run free, fantasizing about the future they want to share, what do they dream about? They're New Yorkers—what else *could* they dream about?

There's a place for us, somewhere a place for us . . .

HERE'S ANOTHER New York story.

In 2001, the owners of the Drama Book Shop received word from the landlord that it was time to go. This was not unprecedented. In the eighty-four years that the Book Shop had served as the go-to place for New York theater folks to buy books, look up scripts, and fraternize, it had been dislodged repeatedly by rent increases or by a builder's desire to plant a high-rise on the spot. (The New York state motto, *Excelsior,* means "ever upward," as if real estate developers needed the hint.)

The new location was less than picturesque: a dicey stretch of West Fortieth Street, just off Eighth Avenue. But it had its compensations. Unlike the previous spot, a cramped space on an office building's second floor, the new store was tall and light-filled, with a mezzanine and plenty of corners where actors could deep-breathe before auditions. But the real action was out of sight. To find it, you had to walk down one flight of stairs, then turn right. There you could gaze upon that rarest of New York sights: *open space.*

Specifically, it was a rectangular room with low ceilings, bare walls, and infinite possibilities. Or so it seemed to Allen Hubby, who was then a co-owner of the store, when he set eyes on it.

"The Book Shop had always been a valuable resource to the theater community," he says, "but we really thought the new space would allow us to be a *member* of the theater community—a real participant."

To fulfill that potential, the space needed a theater company. Luckily, Allen knew of a theater company that needed a space. Four young friends—Tommy Kail, John Buffalo Mailer, Neil Stewart, and Anthony Veneziale—had begun producing plays and readings together as Back House Productions. They were scrappy and itinerant, working in different places around the city, which is the only thing a new company can do. But they were making good on the hopes they'd nurtured as Wesleyan undergrads, all those late nights they'd spent "sitting up and talking about our big theater dreams," as Tommy puts it.

Thanks to Allen, Back House became the resident company of the bookstore's basement space, which was now called the Arthur Seelen Theatre. It would be responsible for programming plays, readings, and other events there. Needing to paint the place seemed like a small price to pay, considering *the bookstore was not charging them any rent.*

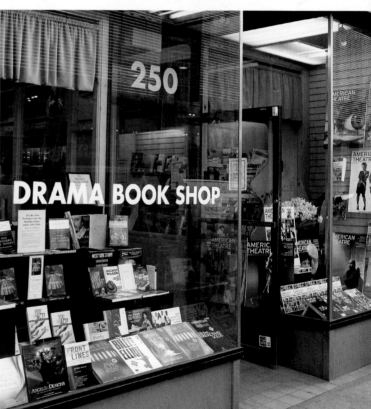

LIN CAME BACK TO THE BOOKSTORE AND KEPT COMING.

Even as they filled up the theater's calendar, they kept thinking about a project that John and Neil had seen two years earlier: *In the Heights.* Tommy, who was beginning to piece together directing gigs, listened to the demo CD. He liked it, too. The four of them were so enthusiastic about the idea that they announced it on their website.

Lin still recalls how he felt when he saw it: "A little bit *what the f---?*"

He had talked with them about doing the show, but they hadn't reached a formal agreement. So what was it doing on a website?

"It almost blew up," says Tommy. "It was a whole thing."

Lin was irritated, even after they took the announcement down. But what was he going to do—brush them off? These guys were the only ones showing the slightest interest in his work.

So, a week after graduation, in June 2002, he took his first walk down the bookstore stairs. He noticed that the walls were half black; he noticed an upright piano. He sat down with them at a folding table. They started to talk—and kept talking for hours.

That was the day, Lin says now, when "Tommy and I locked in." The weird symbiosis of creative partnership—somebody who draws out your best even as you draw out theirs, who sees things the way you do (but not *exactly* the way you do), who goes where you're going without needing a map, whose opinions you rely on because they're right even when they're wrong, who makes you work so hard because most of the time it doesn't feel like work—why try to explain it? Just go try to find it. And if you do, hang on.

LIN CAME BACK TO THE BOOKSTORE and kept coming. Whenever he wasn't working at various jobs to pay rent, like substitute teaching at his alma mater, Hunter College High School, he'd bring songs, scenes, ideas. He'd also bring Bill.

The story (as Lin tells it) is that during his junior year at Wesleyan, he saw a student production of *Once on This Island,* and when it ended, he walked up to the music director, Bill Sherman, and said, "I don't know you, you don't know me, but we're going to work together for a really long time."

This struck Bill as presumptuous. *Who is this guy?* he thought. "But soothsayer Lin—that's what turned out to happen," he says, twenty years of near-constant collaboration later.

"I WAS ON THE OUTSIDE OF EVERY COMMUNITY."

Bill wasn't a big musical-theater guy, being more of a hip-hop fan. And he didn't hold himself an expert on Latin music, being a Jewish kid from Long Island. But he'd collected a degree in music, and he'd led a band of his own, so he understood how to work with musicians. And by the time he started taking four-hour lunch breaks from his IT job to hang out at the Book Shop, he understood how to work with Lin.

"I'd say three words, and he'd say, 'Got it,'" says Lin.

Later that summer, they decided to hear the show out loud. Tommy proposed that Lin play Usnavi. He suggested it without any particular fanfare—it just made sense to him. Lin knew the material better than any actor who might be willing to learn it, and he was charming enough to coax an audience past all the parts of the show that didn't yet exist.

Lin was happy to do the role, but that doesn't mean he identified with it. Usnavi was the guy who was cool with everybody, the heart of his community. Lin . . . *wasn't*.

"I was on the outside of *every* community," he says. *Which ones?*

"I'm talking about in Washington Heights. I'm talking about at Hunter. It was sort of like, 'I'm over here.'" He gestures way off to his left.

Lin could relate to those old legends of Broadway—the Gershwins and Berlins, the ones who were raised in New York by parents from someplace else and had to figure out a life. He grew up in a Puerto Rican family on the border of Inwood and Washington Heights, a distinctly Latino part of the city. As a kid, he had friends in the neighborhood—they'd play in the streets. But then he went to Hunter, the prestigious selective-enrollment public school on the Upper East Side. His life was dividing. He lost the neighborhood friends. The new ones from Hunter were wealthier and more worldly. So where did he belong?

Being Usnavi, somebody who understands everybody's stories, "that was aspirational for me," Lin says. "I didn't feel like an authority on *anything*."

"TO HAVE COHORTS, TO HAVE A PLACE TO GO—IT MEANT EVERYTHING."

Nina, on the other hand—the odd one out, the character who's in the neighborhood without feeling like she's of it, surrounded by familiar faces but still looking for a sensation of home—*that* he understood. His identification with her was especially close that summer, coming back from college just as Nina does in "Breathe."

Maybe his identification with her helps to explain why "Breathe" would take him *years* to write. It definitely explains why he loved the bookstore so much. What a strange thing it was, to bring all of himself to a place and feel like he belonged.

"To have cohorts, to have a place to go—it meant everything," he says.

▲ Bill Sherman

Breathe

1. One of the most fun things to do while writing this score was the "standards"— songs that don't exist but needed to feel like they've existed forever. I always imagined the "sigue andando" hook as an old bolero that Nina's heard a hundred times and is riffing on to express this new moment. Another one is the song "Siempre," an imagined bolero to which I only ever wrote one verse and chorus, which you can hear in the dinner scene and the finale. I can't tell you how many people have come up to me swearing up and down, "My grandparents used to listen to 'Siempre'!" No, they didn't. I made it up! But it means I did my job.

2. My parents show up on screen at this point in the movie. Howls of inappropriate laughter from our family at this moment every time.

3. I was so moved by the way Jon Chu approached this song in the movie. Nina sees younger versions of herself on these blocks. As someone who has logged forty years in the same neighborhood, I find it incredibly powerful and true.

PIRAGUA GUY: Sigue andando el camino por toda su vida. Respira.

NINA:
Breathe.

PIRAGUA GUY, SONNY, MAN, USNAVI:
Y si pierdas mis huellas que dios
Te bendiga.
Respira. ❶

NINA: This is my street.
I smile at the faces
I've known all my life. They regard me with pride.
And everyone's sweet,
They say, "You're going places!"
So how can I say, that while I was away, I had so much to hide!
Hey guys, it's me!
The biggest disappointment you know.
The kid couldn't hack it, she's back, and she's walkin' real slow.
Welcome home.
Just breathe . . . ❷

ENSEMBLE (DANIELA, CARLA, WOMEN, PIRAGUA GUY, SONNY, MAN, USNAVI): Sigue andando el camino por toda su vida.
Respira—

NINA:
Just breathe—

ENSEMBLE:
Y si pierdes mis huellas que dios
Te bendiga.
Respira—

NINA: As the radio plays old forgotten boleros
I think of the days when this city was mine.
I remember the praise ❸

NINA:
Ay, te adoro,
  te quiero.
The neighborhood
  waved, and
Said, Nina, be brave and
You're gonna be fine.
And maybe it's me,
  but it all
Seems like lifetimes ago ¡Respira!

ENSEMBLE:
Te adoro

Te quiero
¡Respira!

NINA: So what do I say to these faces that I used to know?
"Hey, I'm home"?

WOMAN: Mira Nina

NINA: Hey . . .

CARLA, WOMAN, DANIELA, PIRAGUA GUY, MAN: No me preocupo por ella.

NINA: They're not worried about me. ❹

CARLA, WOMEN, DANIELA, PIRAGUA GUY, MEN: Mira, allí está nuestra estrella.

NINA:
They are all counting
  on me to
Succeed,
I am the one who
  made it out!
The one who always
  made the
Grade
But maybe I should
  have just
Stayed home . . .

ENSEMBLE:

Ella sí da la talla . . .
Ah! Ah, aah

Mira Nina

NINA: When I was a child I stayed wide awake, climbed to the highest place
On every fire escape, restless to climb. ❺

ENSEMBLE: Respira . . .

NINA:
I got every scholarship,
Saved every dollar,
The first to go to
  college,
How do I tell them why
I'm coming back home,
With my eyes on
  the horizon

ENSEMBLE:

Respira . . .
Ahh

NINA: Just me and the GWB asking, "Gee, Nina, what'll you be?" ❻ ❼
Straighten the spine.
Smile for the neighbors.
Everything's fine.
Everything's cool.

The standard reply:
"Lots of tests, lots of papers."
Smile, wave goodbye,
And pray to the sky, oh God . . .
And what will my parents say? **8**

ENSEMBLE: Nina . . .

NINA: Can I go in there and say,

ENSEMBLE: Nina . . .

NINA: "I know that I'm letting you down . . ."

(ABUELA CLAUDIA appears at the stoop.)

ABUELA CLAUDIA: Nina . . .

NINA: Just breathe . . .

(She exits into ABUELA CLAUDIA's apartment.)

4. Maybe some of the most sophisticated rhyming occurs in this bridge as Nina is simultaneously translating what her neighbors are singing and matching their vowels—estrella/they are, talla/I am. This section was created between Off-Broadway and Broadway and makes all the difference in the world, amping up the pressure from the neighborhood and adding a multilingual twist.

5. I remember writing this line on a beach, singing the words to myself over and over until the internal assonance had that cascading rhythm just right.

6. My first memory of the George Washington Bridge was walking with my Abuela Mundi to my piano lessons. We'd emerge from the train station, and it somehow loomed over the street despite us being at the highest point in Manhattan. I now live across the street from where I took those lessons, and the perspective of the bridge that loomed over them—and over our set in Anna Louizos's beautiful design—is outside our window. My kids call it their bridge. It is one of the few constants in an inconstant life.

7. My wife, Vanessa Nadal: "When I saw the set for the first time, I gasped! I was floored. It's my view! My uptown, off the map view!"

8. Translating the stage musical to the screen led us to make changes big and small. As you'll read later in the book, Nina's family is different in the movie, so I had to rewrite this lyric. And I'm grateful for the chance, because it gave me another way to define Nina. So in the movie, she sings:
And how do I dare to say?

RIDE WITH ME

CHRIS JACKSON HAD PLANS to see a friend. It was an afternoon in fall 2002.

When he arrived at the little deli in Midtown, that friend, Jené Hernandez, was saying goodbye to somebody Chris didn't know. White dude, curly hair.

Chris didn't feel too chatty that day, so he brushed the guy off: a chin nod, "'Sup." He didn't think much about it.

Chris wanted to see Jené to learn more about a new project she'd described. Coming off four years in *The Lion King* on Broadway, Chris was skeptical of auditioning for people he'd never heard of, especially in the basement of a bookstore. But he was also unemployed. A show that was supposed to keep him working until the end of the year had just closed without warning.

He'd been dealing with injuries. He was disillusioned with acting. He felt isolated from the whole profession. "Like somebody who had been through a bad relationship," he recalls.

A day or two later, he walked his skeptical feet down the stairs of the Drama Book Shop, a place he never even knew existed. He turned right, opened the door, and introduced himself to the three people waiting for him: Lin, Bill,

and the curly-haired dude, who was Tommy Kail.

Asked many years later how he felt in that moment, he says, "Ohhhhh!"—a one-syllable mix of shock, shame, and determination to laugh in spite of it all.

(Tommy, for his part, doesn't recall feeling that Chris had been unfriendly when they were introduced. "I'd met so few actors at that point, I didn't know any better," he says.)

It was time to audition. Lin played the piano. Chris sang the song. Tommy and Bill seemed happy.

Chris thanked everybody and got ready to leave, because that's what you do after an audition. You leave.

Except somehow he didn't feel like leaving. And somehow neither did they.

"We kicked it," says Chris. The four of them spent an hour shooting the shit, making one another laugh, generally having fun. "And I hadn't had fun in the theater in many years."

By the time Tommy got around to saying something along the lines of, "All right, we're going to move forward with you," the audition felt like an afterthought. Chris had found the closest collaborators he'd ever have—his best friends for two decades and counting.

Doreen Montalvo ▶

IN 2002 AND 2003, more and more actors had an experience like Chris's: the uncertain walk down the stairs (or up to the mezzanine), the audition, the casual invitation to stick around. Some heard about the peculiar project from their agents; others heard about it from friends. It's how people like Janet Dacal, Henry Gainza, and Doreen Montalvo first got connected with the show.

Actor by actor, rehearsal by rehearsal, something started to grow in that space. The featureless, windowless black box in the basement started to develop a character. It had a *vibe*.

Ask the actors about it now—about what they remember all these years later—and they'll say first that they just enjoyed it. "I couldn't wait to be in a room with those guys," says Janet. "We were all so young. We were just making it up as we went. But it was a very safe place to create and try things and make mistakes and figure them out."

The second thing they'll say is how different it felt to be performing a story about Latino characters, written by a Latino writer. "We'd sit around a table as new songs were brought in, and every time it would be like, 'Oh my God—this is about *us*. I've never experienced this before,'" says Doreen.

For all the joy that *Heights* had begun to bring to young artists, this is still a story about show business. That means heartbreak all around. Every time Tommy held auditions, more actors left disappointed than got cast. Nor was getting an offer a guarantee of a long stay. Sometimes an actor got a better job and decided to leave. Other actors seemed like the right fit for a role but turned out not to be and weren't invited back. A few actors gave beautiful performances in roles that one day ceased to exist. It wasn't just actors, either. People came and went from all corners of the production in this show's very long life.

Recuerdo
NÚMERO UNO

CHRIS JACKSON
BENNY IN THE ORIGINAL OFF-BROADWAY AND BROADWAY CASTS

I don't remember exactly when "Benny's Dispatch" came along— I just remember I always loved singing it. Lin writes songs that he knows I'm going to love. He hears my voice in his head clearer than I hear it in my own. I couldn't be prouder of that song. It was the first song ever written for me on a Broadway stage.

I kept my dispatch mic. Yeah, I walked out with that one. It reminds me of how much fun we had and how much it meant to me that Lin and Tommy trusted me with "Benny's Dispatch." By the time I was singing it on Broadway, a maturation process had culminated for me. I just felt like, "These guys depend on me. They're my friends. They're my brothers. I'm not going to let them down."

Henry Gainza, Lin-Manuel Miranda, and Chris Jackson in a photo taken by Anthony Veneziale

AND THEN THERE'S Veronica Vazquez.

In early 2003, she auditioned to play Nina. It went so well that she was invited to return for a "chemistry read" to see how she sounded singing a duet with Benny—that is, with Chris Jackson.

Veronica loved Chris's voice on the demo recording she'd been sent. She had a hunch that their shared background in singing R&B would make for great vocal chemistry. And then she set eyes on him. "Goo-goo eyes," she calls them.

Chris was astonished by her—how beautiful she was, how she carried herself. And then he heard her sing. "Her voice made my heart beat fast," he says.

They sang "Did I Wake You?," an early ballad for Benny and Nina.

She got the part.

Veronica and Chris played it cool, but over the next few months, their castmates could see the mutual attraction. In May 2003, Lin and Tommy wanted to try out material for an audience at Repertorio Español. But Veronica was concerned. She pointed out to Tommy that the script called for Nina and Benny to kiss, but they had never rehearsed it. This was going to be awkward.

"That's *exactly* what I want," Tommy replied.

The presentation started. The moment for the kiss arrived. Chris—"being super a gentleman," Veronica says—was hanging back. So she grabbed his hand, pulled him close, and they both leaned in.

Chris Jackson and Veronica Vazquez

Their castmates, arrayed in chairs behind them, gasped. Nothing about it was awkward.

The hand-grab is part of the show's lore now. It's family lore, too, for Chris and Veronica Jackson, for their son, CJ, for their daughter, Jadelyn.

RIDE WITH ME

Benny's Dispatch

BENNY: Check one two three. Check one two
three.
This is Benny on the dispatch. Yo. ①
Atención, yo, attention,
It's Benny, and I'd like to mention
I'm on the microphone this mornin'.
Honk ya horn if you want it.

**(Car horns blast. NINA exits ABUELA CLAUDIA's
apartment, enters the dispatch.)**

1. The beat for this song
was originally written
for an early tune called
"The Long Way Around,"
wherein Benny picked
Nina up from the
airport and took her
home via a scenic route.
Two people sitting
in a car is never fun
onstage, so I rewrote it
as Benny's first time on
the dispatch mic, which
felt like a fun way to
show his joy in his work,
his lyrical cleverness,
and his New York
knowledge.

2. My bus ride to school
took me from Dyckman
Street all the way to
the Upper East Side,
and traffic determined
whether to take the
West Side (and choose
highway traffic or local
along Riverside Drive)
or cross to the East
Side, where one can
clearly see the Deegan
traffic and Yankee
Stadium run parallel
to the FDR across the
Harlem River. So I know
these directions cold.

BENNY: Okay, we got traffic on the West Side
Get off at Seventy-ninth, and take the left side
Of Riverside Drive, and ya might slide.
West End's ya best friend if you catch the
  lights.
And don't take the Deegan, ❷
Manny Ramirez is in town this weekend. ❸
Sorry, Dominicans, take Route Eighty-seven,
  you ain't getting back in
Again . . .
Hold up a minute . . .

(He puts down the radio.)

NINA: Benny, hey— ❹

BENNY: Nina, you're home today!

NINA: Any sign—

BENNY: Of your folks? They're on their way!

NINA: Anyway—

BENNY: It's good to see your face—

NINA: Anytime—

BENNY: Hold up a minute, wait!
You used to run this dispatch, right?

NINA: Once or twice—

BENNY: Well, check the technique! Yo!

(Into the dispatch)

There's a traffic accident I have to mention
At the intersection of Tenth Avenue and the
  Jacob Javits Convention Center.
And check it, don't get stuck in the rubber-
  neckin'
On a Hundred Ninety-second,
There's a double-decker bus wreck ❺
And listen up, we got a special guest!

BENNY:	**NINA:**
Live and direct from	Benny . . .
a year out west!	

BENNY:	**NINA:**
Welcome her back,	Benny . . .
She looks mad stressed!	
Nina Rosario, the	
barrio's best!	
Honk your horns . . .	

(We hear a series of syncopated horn blasts, as BENNY
continues to sing.)

She's smiling . . . Say hello!

(NINA steps to the microphone.)

NINA: Hello . . .

(We hear the cacophony of the most beautiful horn
chart ever written.) ❻

Good morning!

(NINA catches herself having fun, abruptly stops.)

I better find my folks.
Thanks for the welcome wagon.

BENNY: Anytime. Anytime, Nina.

(NINA heads for the door. BENNY stops her.)

BENNY: Wait here with me. ❼
It's getting hot outside, turn up the AC.
Stay here with me.

(She sits beside him. BIG BUTTON!) ❽

3. This was always in
honor of Washington
Heights native Manny
Ramirez. For the movie,
I updated it to a more
recent Dominican hero,
Big Pápi Ortiz. Both
Dominican phenoms
played for non–New
York ball clubs, creating
friendly arguments
for the neighborhood
forever.

4. I just really like
Nina's
  Benny, hey—
  Any sign—
  Anyway—
  Anytime—

She's being interrupted
by Benny but rhyming
in her own world, with
herself.

5. There are *no* double-
decker buses this far
uptown—we're too
mountainous. So I
assumed the existence
of one would instantly
cause a calamity.

6. I wrote this stage
direction as a gauntlet
to throw down to
Bill Sherman and
music director Alex
Lacamoire. They
came back with a
very Beatlesque "Sgt.
Pepper"–sounding
thing. But then our
choreographer, Andy
Blankenbuehler,
preferred the synth
horns I put on the
demo. The final product
is somewhere in
between.

7. The bass line for this
last section will grow
to full flower in Benny
and Nina's final song,
"When the Sun Goes
Down." Here's the first
hint of it.

8. "Button" is the
musical theater term
for the bump at the end
of a song. It lets the
audience know when
it's time to applaud.

CHAPTER *Four*

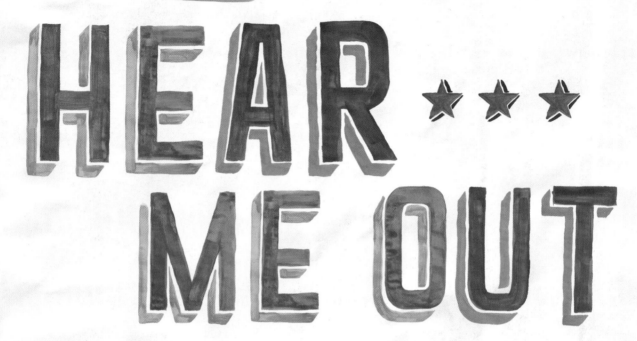

OTHER NEW YORK ANTHEMS are more triumphal—and many are better known—but none rings truer than "Another Hundred People." It is one of Broadway's enduring contributions to city anthropology.

In this song from Stephen Sondheim's *Company*, a character sings about "a city of strangers." She doesn't mean it as a complaint. With wry humor, she describes a place so packed with people that life consists of chance encounters and missed connections. Somebody is always coming and somebody is always going and every now and then you spot a friend.

When young artists arrive in such a place and say they're looking for their big break, they really mean they're hoping to find the right person at the right moment amid the city's whirl. Or that the right person will find *them*. Because a couple such breaks can make all the difference in the fortunes of a project, a career, even a life—as long as you play them right.

For example.

In the spring of 2003, the actor Andy Gale ran into a friend on Forty-second Street. The friend, Nevin Steinberg, calls it "one of those happy New York bump-intos." It wasn't a shock that they would (as Sondheim's song puts it) "find each other in the crowded streets." They had worked together years earlier, Nevin doing sound for a show that Andy was acting in.

While catching up—where've you been, where're you going, etc.—Andy mentioned that he was coming from (or heading toward—neither of them remembers) the Drama Book Shop.

"There's this show, *In the Heights*," Andy said. "You're going to want to be part of it."

Nevin was intrigued.

While *Heights* was germinating in the bookstore basement, Andy, who is a teacher as well as an actor, gave Tommy encouragement and advice. He talked about how to make an actor feel comfortable and how to learn the most from an audition—the little insights that he'd accrued in a career that started before Tommy's birth. He had no formal role in the show; he just wanted to see young people he liked and admired have every chance to succeed, even when it meant not succeeding right away. "They needed to take missteps, which would lead them to more creative steps," he says. "That's part of the process—to try things out in a way where it would be safe to say, 'Well, that really doesn't work.'"

"You should meet those guys," Andy told Nevin. "It's gonna be really special. Also a challenge. They're going to need somebody like you."

Andy arranged for Nevin to visit the bookstore basement, and he set up a meeting with Tommy. (In fact, he had begun setting it up months earlier, mentioning a sound designer that Tommy ought to know: Nevin Steinberg.)

Down the steps Nevin went. He met Tommy, Lin, and Bill. He watched some of their work. He found it to be "an amazing and strange thing."

"I had never heard anything like it: a piano and a guy rapping about his neighborhood," Nevin recalls. "And my career was new musicals. This is what I *do*."

He could see why Andy thought the show was still in its early days. It wouldn't need a sound designer for a while yet. But he was already hooked, and not just by the show's novelty: "It was the sense of humor, and the heart, and the rhythm," he says. And so, with no formal role, he began contributing.

A few days later (or maybe weeks—neither of them remembers), Nevin was riding the 1 train downtown. The door opened, and in stepped Kevin McCollum. They had known each other for years. At the time of this second "happy New York bump-into," Nevin was working on the Broadway transfer of *Avenue Q,* a new musical produced by Kevin and his business partner, Jeffrey Seller.

"I HAD NEVER HEARD ANYTHING LIKE IT: A PIANO AND A GUY RAPPING ABOUT HIS NEIGHBORHOOD."

After the ritual round of catching up—where've you been, where're you going, etc.—Nevin felt the same impulse that Andy had.

"I just saw a thing that's really cool," he said. "It's new and it's very early, but I think there's something there, and I think you'd be excited by it, and by these people."

Nevin told Kevin the same thing that Andy had told him: "You should meet them because they're going to need you."

Kevin was intrigued.

Ever since he and Jeffrey had produced *Rent,* the rock musical that revolutionized Broadway and launched both their careers, he had kept an eye out for adventurous voices. "I'm all about new musical vocabularies," Kevin says. "Musicals are best when they surprise. They have to go beyond what came before."

One night shortly after running into Nevin on the train, Kevin took his advice and went to the tiny Lion Theatre in the Theatre Row complex on Forty-second Street. He sat by himself: Jeffrey was checking out a different show that night. He didn't know what to expect when the workshop presentation began. But out came Chris and Veronica, and Janet and Doreen. And out came Lin.

"I wasn't quite sure what was happening," Kevin recalls. A lot of plots were competing for attention, some more compelling than others. But one factor was undeniable: "Every time this character Usnavi spoke, I was really hooked in."

"IT WAS INFECTIOUS— THE PASSION, THE TALENT, HIS CHARM."

At intermission, Kevin had his own "happy New York bump-into"—more consequential than the previous two. He ran into Roy Furman, a fellow Broadway producer, who was seeing the show with his wife and their daughter, Jill.

They asked Kevin what he thought.

"I really dig that guy," he said, meaning Lin. "Every time he comes onstage, I want to know more."

Jill was intrigued.

Three months earlier, she'd had the exact experience that Kevin was having. *Who is this guy?* she had asked herself, watching Lin rap his way through a presentation in the bookstore basement.

"He was so ridiculously talented," Jill recalls. "It was infectious—the passion, the talent, his charm."

At the time, Jill was associate producing shows with her dad, looking for a way to strike out on her own. She was seeking the same thing that Nevin and Kevin were seeking: a genuinely new voice, from a writer who inspired her. She thought she had found it in Lin.

So—like Andy, like Nevin—she had begun contributing to the show, trying to help it along. "It felt like she moved into the bookshop," recalls Allen Hubby. "She was there every day, it seemed like."

With intermission winding down, Roy proposed the four of them have dinner after the show. That night, dining together at Orso (they ordered pizza—that part everybody remembers), Jill and Kevin made a plan. They would work together to develop *In the Heights* and find out what it could become. They would begin by inviting the guys to sit down with them in Kevin's office the following week.

Neither of them thought a Broadway ~~n~~ was imminent, though Jill made it her personal mis ~~propel~~

Heights there with the least possible delay. ("I was the biggest pain in the ass," she says.) Kevin wanted Jeffrey to be enthusiastic about the show, so he *didn't* bring him into the meeting. A script and CD weren't going to capture the thrill of watching Lin and his castmates live. He told Jeffrey he'd get the show into shape, then set up a reading. And then Jeffrey would see.

To Lin, all of this was amazing, surreal, and *fast*. "Within a year, I'm already working with the guy I've read about in the big black *Rent* book," he says. "It really felt like, *I'm on my way.*"

LIN'S DEVOTION TO JONATHAN LARSON meant a lot to Kevin, as it would to Jeffrey when they met a few months later. Larson's sudden death—at age thirty-five, the night before *Rent*'s first preview in 1996—continued to reverberate around the New York theater world in 2003. By that point, the influence of *Rent* had begun to emerge. "It was so unfair he couldn't be here to see it," Kevin says.

Still, Kevin believed it was "not necessarily a good thing" that a musical would reflect too much of Larson's influence. That's why he wasn't completely sold on the love triangle in *Heights*. Lincoln's furtive love for Benny and his stifled dream of becoming a songwriter felt a little too familiar. "We already have *Rent*—we don't need another," he says.

Usnavi, on the other hand: Here was something different. He captured Kevin's attention partly because of Lin's charisma, but also because the story of a young man dreaming of his island home reflected Kevin's own experience. He had grown up in Hawaii, getting involved with his mother's theater group, absorbing the Broadway cast albums that she brought home. When he was fourteen—an only child being raised by a single mother—she died of cancer. He went to live with his aunt and uncle in the Chicago suburbs.

It was cold; he missed his friends. Like Usnavi, he dreamed of going home. But there was nothing left for him there.

That experience would shape Kevin's taste in shows—and his approach to developing them. "Musicals are about finding your family against all odds," he says. "Look at *Rent*, or *Avenue Q*—it's all about finding your home." It's what had drawn Kevin to *Heights* and made him want to help Lin succeed.

But there was a vast distance between the producer atop one of New York's peaks and the upstart writer scratching in the bookstore basement—so vast that one of Kevin's attempts to help got garbled along the way.

Kevin could see that Lin hadn't solved the show's story, a tangle of too many characters and plots. In one early meeting, he raised the possibility that Lin might benefit from having another collaborator. This was, after all, the way most musicals work. A composer writes the music, a lyricist writes the lyrics, a librettist writes the book—the dialogue between songs. Sometimes a writer will do two of those things. Jonathan Larson was one of the very rare talents to do all three.

Lin had already taken off one of his hats when he entrusted the show's direction to Tommy. Should he take off another? "I didn't know what he was best at," Kevin says, so he proposed a few ways that Lin could bring on another writer. Proposing is all Kevin could do: He and Jill had already agreed that the decision to collaborate or to go it alone was entirely Lin's.

Looking back, Lin can see that "it was offered in a spirit of 'What else do you need?'" But at the time, hearing what he took to be a suggestion (from a producer of *Rent*, no less) that *Heights* might be better off if he wrote only the book and lyrics—and let someone else write the music— sent him spiraling.

Was he a composer? Or a lyricist/librettist? Or both? Or neither?

He didn't have trophies to reassure him or a fat binder of glowing reviews. He was still a decade away from *Hamilton* and *Moana* and "Love is love is love is love." He was a twenty-three-year-old would-be Broadway writer whose chief connection to Broadway was his parents' cast albums.

Lin and Tommy would reach a point in their collaboration, and their friendship, where they talked almost every day. But in 2003, they were still getting used to each other. So Lin didn't share what he was feeling. Still, Tommy could tell something was up. After a year in which material came flying out of Lin, weeks went by without a new song. Then months.

"He just had this approach avoidance to his keyboard," Tommy recalls. "It felt like he was having to climb a hurdle to get onto a chair that he'd sat on for so many years."

Tommy tried to be encouraging and keep Lin going. But as any writer will tell you, whether you're bursting with confidence or racked by doubts, the easiest thing in the world is *not* to write.

Lin started to make peace with the idea of not composing the show's music. He asked people to recommend musicians who might work with him. He got as far as picking up the phone to call one of them.

He got that far and no further.

"I hung up the phone and said, 'F--- *this,* I'm the composer,'" Lin says.

It had taken months of soul-searching, but he had come to realize two things about the show and about himself.

The first was: "If I don't know how to write this music, then I don't know how to do anything."

The second was: He *did* need a collaborator on *Heights,* but not to write the music.

In early 2004, he told Kevin and Jill, "I'd love to have a book writer to help me unlock this story."

▲ Quiara Alegría Hudes and Lin-Manuel Miranda

"I DON'T WANT TO say anything—you should just meet her," Jill told Lin.

"You know what, I'm not going to say anything," Tommy told him. "You should meet her."

Why won't anyone say anything? Lin wondered.

This is not how Jill and Tommy had reacted to the other potential librettists they'd been meeting. But he took their advice and made plans to sit down with Quiara Alegría Hudes.

He showed up for their dinner at Market Café (a quiet place on Ninth Avenue—it's gone now) with a little trepidation. Quiara had a degree in music composition from Yale and an MFA in playwriting from Brown. She wrote serious, lyrical plays. Imagine his surprise—and relief—when she turned out to be warm and kind. "A goofball," even.

They found common ground. Lots of it.

As Quiara recalls the night, "He started talking about his cousins, I started talking about my cousins. He started talking about his abuela, I started talking about my abuela. He started talking about his parents, I started talking about my parents. By the end, we said, 'We might as well be cousins.'"

Lin could see that Quiara had shared his struggle to reconcile different sides of himself. In fact, her challenge was even more acute than his. Quiara's father, who is Jewish, and mother, who is Puerto Rican, separated when she was in first grade. When her mother fell in love with a

man from Puerto Rico, her family divide became a cultural divide. "I felt like a constant migrant in my own life, ping-ponging between two worlds," she says.

But the circumstances of how she grew up, in Philadelphia, opened up differences with Lin—so much so that she was nervous about the meeting. When Jill first approached her about the project, she had sent a script and CD of *In the Heights*. In that draft, a dinner scene included "the encyclopedia game," in which Kevin tested Nina to see how much she was really learning at Stanford. Quiara was intimidated by the idea that it might have been drawn from life. *That's something that college-educated families do,* she remembers thinking.

A certain defensiveness bubbled up in her, a certain embarrassment. She might have a college degree, but she was the first person in her immediate family to get one. Quiara's stepfather was one of the smartest people she knew, but he had left school at sixteen to get a job and help support his family. In fact, Kevin Rosario—even in that early draft—bore a remarkable resemblance to him. Sedo Sanchez has always been a big personality, with a lot of energy and years of experience running a series of businesses in the barrio. He was proud to tell a story about shining shoes as a boy and how he would always invest his nickels in more rags, more polish. He and Quiara's mother supported her, no matter what path she chose, because they knew she couldn't follow in theirs.

Quiara liked Lin's script and loved his music but wasn't sold on joining the project. Her time was already scarce. She was temping to pay the bills, since she and her law-student husband were putting rent on their credit cards. She wasn't eager to spend her limited writing time on a musical aiming for Broadway, which didn't captivate her the way it did Lin. "My parents never played a cast album," she says. She grew up not knowing what one was.

On top of everything else, Lin had already written a hundred-page script. What was left for her to do?

"This is your thing," she said. "I don't want to come and trample on your thing. How would this work?"

A photo of Lin taken by Quiara during their first walk around Washington Heights

"I don't know," Lin said. "Let's find out."

Quiara came away thinking about the differences in their families, the special perspective that she gained from how she grew up. The center of the story, the Rosario family, was "a pretty stable American notion of a family," Quiara says. "And I was like, 'Okay, but . . .'" She had a tactile sense of all the things that can strain a family—and split it apart.

She thought about Vanessa, who had been in the show from its earliest days: the savvy woman who lights up the club and dreams of getting out. Lin had recently written "It Won't Be Long Now," putting her aspirations in song. Quiara could imagine what happens to her when she's offstage, all the pressures she faces. "I definitely pushed that she has an unstable family life," Quiara says.

She thought about how class diversity operates even among the residents of a single block in the barrio. "They sing in the opening number that they're making ends meet, but what Kevin Rosario does is a different sort of making ends meet than Vanessa. If Nina can't make a tuition payment, her father figures it out. But if Vanessa can't pay rent, she's out. There's not a backup plan, you know?"

And she thought about Lin and how much fun they'd had at dinner. "His enthusiasm toward life is contagious," she says. She wanted to keep talking with him about the show.

New York doesn't make promises to young dreamers. You can find guidebooks when you get here, but no instructions. It'll put people in your path, seven or eight million of them, but you need to figure out for yourself what to do with them. When a situation demands it, the city will also help you get away from them.

Quiara and Lin walked to the subway entrance at Fortieth Street. He said goodbye, then went down the stairs. This was a ruse. He walked past the ticket booth and came back up on the far side of Eighth Avenue, where Quiara couldn't see him. He wasn't going to wait till he got all the way back uptown to make this call.

He dialed. It rang. Tommy answered.

Lin said, "She's the one."

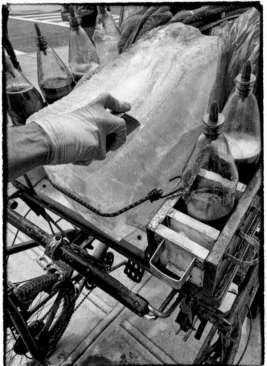

LIN SAID, "SHE'S THE ONE."

HEAR ME OUT

It Won't Be Long

1. Truth be told, there *are* no elevated trains in Washington Heights proper: The 1 emerges from underground at 200th Street, which is technically Inwood. But this was *my stop* growing up, and while writing *Heights*, I lived a block from these train tracks. What I'm saying is this technically means Vanessa lives *just* uptown from the block in our show and commutes twenty blocks.

2. Our first day of filming the movie was downtown at the Astor Place subway stop. I used to do an after-school theater program in high school right next to that stop, and spent countless hours sitting on the floor in the humor section of the now-extinct Astor Place Barnes & Noble. Suddenly, here we were with a movie crew, shutting down foot traffic and filling Astor Square with dancers. It's amazing how many versions of your life can unfold on the same few blocks.

We'd come to Astor Place to shoot a story line that was new for the movie version: Vanessa dreams of being a fashion designer and fights to break into the field. The dialogue in the next part of the song plays very differently in the two versions, though in both cases, she finds her way back to the bodega—and to Usnavi.

3. Quiara and I got the text from our company manager, Brig Berney: "Chita Rivera and her daughter are at tonight's performance." I was no longer performing in the show, so we *raced* over to the Richard Rodgers and hid in the balcony to watch her reaction. Her jaw dropped, and she and her daughter just started elbowing each other and grinning. So did Quiara and I.

4. There's a great anecdote about the making of *Fiddler on the Roof*. Bock and Harnick were turning out song after song, but they were still without an opening number, and Jerome Robbins finally pinned them down with Joe Stein and said, "What's this show about? In one word?"

"Tradition."

"That's your opening number."

Well, for *Heights*, that word is "Home," in all its permutations. Usnavi defines home as a place he barely remembers, and Vanessa defines it as something to escape.

This is one of many lessons we would learn from *Fiddler*. Keep reading.

VANESSA: The elevated train by my window doesn't faze me anymore.
The rattling screams don't disrupt my dreams
It's a lullaby, in its way.
The elevated train drives everyone insane but I don't mind, oh no. ❶
When I bring back boys, they can't tolerate the noise
And that's okay, cuz I never let them stay.
And one day, I'm hoppin' that elevated train and I'm riding away!
It won't be long now!

(Men whistle at VANESSA on the sidewalk.)

The boys around the way holler at me when I'm walking down the street.
Their machismo pride doesn't break my stride—
It's a compliment, so they say.
The boys around the way holler at me every day but I don't mind, oh no.
If I'm in the mood, it will not be with some dude
Who is whistling cuz he has nothing to say
Or who's honking at me from his Chevrolet.
And one day . . . I'm hoppin' in a limousine and I'm driving away!
It won't be long now! ❷

(VANESSA approaches USNAVI outside the bodega.)

Ay, Usnavi, help! SOS!

USNAVI: Good morning, Vanessa!
If it isn't the loveliest girl in the place.

(She wipes his cheek.)

VANESSA: You got some schmutz on your face.

SONNY: Good morning!

SONNY, USNAVI: Good morning!

(VANESSA kisses SONNY on the cheek. She grabs SONNY to dance.)

USNAVI: Vanessa . . .

SONNY: Vanessa . . .

USNAVI, SONNY: Vanessa . . .

DANIELA (SCREAMING FROM THE SALON): *VANESSSSSAAAAAA! I'm thirsty, coño!*

VANESSA: *Can I get a Pepsi and some packing tape?*

SONNY: *Uh, my cousin over there with his tongue hanging out has been meaning to ask you . . .*

VANESSA: *Yes?*

SONNY: *What a lady such as yourself might be doing tonight?*

VANESSA: *Does your cousin dance?*

SONNY: *Like a drunk Chita Rivera.* ❸

VANESSA: *Okay . . . After Nina's dinner, we can hit a few clubs and check out the fireworks . . .*

(USNAVI awkwardly hands her a bag. She exits.)

USNAVI: Oh snap! Who's that? Don't touch me I'm too hot! Yes!
¿Qué pasó? Here I go! So dope! ¡Y tú lo sabes!
¡No pare,

SONNY, USNAVI: Sigue, sigue!

USNAVI: Did you see me?

SONNY, USNAVI: Freaky freakit!

USNAVI: What a way to begin the weekend, Sonny, anythi̶ want is free, man!

Now

And my dearly beloved Dominican
    Republic
I haven't forgotten

SONNY, USNAVI: You!

USNAVI: Gonna see this honey, make a
    little money,
And one day I'll hop

SONNY, USNAVI: Jet Blue!

USNAVI: But until that fateful day, I'm
    grateful
I got a destination.
I'm runnin' to make it home, and
    home's what Vanessa's runnin'
    away
From! ❹
I'm runnin' to make it home, and
    home's what Vanessa's runnin'
    away
From . . .

(USNAVI is at the bodega door, VANESSA at
the salon door. She sings to him.)

VANESSA: The neighborhood salon is
    the place I am working for the
    moment.
As I cut their hair, ladies talk and
    share—
Every day, who's doing who and why.
The neighborhood salon doesn't pay
    me what I wanna be making
But I don't mind.
As I sweep the curb, I can hear those
    turbo engines
Blazing a trail through the sky.
I look up and think about the years
    gone by.
But one day—I'm walkin' to JFK and
    I'm gonna fly!
It won't be long now!

A THOUSAND
★★★ GAMES

ALL SORTS OF MOVIES and plays influenced *In the Heights,* but Lin describes only one of them as the show's "blueprint": *Fiddler on the Roof.* The circumstances of the two musicals vary in notable ways—there are no marauding Cossacks in Washington Heights, as there were in the shtetl that Bock and Harnick put onstage. Still, both shows depict life in a community under pressure from forces both within and without. Lin, Quiara, and Tommy paid repeat visits to a Broadway revival of *Fiddler* while working on *Heights.* Afterward, more than one of their creative disagreements were settled by somebody citing what *Fiddler* had done.

(Broadway is a compact enough village that when *Fiddler*'s librettist, Joseph Stein, came to see *In the Heights,* Lin got to tell him how grateful they were—and how much they stole. Fortunately, Stein had liked the show. "You're welcome," he replied.)

Thanks to Jeffrey and Kevin's involvement in *Heights,* the show had a useful point of reference much nearer at hand. *Avenue Q,* another McCollum/Seller production, was like a "big sibling" to *Heights,* according to Lin. It featured irreverent puppets, a lively score, and one of the funniest scripts in years. On their way to winning a Tony Award

for Best Musical (Jeffrey and Kevin's second, after the one for *Rent*), that show's creators had spent a vital couple of weeks in Waterford, Connecticut, at the Eugene O'Neill Theater Center. Since 1964, the O'Neill has given composers and playwrights a chance to develop projects away from the distractions of summer in the city.

With the example of *Avenue Q* before him, Lin had applied to the O'Neill in 2003. He'd been rejected. After Quiara joined him, they tried again and got in—one of three musicals accepted out of three hundred applicants that year. Twelve actors and the show's creative team would spend two weeks there in July 2005 trying to solve the problems that remained to be solved.

By then, Jeffrey had seen a presentation of *Heights* and decided "I'm in" before the opening number even ended. He always looks for shows that sound new: *Rent* before this, *Hamilton* after. Lin's juxtaposition of rap and traditional Broadway songs more than qualified. "When the ensemble came in behind Lin singing 'In the Heights,' I just got chills all over my body," he says.

With Jeffrey, Kevin, and Jill all backing the project, the creative team had reason to hope that the O'Neill would be the last step before a full-fledged Broadway-bound

Tommy Kail and Lin-Manuel Miranda at the O'Neill ▶

production. It was an ambitious plan, but it wasn't crazy. "Everything had been crescendo up till then," recalls Bill Sherman.

Lin hoped so, and not just for the obvious reasons. "I had my employment worked out exactly through summer, and that was it," he says. No production, no job.

AFTER THREE YEARS in a windowless underground box, the O'Neill offered a startling change of scene: the eleven grassy acres, the huge blue sky, the hill rolling down to the Long Island Sound. It was like summer camp for grown-ups, or a college where everybody majors in putting on shows with your friends.

"We were working our asses off," recalls Javier Muñoz, who played Usnavi so Lin could focus on writing. "But it was an absolute joy."

By day, they would rehearse in a converted barn and eat meals together in the cafeteria. By night, they would walk down to the water and watch the shooting stars. After the freestyle rapping on the beach came the salsa dancing

in the barn. Lin would plug in his iPod and play DJ. The other two hundred people on the campus were welcome to join those parties, and many of them did. According to Preston Whiteway, who worked at the O'Neill that summer and later became its CEO, nobody had done anything like those parties before, but every summer since, the staff has tried to recapture their joy and their camaraderie—"that sense of an O'Neill family, that we're all in this together."

"WE WERE WORKING OUR ASSES OFF. BUT IT WAS AN ABSOLUTE JOY."

The actors could relish the experience in part because they were there to serve the writers. Which was lovely for them—but it put more pressure on those writers.

Quiara had been writing the libretto for nearly a year at that point, a time she recalls as "a lot of play, a lot of exploration, a lot of discovery." She and Lin were integrating their styles, figuring out which parts of the story should be spoken and which ought to be sung. From her first listen to the demo CD, she had sensed that the density of Lin's lyrics meant that her book scenes needed to be short. But, paradoxically, fewer lines meant a bigger challenge—each scene still needed to feel satisfying. "That was something I struggled with, with so little real estate," she recalls.

She recognized that the O'Neill offered them an opportunity that would not be coming again: "It was definitely like, 'This is a turning point, but we don't know to what.'" So she used every second of it. She never slept more than four hours at a stretch. She would wake in the middle of the night to write when nobody was around—well, almost nobody. One night, a well-dressed woman walked through the room and smiled hello; Quiara smiled back. Then she remembered that every door in the room was locked. A sleep-deprived hallucination, she thought—until somebody told her about the nice lady ghost known to haunt the grounds.

Lin was equally stressed, though he didn't get a ghost story out of it. He wrote song after song—"Blackout," "Alabanza," multiple songs for Nina—trying everything he could to get the balance of Lincoln's and Nina's stories right. By that point in the show's development, Lincoln had shed his secret love for Benny. Now his major conflict was with his father, who wanted him to take over the family car service despite his dreams of becoming a songwriter. A lifetime of finishing projects late at night had taught Lin that he could wake himself up by taking a shower. It didn't work at the O'Neill. He spent two weeks "just tired and wet."

Lin's home-movie footage captures another sign of the pressure they were feeling: the rare sight of Tommy Kail looking tense. "It was really the first time that Jill and Jeffrey and Kevin were focused on us, so that was a new experience for me," he recalls. "It just felt like the stakes and the temperature both got raised."

It helped that they had another set of shoulders to carry the weight. A few months earlier, Alex Lacamoire had joined Bill as co-orchestrator and music director. Lin, inveterate fan of cartoons, was reminded of another five-person team of heroes who come together to do great things. "We're Voltron!" he declared.

Before the cast and creative team presented the revised show, they gathered for a big class photo. Look closely at the spot between Lin and Tommy in the photo on page 44: It's Voltron.

THE CROWD STREAMED INTO THE BARN; the actors stepped up to music stands; the new and improved show began.

With Lac (as Alex is known to friends and colleagues) at the piano, the music had never sounded better. With Robin De Jesús playing Sonny, the dialogue got more laughs. With Huey Dunbar lending Lincoln what Lin calls his "gift-from-God voice," "Alabanza" brought the house down. "It turned that space into a cathedral," recalls Chris Jackson.

The presentations generated such strong word of mouth that the O'Neill added an extra performance— a nearly unprecedented move. The cast performed five times and got five standing ovations, which was also unusual.

Everybody seemed to love it—except the people who needed to love it most.

A few hours after the final presentation, Voltron (Lin, Quiara, Tommy, Bill, and Lac) and the producers (Jill, Kevin, and Jeffrey) assembled for what several of them, many years later, would independently describe as "the come-to-Jesus meeting."

"THIS IS A **TURNING POINT,** BUT WE DON'T KNOW TO WHAT."

43

They sat at a picnic table in the sun.

The participants' memories of what happened next don't line up in every particular, but the thrust of the meeting is clear. Quiara distills the producers' message this way: "You've done your work and it doesn't work."

A standing ovation in Waterford was one thing, but Broadway—the only goal worth chasing at that point—was another. Lin, who had gone into the meeting "hoping against hope" for a production, quickly realized he wasn't going to get one.

Jill might or might not have said out loud what she recalls feeling that day: They had taken "one step forward, two steps back."

Kevin said that they were still trying to cram too many plots and characters into the show. It wasn't clear which stories were important to them. Until they figured it out, they weren't ready to move ahead.

"CAN YOU KILL OFF ONE OF THE MAIN CHARACTERS?"

Somebody—most likely Jeffrey—made a comment that, under the circumstances, had more force than a mere suggestion: Lincoln needs to go.

Bill, already stung by what he describes as "the slap of truth in the face," had trouble understanding what he'd just heard. "I remember thinking, *We've had Lincoln since college—what are you talking about?* In my head, I'm like, *Can you kill off one of the main characters?*"

All the while, Tommy was processing his feeling of surprise. He'd known there was more work to do, but he hadn't expected the producers' dissatisfaction to be so cut-and-dried. Here was a delicate situation. He had four collaborators in confusion and distress and three producers looking for a response. Luckily for all seven of them, Tommy had an intuitive sense, even at that early age, for keeping people steady—a kind of gyroscope for whatever was going on around him.

In distilled form, the response he offered was: "I got it."

He and the team understood the reaction, they were grateful for it, and there was no question that they would go back to work and make the kind of progress that the producers wanted to see.

It was the perfect response, even though—or, maybe, *especially because*—none of them knew how they were going to do it.

I'm Out [1]

LINCOLN: Run away from home
Ignore your mother's screams and leave today.
You should have done this years ago.
Why are you still at home
Shoving down all the things you need to say?
Suffering for no reason. A lonely son.

I've
Wasted my life
Writing at night
Driving by day
But now it's clear
Year after year
Long as I'm here
It's safe to say
I'll never be
The son that you wanted
Or even the son you accepted
So that's gonna be how we left it.
You screaming at me and me . . . walking out.

So I'm out.
Out of ways to make you happy.
I'm running out. Yes, I'm out.
So I know it's time to go.
And I love you but you'll never see me the way I see myself
When I'm alone
With a notebook and a microphone. [2]

When I write a song
I am somewhere far beyond this place.
Everything feels electric, connected . . . [3]
When I write a song
I imagine you [4]
Nodding your head in time
List'ning the way you listen to your boleros.
I wanted to cry
When you stood by me
And you handed me your keys:
"Lincoln, take these."
I couldn't breathe.
I never cease to let you down.
I'll never live
Up to your expectations.
So this is the situation:
You're getting upset and I'm getting out.

I am out.
Out of patience with this family.
I'm running out. Yes, I'm out.
And it's time, it's way past time!
After twenty-four years of only hearing you shout
It's crystal clear you don't know what I'm about.
So Mami, Nina, sorry, see ya, please no crying allowed.
I'll be back when I've made you proud!
And I'm out! [5]

1. "I'm Out" is an excellent example of a perfectly cromulent song that would be a standout in any musical but didn't make the cut for *In the Heights*. It's dramatically effective; its rhythms are rooted in the same Latin world as the rest of the show, particularly the ending. So why did we drop it? Mainly because it's sung by Lincoln Rosario, Nina's brother, who didn't survive the O'Neill workshop in 2005. That said, I think the character hung around as long as he did because he had excellent songs like this one.

When I look back at this, what jumps out at me is how *adolescent* the lyrics feel. I don't mean that in a pejorative way: It's anguished, it's Lincoln attempting to bridge a father-son divide and failing, it's passionate. It also feels particular to *my* adolescence: You will not find a bigger fan of my work these days than my father, but during my teen years, he was *really* pushing me toward law and struggling with my mediocre grades in any classes besides English and music, and that feeling of "maybe we will just *never* understand each other" feels very particular to my teen years. (You'll get his side of the story in the next chapter.)

All this to say, while I admire Lincoln's passion, this feels like a song for a teenage character to sing, not someone in his mid-twenties. Which makes sense! I *was* a teenager when Lincoln came into existence!

This is also perhaps a good place to mention that every chapter title in this book is the name of a cut *Heights* song. And there are enough cut song titles for two more books.

2. I think this line is the realest thing in the song. Everything else is just okay.

3. This isn't quite autobiographical, because I have felt as many different ways writing songs as I have had days. I've worked for years on one song and written two songs from scratch on the same day. Sometimes it feels as easy as falling; other times it's like moving furniture with no end in sight, or a crossword puzzle where the clues keep changing. I suppose, on the *best* days, it feels like this—when every moment your hands touch the keys or the keyboard, you feel options opening to you, you feel present, you feel nothing but possibilities.

4. Your first audience is yourself. You have to tell yourself the story of your song—and make yourself feel and understand it—if you have any hope of making anyone else feel and understand it. Stephen King talks about an Ideal Reader: I rarely imagine that person *as* I'm writing, but once I have *written* something, I sometimes imagine its effect on an audience. Most often, it's my wife: I like her taste, and I know if I've made her laugh or cry, I've cleared the highest possible bar. I love the detail of Lincoln imagining his father's reaction to his song, because it tells us how much he's yearning to communicate with him and that every conversation isn't scratching the surface of all the things he needs to say.

5. There's a temptation to imagine the show if Lincoln's character had stayed, but it's simply impossible. The moment we cut Lincoln, Nina inherited his fraught relationship with Kevin, and it instantly made Nina so much richer and more complex. Lincoln died so Nina could *thrive*. Thanks, Lincoln.

CHAPTER Six
SIEMPRE

"WHAT'S THAT SUSHI SIGN?" says Luis A. Miranda, Jr. Through the window of the car, he sees a restaurant hawking an unlikely mix of cuisines. "Oh my God—mofongo and sushi. That's when you know life has changed."

In early 2020, when he offers a guided tour of Washington Heights, Luis has seen forty years of the life of the place: long enough to recognize a new twist in an old story. This neighborhood is always cramming different cultures together. Before World War II, European immigrants, particularly the Irish and the Jews, shared these blocks, not always peaceably. (Luis points out traces of this old-world legacy, like the signs in Greek at the Highbridge Park pool.) After the war, many old-timers fled for the suburbs, clearing the way for a new mix of cultures. Between 1970 and 1980, the proportion of residents hailing from Latino homelands leapt from less than two percent to nearly forty percent.

That's when the Mirandas arrived.

"It was terrible," says Luis.

That doesn't mean he disliked it. He loved it; he still does. Anyway, the things that made it "terrible" back then—crime, unemployment, fewer cafés and restaurants than he was used to—made it attainable for him and his wife, Luz Towns-Miranda. In 1981, they were finishing their graduate studies at NYU, a young couple needing to accommodate a growing family. They found a little house on the border of Washington Heights and its northern neighbor, Inwood.

They arrived just in time to celebrate the second birthday of their son, Lin-Manuel.

If the Mirandas had chosen to stay in Greenwich Village, or had moved to New Jersey, it's difficult to imagine that Lin ever would have written a musical about Washington Heights. But this is only one of the ways his family influenced the show. Their lives and their stories shaped it in deeper and subtler ways, too—one story line in particular.

THE RESTAURANT ON DYCKMAN STREET—which does not serve sushi—is empty when Luis walks in, the lunchtime rush not having begun. Over the next hour, the tables fill up. People cross the room to greet him. A handshake, a kiss. A word about this, a joke about that. All in Spanish.

"That's the feeling I wanted when I moved here," he says. "It feels like home."

Luis grew up in Vega Alta, Puerto Rico, a small town half an hour west of San Juan. It was small enough that everybody knew everybody, the sensation he would later feel in Washington Heights. By nineteen, he was thriving: a college graduate with a good managerial job, married to his high-school sweetheart. But it wasn't enough. In 1973, he announced a decision that baffled his family: He was moving to New York. He wanted to get his Ph.D. at NYU. Then he would come home.

THIS NEIGHBORHOOD IS ALWAYS CRAMMING DIFFERENT CULTURES TOGETHER.

46

Luis Miranda, Sr.—Lin-Manuel's Abuelo Güisin—at the credit union he ran in Vega Alta (pictured here with his right-hand man, Agustin Flores)

Washington Heights in 1985

The move wasn't easy. He didn't speak English. He needed to find a job. The long-distance marriage didn't last. But after four years in the city, the plan seemed to be on track. He had started dating Luz, who was also from Puerto Rico. They decided to return to the island together.

Luis went as far as shipping his furniture home. But then they didn't leave.

Though Puerto Rico went on exerting what he calls "a constant pull in my head," he felt that they belonged in New York. The decision meant that Lin would grow up in a household inhabiting two worlds: Daily life was in New York, but family ties bound him to Vega Alta, where he spent a month every summer. He had heard the story of Luis shipping the furniture home. He knew how real a possibility it was that he could have been born there. The bridge section of "When You're Home," when Nina wonders what would have happened if her parents had stayed in Puerto Rico, is very much drawn from life.

Considering how much of Lin is in the character of Nina, Luis sees pieces of himself in the character of Nina's father, Kevin. The role is "probably" based on him, he says—particularly the part about sacrificing for the children. He and Luz were determined to send Lin and his sister, Luz, to college and do it without burying them in debt.

So they took multiple jobs, putting in a full day at an office, then teaching college courses at night. It was unrelenting; it went on for years. "Horrible," he says.

But Luis says that he's hardly the only model for the character. Washington Heights, like Vega Alta, comprises many small businesses and the families who run them. He points them out on the tour: the bodegas, the salons, the shop where he buys his guayaberas. Didn't all these families have kids, and didn't they all make sacrifices?

"Kevin," he says, "is also the story of everyone we knew in the neighborhood."

THE FATHER who makes great sacrifices for his children is a familiar story. We've all seen a million movies in which he imposes his will on his children, pushing them to redeem all that's been done on their behalf. The O'Neill version of *In the Heights* was an extreme version of the tale: Kevin didn't just discourage Lincoln's dreams of becoming a songwriter; he pressured him to stay home and take over the family business.

Lin's parents never pushed him to give up his dreams of writing and acting. But Luis repeatedly cautioned prudence. He wanted his son to hedge his bets.

"I said *look at Rubén Blades*," Luis recalls. "There is no bigger salsa star than Rubén Blades. And he's a lawyer! From an Ivy League school! So if this shit doesn't work, you'll try a couple of cases."

Luis knew how limited the opportunities were, especially for Latino actors. Back in Vega Alta, he had watched his uncle, a remarkably gifted actor, struggle to make ends meet. Yet at a crucial moment for Lin, which turned out to be a crucial moment for the show, Luis's belief in his own advice was put to the test.

In 2003, after Lin had been substitute teaching at Hunter for a year, he received the offer that young educators dream of receiving: to teach seventh grade full time. It was a chance to do a job he loved, one that came with lifetime security. No more scratching out rent payments, relying on checks for jingles that Luis had hired him to write for political clients. ("Out of pity," Luis says.) But if he took the job, he'd have less time to work on the show. Lin could imagine what he would later call "the *Mr. Holland's Opus* version of my life," where the show never got done.

He didn't know which path to choose. So he asked his dad.

You can see how Luis, after a lifetime of chanting *Rubén Blades, Rubén Blades,* would rush to tell Lin to take the job. But somehow he couldn't bring himself to say it. Taking the job would make sense. But if Luis had done what made sense, he never would have left Puerto Rico. How could he argue against everything that had happened in his life since he was eighteen?

"I said, you have to do what feels right," recalls Luis. "And if what feels right is to continue writing *In the Heights,* then that's what you have to do." And that is what Lin did.

The version of Kevin Rosario that audiences saw at the O'Neill, the one who imposes himself on Lincoln and tries to shoot down his dreams, is not the Kevin that audiences see today. After the O'Neill, with Lincoln gone, Kevin no longer tries to keep his child close to home—he does the opposite. He wants Nina to take flight. He wants her not to give up on herself. In this version of the show, the sacrifices of the parents are made in the service of *their child's* dreams, not their own.

Lin and Quiara hadn't seen that dynamic in a million movies. But they had seen it.

"IT IS THE MOST cluttered place you will ever see," Luis says.

He's talking about the house that he and Luz bought in 1981, the place they still call home, the last stop on the tour. It isn't really cluttered; it's lived-in. Coffee in hand, Luis shows a guest the living room—really two compact rooms with a wide opening between them.

It takes some imagination to picture the scene he's describing, from twenty years ago.

During Lin's unhappy winter break in his sophomore year at Wesleyan (girlfriend abroad, crushing deadlines to finish the show), his parents thought of a way to cheer him up. They proposed that for his twentieth birthday, which was a few weeks away, they forgo the usual party and invite friends over to listen to his show.

Luis points out the spot where Lin and a few co-stars sang the songs he'd been writing about the neighborhood. He waves an arm to indicate where all their friends had crowded into chairs, listening.

It worked; Lin *did* cheer up. Applause, like the sight of friendly faces, is medicinal.

A few months later, *In the Heights* would have its first public production at Wesleyan. But you could fairly say that the show's true world premiere was here in this living room, and its first producers were Luis and Luz Miranda.

Luis sips his coffee. "I always believed the show was going to work."

Inútil [1]

KEVIN: This isn't happening.
Inútil. Useless.
Just like my father was before me.
Inútil. Useless.
And every day
He cut the cane.
He came home late and prayed for rain. Prayed
    for rain.

And on the days
When nothing came
My father's face was lined with shame.
He'd sit me down beside him and he'd say,
"My father was a farmer,
His father was a farmer,
And you will be a farmer." [2]

But I told him, "Papi, I'm sorry, I'm going farther.
I'm getting on a plane
And I am gonna change the world someday."
And he slapped my face.
He stood there, staring at me, useless.
Today my daughter's home and I am useless.

And as a baby she amazed me with
The things she learned each day. [3]
She used to stay on the fire escape
While all the other kids would play.
And I would stand beside her and I'd say:

"I'm proud to be your father,
Cuz you work so much harder
And you are so much smarter
Than I was at your age."
And I always knew that she would fly away
That she was gonna change the world
    someday. [4]

I will not be the reason
That my family can't succeed.
I will do what it takes,
They'll have everything they need.
Or all my work, all my life,
Everything I've sacrificed will have been
    useless. [5]

1. It is hard for any musical theater writer to write a song for a father when "Soliloquy" from *Carousel* already exists and casts such a long shadow. Again, the answer is always specificity. Once I stumbled on the word "inútil," I knew Kevin had his own lane to express himself at this moment.

2. Parents overcorrect. We remember the worst injustices of our childhood and we say, "I'm never doing that to my kid." Kevin's father's sin was to say, "You're going to be just like me."
    Kevin's is, "You're not going to be anything like me." We overcorrect.

3. When I watch the show now, this song moves me the most. It required me to make a leap of empathy into fatherhood that I had not yet experienced but can clearly recognize from the other side, with two children of my own who run rings around my expectations and amaze me daily.

4. The best Kevins really get swept up in this section, caught up in their dreams for Nina, and that "world some . . . day" lands in the pit of the stomach, as the right-hand piano figure of Kevin's distress returns.

5. So it's not "Soliloquy." But it does the job, tracing the arc of his life to the inevitability of his making this decision.

CHAPTER Seven

FREESTYLE

LIN OPENED HIS EYES.

Tommy, wide awake in the bed next to him, started popping off ideas for how to fix Act Two.

"Tommy," Lin said, "it's six A.M."

Tommy considered this for a moment, then said: "What if I just rip off this blanket and I'm a mermaid?"

A week after leaving the O'Neill, Lin and Tommy flew off to Scotland. They had been invited to perform at the Edinburgh Fringe Festival along with other members of Freestyle Love Supreme, the improv hip-hop group that had grown up alongside *In the Heights:* Anthony Veneziale, Chris Sullivan, Arthur Lewis, Chris Jackson, and Bill Sherman. Looking back, Tommy considers it a stroke of good fortune that the first thing he and Lin did after leaving the stress of the O'Neill was spend a few weeks using what he calls "the part of our brain that was non-scripted."

IN SHORT:
BENNY WAS GROWING UP.
IN 2005, ALL OF THEM WERE.

"I remember being very free. You're on the other side of the world. You can say anything, you know? It just felt like, 'All right: What if her name *wasn't* Nina?'"

Nina ultimately stayed Nina. But *Heights* didn't stay *Heights.* The removal of Lincoln marks a turning point in the history of the show—and in the maturation of its creators. Tommy thinks that their willingness to cut loose such a huge character demonstrated something important to the producers: "that we were unafraid." They were willing to sacrifice things they loved for the greater good of the show.

It also opened up possibilities for richer and more complex stories. "There was more real estate available," Tommy says.

But what should those stories be?

One shift was already under way. In early versions of the show, Benny followed his mother's advice: He never gave his heart away, just pursued one girl after another. He lived to party. He was "basically the Latin lothario," as Lin puts it. But around this point in the show's development, its creators noticed that they had a more interesting model for Benny.

Chris Jackson laughs when asked about this now. "It's a good question: Where does he end and I begin?"

Bit by bit, Benny was beginning to resemble the actor playing him. He stopped being Latino and became Black. Other Chris-like qualities followed. He focused on his career. No more fantasizing about tricking out his car (which he did in an early version of "96,000"); instead he thought about business school. He didn't go to the club as much. He even put on a tie.

In short: Benny was growing up. In 2005, all of them were, Chris more than most.

Much as he loved performing with the Freestyle guys, it was awful to be half a world away from his family. Veronica had given birth to their son a few months earlier. The financial pressure on them was real, and mounting. "We had no money—like, *none*," he recalls.

Members of Freestyle Love Supreme on tour in Scotland, as seen in the documentary *We Are Freestyle Love Supreme*

"WE HAD ★ NO MONEY— LIKE, NONE."

Chris didn't know what the future held for *In the Heights,* but he didn't want to give up on the show. In Scotland, he got used to seeing Lin on his laptop. "And I'd just walk past him," he says. "I knew what he was working on."

Tommy remembers going for a walk with Lin in Edinburgh, kicking around ideas. They passed through a tunnel covered with graffiti, then came out the other side, someplace in the middle of a very foreign town. One of them said what both of them had been thinking: "Look at where we are, talking about Benny and Nina."

It was the farthest either of them had ever been from home.

WHEN EVERYBODY REUNITED in New York that fall, the time had come to solve, once and for all, a puzzle that had persisted since Wesleyan: Who is Nina Rosario? What does she want?

Up through the version at the O'Neill, she was a successful young woman, thriving (if a little uncomfortable) at her fancy school. Washington Heights was where her real trouble lay: That's where her parents feuded with her brother and where the salon ladies picked on her, called her a gringa, said she couldn't dance. When she left the neighborhood for a prestigious fellowship at the end of the show, her parents were sad, but she seemed relieved.

Now that Lin and Quiara had an opportunity to rethink Nina and make her more than Lincoln's sister and Benny's crush, they contemplated the pressures that face young Latino overachievers. At Wesleyan, Lin had known fellow Latino students— many too many of them—who said they were going to take a little break from school but never came back. Quiara was—is—haunted by a tall stack of folders she had seen on a dean's desk at Yale, composed mainly of files about Latino classmates who were facing one or several difficulties (academic, psychological, family-related, financial) that jeopardized their ability to remain at school.

After the O'Neill, Nina's predicament reversed itself. Washington Heights was still an uncomfortable place for her, but it was much less alienating than Stanford, which felt like no home at all. Quiara describes Nina's new

▲ Mandy Gonzalez, who played Nina on Broadway

dilemma this way: "If you get the thing you're going for, and you still don't have a place in the world, does it mean you'll *never* have a place in the world?"

That feeling of dread isn't limited to young overachievers, Latino or otherwise: It's shared by many people who try to, or need to, change their situation. It's part of the burden they carry as they search for a home.

THE THIRD MAJOR SHIFT after the O'Neill wasn't about any one character; it was about all the characters. It went to the heart of what *In the Heights* wanted to be.

That heavy question had come up in Lin and Quiara's get-to-know-you dinner in 2004. "What's the show *about?*" he had asked her. And Quiara had replied, "I think it's about the community, not just one character or one conflict."

She liked the stories that the show was telling at that point—the Lincoln-Benny-Nina love triangle, Lincoln's pursuit of his songwriting dreams—but she felt that the essence of *In the Heights* might be someplace else. A richer story, she thought, would include the full web of relationships among these residents of Washington Heights, whether they be friends, relatives, or neighbors.

Different desires pulled each of the characters in a slightly different direction, but it also seemed to Quiara that they faced a common threat, the oldest New York threat of all: the danger of losing the ground on which they stood. Gentrification didn't factor into the show at all in its Wesleyan incarnation. But by the time Quiara got involved, new money was putting pressure on everyone and everything. Rents were going up; outsiders were moving in. With Lincoln out of the way, they had enough space to grapple with the changed reality of Washington Heights. After the O'Neill, the show would become what Quiara had described to Lin at their dinner: "This is a story about what happens to a community as they rise or fall together."

As a practical matter, *Heights* would tell "a story about three businesses," in Quiara's words. The show would continue to dramatize the Rosarios and their car service. And it would continue to showcase Usnavi and his bodega, the crossroads for all the characters. But it also put new attention on Daniela's salon, which began to feel the same pressure as the rest of the block.

You can measure the scale of the change by Andréa Burns's reaction. When she created the role of Daniela in a 2004 reading, the salon ladies served as comic relief. "This is the party side of the stage," she says. Coming back to the project after the O'Neill, she was surprised to find that Daniela and Carla had gained dramatic weight. Now they needed to make the audience laugh *and* sympathize with their plight.

Andréa didn't know if it would work. "I remember talking to Tommy: Is this going to play? How are we going to do Anatevka?"

She would need the reaction of a paying audience to know the answer. And she wouldn't get one of those for a while.

Three months after Lin and Tommy returned from Edinburgh, Jill, Kevin, and Jeffrey arranged a reading. The producers wanted to see if the members of Voltron had delivered the changes that they had promised. They, too, were going to rise or fall together.

THEY CONTEMPLATED THE PRESSURES THAT FACE YOUNG LATINO OVERACHIEVERS.

No Me Diga

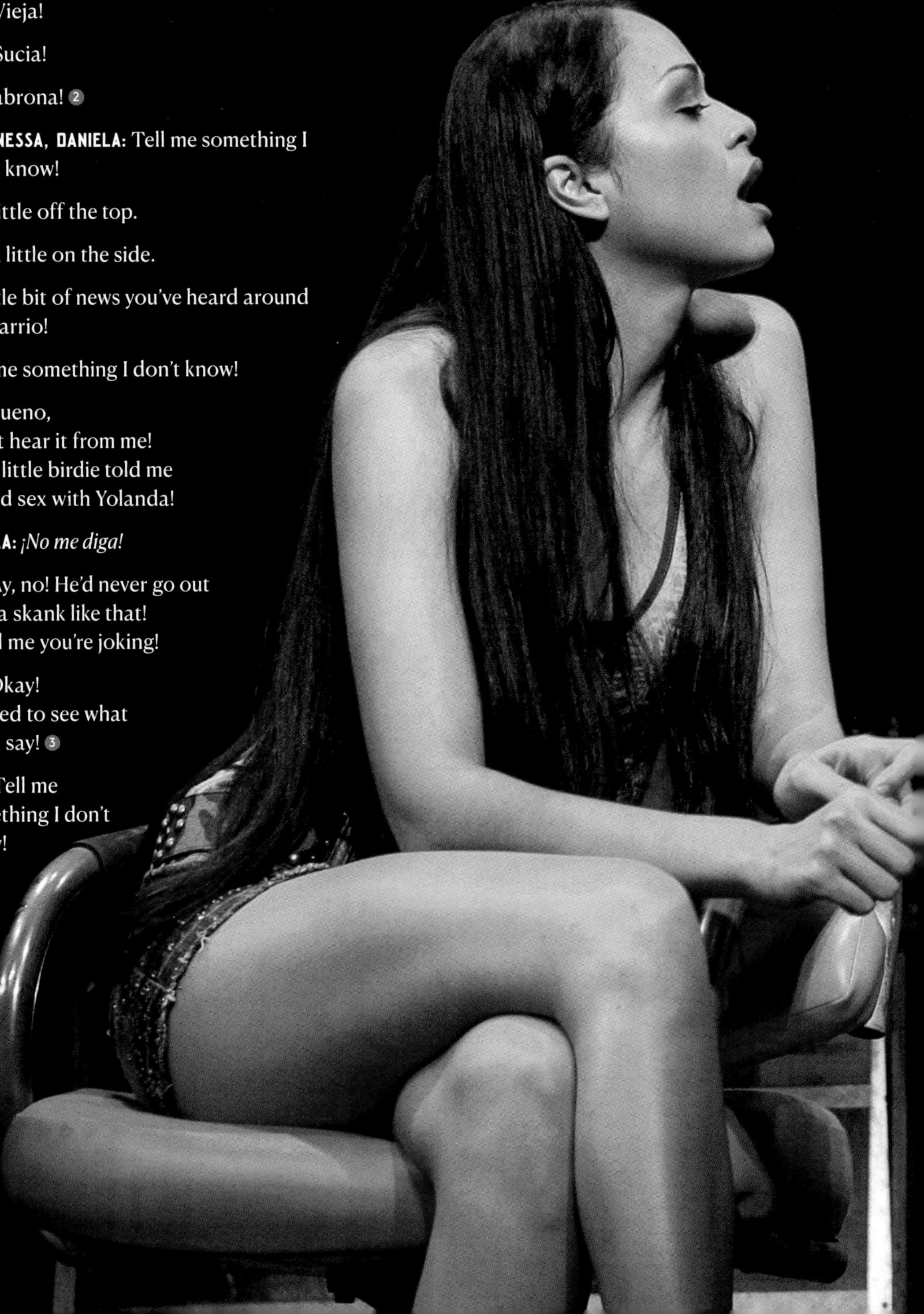

1. My favorite question from a non-Latino amateur production of *Heights:*
"So who's Linda?"
"Who?"
"Y'know, Gorgeous Linda in the salon?"

2. My Abuela Mundi cursed a *blue streak*. The result: I didn't know which words were curse words in Spanish as a kid, regularly scandalizing my elders on my trips to Puerto Rico. I feel like I've passed that karma along by slipping "cabrona" into something that gets done at so many schools.

3. It's always bugged me that this verse has such a subtle punch line: It's a piece of gossip that is a lie. It's funny, and we get a hint of Vanessa's dormant feelings for Usnavi, but I wish it had more of a snap. One day I'll get around to rewriting it.

DANIELA: Gorgeous!

CARLA: ¡Linda! ❶

CARLA, DANIELA: Tell me something I don't know!

VANESSA: ¡Vieja!

DANIELA: ¡Sucia!

CARLA: ¡Cabrona! ❷

CARLA, VANESSA, DANIELA: Tell me something I don't know!

CARLA: A little off the top.

DANIELA: A little on the side.

NINA: A little bit of news you've heard around the barrio!

ALL: Tell me something I don't know!

DANIELA: Bueno,
You didn't hear it from me!
But some little birdie told me
Usnavi had sex with Yolanda!

NINA, CARLA: *¡No me diga!*

VANESSA: Ay, no! He'd never go out with a skank like that!
Please tell me you're joking!

DANIELA: Okay!
Just wanted to see what you'd say! ❸

COMPANY: Tell me something I don't know!

4. Love the innuendo here, and Andréa Burns always sold it by honking that horn break with a firmly planted fist.

5. Here's the real punch line.

CARLA, NINA, DANIELA (AT VANESSA): Mmm-hmm-mmm . . .

VANESSA: *What? I don't care!*

COMPANY: ¡Ay bendito!

DANIELA: So, Nina, I hear you been talking to Benny.

NINA: And what do you hear?

DANIELA: I hear plenty.
They say he's got quite a big . . . taxi! ❹

CARLA, VANESSA: ¡No me diga!

NINA: Okay! I don't wanna know where you heard all that!

CARLA: I don't think I know what you mean . . .

DANIELA: Carla! He's packing a stretch limousine!

(CARLA gets it. They all laugh.)

VANESSA, DANIELA: Tell me something I don't know!

CARLA: Long as he keeps it clean! ❺

NINA, VANESSA, DANIELA: Ay dios mío . . .

(The women hoot and holler.)

DANIELA: Nina, seriously, we knew you'd be the one to make it out!

VANESSA: I'll bet you impressed them all out west, you were always the best,
No doubt!

CARLA: We want front-row seats to your graduation—

DANIELA: They'll call your name—

DANIELA, CARLA, VANESSA: And we'll scream and shout!

(They cheer for NINA. The music stops.)

NINA: *You guys, I dropped out.*

DANIELA, CARLA, VANESSA: *¿¡No me diga?!*

NINA: *I should go.*

(Nina exits.)

DANIELA: *That's a shitty piece of news.*

CARLA: *That girl never quit anything.*

VANESSA: *What the hell happened?*

DANIELA: *I don't know . . .*

DANIELA, CARLA: *I don't know.*

DANIELA: *I don't know!*

CARLA, VANESSA: Tell me something I don't know!

COMPANY: ¿Qué sé yo?

The SALON LADIES

By QUIARA ALEGRÍA HUDES

FROM THE MOMENT Lin and I met, I pitched him on a lens of strong women and female empowerment. He was game and a half. He was already composing "It Won't Be Long Now" and "Paciencia y Fe," so it was clear that ambitious young women and strong matriarchs were at his core. I was jazzed to flood the piece with resilient, hilarious, and brilliant mujeres like my primas y tías in the 215. I'm so over the stereotype of the fiery Latina, the gorgeous bombshell. Get real. Walk into any barrio salon and you see something much more grounded, working-class, down-to-earth, and actually beautiful. You see girls getting ringlets and updos for special occasions like quinceañeras or sweet sixteens. You see white-collar professionals getting blowouts because frizz is "unprofessional." You see curl grrrls who are all about their hair's natural texture. My worst nightmare of the salon was that it would become a lie, a male fantasy.

On Broadway, Andréa Burns's Daniela was whip-smart, confident, no-nonsense, and a warm leader. She and Janet Dacal, who played Carla, grew extremely close during the process. Janet developed a version of Carla that was easygoing, bubbleheaded, and guileless. Onstage, they gave the impression of two women who'd worked together forever, becoming best friends and foils. It was a vision of feminine friendship I loved.

During tech at the Richard Rodgers Theatre on Broadway, oh man, I wept watching Andréa rehearse "Carnaval del Barrio." Tommy and Andy, our director

and choreographer, were spacing out the actors onstage so Howeil Binkley could light them properly. Tech involves repeating a moment over and over until the light on every actor is perfect. *Go back and do it again* so this spotlight and that sidelight can be adjusted. The repetition can be tedious. There's a moment six minutes into the song where the tonality turns minor and gets this intense call-to-arms vibe. Andréa stood so powerfully in that moment, singing over and over, "Esa bonita bandera contiene mi alma entera." *That beautiful flag contains my entire soul.* I could sense history and struggle behind her delivery—a woman who faced many obstacles and hurdles holding her ground and insisting: I am not ashamed, I will not cower, I am proud. In that moment, Lin's lyrics, Andréa's reality, and Daniela's story seemed to merge into a single resilience-love. A love honed and strengthened by struggle. I still get chills at that part of the song.

ONSTAGE, OUR SALON had five or six people in it, max. For the movie, we had the chance to populate it big-time. Make it a real crammed-in hub. I wanted to create a nexus of diverse feminism and a queer-friendly haven. Every body shape, hair type, skin tone should be in those chairs. Multiple approaches to beauty would be welcomed by Daniela, making her a down-to-earth leader and kick-butt business-woman. Traditional femme, earthy and natural, androgynous, butch, or super made-up—Daniela would help all clients achieve their vision for looking fly.

When I cut the character of Camila (Nina's mom) for the movie, one of the unintended consequences was losing the community's married couple. I worried that an audience would say all eleven leads came from "broken homes" and how that might play into old, tired stereotypes. So I decided to make Daniela and Carla our

> MY WORST NIGHTMARE OF THE SALON WAS THAT IT WOULD BECOME A LIE, A MALE FANTASY.

married couple. I was nervous bringing the idea to Lin, but he was like, HELL YES! During principal photography, we ran out of time to film Daniela and Carla waking up together in the opening number. So we lost our scripted visual to establish their marriage. Lin and I were both like, "No! We cannot be subtle about this; we want it to be clear in the movie that they're our 'traditional' family!" So in February 2020, months after we'd wrapped shooting, we were able to film this shot of them waking up together in the morning. We returned to the block in Washington Heights where we had spent all summer. It was cold now. No leaves on the trees. But it was good to be home.

As I adapted the salon for the screenplay, I craved more women, more gossip, more humor, more chaos, more world-views! Cuca was born, an interloping third wheel and foil to the couple dynamic of Daniela and Carla. Dascha Polanco brought an eruption of unapologetic joy to the role. She's a walking party and has the kind of vibrancy that nail and hair clients would line up for.

FOR ME PERSONALLY, LOOKING BACK AT MY CAREER, THE FILM VERSION OF THE SALON IS VERY FULL CIRCLE.

I told casting and costuming over and over: This has to be believably working class. These women work for ten hours on their feet. This is physical labor, not some fashion spread. So put the employees in comfortable shoes, please. I was truly paranoid that the women in my family would see some stiletto-wearing nail techs and get pissed, like, "You know that ain't real! You failed us, Qui Qui!" (That's my family nickname, Qui Qui.) So Daniela wears platform espadrilles. Vanessa changes out of her morning heels for work sneakers. And Cuca rocks these Liberace-style poofy house slippers.

When I see what Jon Chu and Chris Scott (the choreographer) and his team did with "No Me Diga" . . . when I see the actors and dancers, how they're costumed . . . it is one of my favorite visions of Latinx womynhood. It's alive and unapologetic. It's not about chasing an impossible, harmful beauty standard. These women take up space. They are unafraid to be their version of beautiful. I wrote some of

the diversity into the scene before "No Me Diga": a cranky vieja and a drag queen. But casting and choreography populated this vision more fully. I love the little boy who hangs out—so real. They cover his ears when the talk gets too fresh, but he savors being part of their world.

At the end, when the salon gets priced out of the neighborhood, the block loses more than just a business. It's a loss of vivacious grrrlhood, of womynhood in all its delicious messiness. It's a loss of a local news source. It's a loss of intergenerational teaching from the neighborhood's matriarchs. These intangible treasures, so easily erased . . .

For me personally, looking back at my career, the film version of the salon is very full circle. As a professional and a job creator, I relate to Daniela. I'm proud of my career and in particular the roles I've written as a playwright. I try to create good jobs for great actors. Stephanie Beatriz and I met in 2005 when she starred in my play *Yemaya's Belly* and reunited soon after for my play *The Adventures of Barrio Grrrl!* We came up together on shoestring budgets, honing our craft, two twenty-somethings giddy about our dreams. Back then, the sky was the limit! Years later, after I'd established myself, Daphne Rubin-Vega (Daniela in the film) starred in my play *Daphne's Dive* and then my musical *Miss You Like Hell*. We had both racked up career successes and hit our share of roadblocks. We found strength in our accomplishments and yet could be honest with each other about the costs of a theater career. In the industry, we often felt like outsiders. But in the industry, we also found and created communities that sustained us. The first time Jon Chu let me into editing and I saw an early rough cut of "No Me Diga," I saw two actors who've been there with me through a lot of life and creativity. I'm proud of the long arc of our work.

Daniela is at the epicenter, brow-threading a CRANKY
VIEJA.

> CRANKY VIEJA
> I'm too old and the Bronx is too
> far.

> DANIELA
> ¿Que puedo hacer? I was priced
> out y no soy la primera. Mosta my
> regulars already moved to Grand
> Concourse. Hey, built-in
> customers.

A RECEPTIONIST gets her nails done.

> RECEPTIONIST
> My lunch break isn't long enough
> for the trip, Dani.

> DANIELA
> One: Swipe the fare card. Two:
> Ride three stops. Three: Arrive
> at my new location. Ten minutes,
> max!

Cuca pats a wax strip onto A DRAG QUEEN'S upper lip.

> DRAG QUEEN
> Ten minutes? What are you riding,
> a time machine?

> DANIELA
> Our people survived slave ships.
> We survived Taino genocide. We
> survived conquistadores and
> dictators!
> (MORE)

(CONTINUED)

I TOLD CASTING AND COSTUMING OVER AND OVER: THIS HAS TO BE BELIEVABLY WORKING CLASS. THESE WOMEN WORK FOR TEN HOURS ON THEIR FEET.

IN THE HEIGHTS - Rev. 5/29/19 (Pink)   45.
CONTINUED: (2)
> DANIELA (CONT'D)
> You telling me we won't survive
> the D train to Grand Concourse?!

CHAPTER

Eight

I CAN'T STOP DANCING

ONE DAY IN LATE 2006, the distinctive sights of Washington Heights (the bodega awnings, the tenement facades, the George Washington Bridge), having been mashed flat, were lowered from a theater's mezzanine to the orchestra seats below.

▲ Lin-Manuel Miranda and Anna Louizos

It was an unusual thing to see. (Ever seen *your* neighborhood carried around this way?) It was also a sign of progress. The producers, encouraged by Lin and Quiara's rewrites, felt the show was ready to try its final ascent to Broadway. For most new musicals, that means doing an out-of-town tryout or producing the show at one of New York's nonprofit theaters. But Jill, Kevin, and Jeffrey chose a different path to the summit. After an intensive four-week workshop, they decided to mount a commercial production Off-Broadway. In other words: They would do it themselves.

Jeffrey and Kevin were among the owners of a new multistage complex, 37 Arts. It was so new that construction dust was still settling when the show moved in; it was so new that things like loading in the set became a voyage of discovery. (The scenery had to be hoisted up through the lobby atrium before it could be lowered via the mezzanine.)

The first preview was scheduled for January 9, 2007. Critics would review the show a month after that. Those rapidly approaching deadlines meant that Voltron was far removed from the endless brainstorming of the bookstore basement. Lin and Quiara kept trying to solve the remaining story puzzles, and Lac and Bill kept refining

62

the arrangements. But a new set of dilemmas arose now, about the look and feel of what would happen onstage.

Tommy says his approach was very simple: "I wanted it to feel like real life."

Which begs a question. *Lots* of questions.

Musicals are, by nature, preposterous deviations from real life. That's why we enjoy them. Tommy and the creative team needed to reconcile the actual place they wanted to depict onstage with the fantastical nature of the musical form. More important, they had to do it in a way that suited the tastes, talents, and histories of the artists involved.

The hope was that each would bring out the best in the others—and do it in the rapidly dwindling weeks before a paying audience arrived.

EVEN NOW, ANNA LOUIZOS remembers how proud Lin was to show her around Washington Heights. She wanted to see the places where he had grown up as research for her scenic design, and he was excited to share them. Nobody recognized him on their tour: "He was just another kid from the neighborhood."

She was struck by the distinctive beauty of the place. While many New York neighborhoods had been remade in glass and steel, the residents of Washington Heights had preserved a remarkably high percentage of its prewar buildings. She marveled at the pediments and keystones, the cornices and quoining—block after block of flourishes in stone and brick. "That's what gave those buildings character," she says.

Arrayed onstage at 37 Arts, her set included familiar touches from Washington Heights, but reimagined in all sorts of inventive ways to suit the stylized world of musical theater. By exaggerating the perspective of the buildings, she made the neighborhood feel taller and denser; by using scrim for the upper parts of the walls, she let the audience glimpse people moving inside. The translucent backdrop of the bridge and the horizon completed the effect—at once real and ethereal.

She was also mindful of the people who lived in these buildings—not just today, but in generations past. She created a sign for Rosario's Car and Limousine. But behind

"I WANTED IT TO FEEL LIKE REAL LIFE." ★★★

that sign, the audience can glimpse an older one, for O'Hanrahan's Car and Limousine. It was her way of commemorating the Irish phase of the neighborhood's life. Above those signs, painted on the brick itself, is a still *older* sign, for a bakery, to honor the German Jewish immigrants who were the first to call many of these buildings home.

To realize her vision for the neighborhood, Anna had to make clever use of the playing space at 37 Arts. Unlike most comparably sized theaters, this one had only a single way for the actors to get on and off the stage: a staircase leading down from the playing area at stage left. She found a way to incorporate it into the onstage neighborhood, one so true to life it was practically a sight gag: She re-created the entrance to the 181st Street A train stop.

PAUL TAZEWELL didn't need a tour of Washington Heights: He lived there. The characters in the show reminded him of characters in his community—that was his first reaction to the material. His second was: *I know exactly where to shop for this.*

Because *Heights* is a contemporary show, and because his budget wasn't vast, Paul gathered most of the costumes from stores all around town. This being a musical, the clothes had to fulfill very specific functions. They needed to be vibrant, durable, and in colors that would set an emotional tone for each scene. This made them difficult to find. But he let the characters guide his steps. He shopped for the salon ladies' costumes in stores that Daniela and Carla might really have access to.

THE TOP OF THE WORLD

PART ONE

A look inside the creative process of **ANNA LOUIZOS**, Broadway scenic designer

ROUGH NEIGHBORHOOD LAYOUT
(EARLY IDEA FOR SHOW CURTAIN)

O HANRAHANS
LIMOSINE SERVICE

O'HANRAHAN'S RELIABLE CAR SERVICE
212-679154

Rosario's **CAR AND LIMOUSINE**
TEL. 212
555-0824
DEPENDABLE | SERVICIO DE TAXI | ECONOMICAL

Rosario's **CAR AND LIMOUSINE**
TEL. 212
555-0824
DEPENDABLE | SERVICIO DE TAXI | ECONOMICAL

2'-0"

7'-0"

D3/8   REMOVABLE SIGN
SCALE: 1" = 1'-0"

FOUND DOG
CALL 212-555-2436
MEDIUM BLACK
DOG WITH WHITE
SPOTS
FOUND AT 185TH ST. &
WADSWORTH

FOUND DOG
CALL 212-555-2436
CALL 212-555-2436
MEDIUM BLACK
DOG WITH WHITE
SPOTS
FOUND AT 185TH ST. &
WADSWORTH

"HE WAS JUST ANOTHER KID FROM THE NEIGHBORHOOD."

▼ Paul Tazewell

Paul drew inspiration from his neighbors coming and going on 187th Street, but he also learned from the *Heights* cast. More than any other show Paul had worked on, with the possible exception of *Bring in 'Da Noise, Bring in 'Da Funk*, the *Heights* actors lived in the same stylistic world as their characters. He watched what the actors wore to rehearsals, especially the dancers. "They live with their bodies— they know what works best," he says. Rickey Tripp didn't move the same way as Michael Balderrama; Nina Lafarga didn't have the same style as Asmeret Ghebremichael or Rosie Lani Fiedelman. Paul didn't impose the aesthetic of Washington Heights on the company; he refracted it through each artist who called this version of the neighborhood home.

This approach explains the most distinctive costume element in the show: Usnavi's Kangol hat. Paul laughs when asked about it. "Lin used to wear that hat to rehearsal all the time."

LONG BEFORE THE SHOW moved into 37 Arts, Lin could hear its variety and energy in his head: "I want it to sound like walking down Broadway from 185th Street to 175th," he had told Bill.

Nevin Steinberg had loved that musical kaleidoscope from the first time he'd heard it in the bookstore basement. Now that the show was finally ready for a sound designer, he had to make sure the audience would hear all the nuance in the Latin, pop, hip-hop, and traditional Broadway songs.

This was, he discovered, "an impossible task."

In many respects, *Heights* was a traditional musical, a form that usually puts lyrics front and center in the sound mix. But Lin's score tapped into styles that didn't lend themselves to exquisite clarity in every syllable. Nevin didn't come up with some revolutionary solution, he says now: "I just became slightly maniacal about it." Once technical rehearsals started—that is, once the actors started wearing Paul's costumes on Anna's set, in the hectic final days before the first preview—he tuned and re-tuned the sound system, imagining the experience of each of the four hundred audience members.

He also became intensely protective of the show. "I felt like the guardian of something," he says. As one of the most experienced people in the room, and the one with the longest relationship with the producers, Nevin took it on himself to work with Jason Bassett, the production stage manager, and Casey Hushion, the assistant director, to do everything possible to help the show succeed. Which really meant helping its young director succeed.

Tommy was only a few years into his career. He had never run tech for a show at this scale. "You look for the adult in the room, and you realize it's you," he says.

Today, after more than a decade of experience with shows large and small, Tommy doesn't approach tech all that differently than he did back then. "The big difference is that I'm able to quiet any of the noise around my instincts sooner," he says. "I trust them more deeply now— and fully, and quickly."

Whatever audiences might think of the show, no one could say that Tommy hadn't done his homework.

To prepare to direct his first big musical, he had availed himself of the Library for the Performing Arts at Lincoln Center, which maintains a video archive of significant Broadway productions dating back decades.

"I watched every musical that had won the Tony for the last twenty-five years," Tommy says.

He also watched the shows that didn't win Best Musical but could have, like *Dreamgirls*.

He also watched every show that had won Best Play.

"I actually won an award from the library because I watched so many," he says, smiling at his youthful hyper-diligence. "I won an *award*."

EVOKING THE ACTUAL SIGHTS and sounds of Washington Heights got Tommy part of the way toward the realism he wanted. But he also imagined a thrum of activity all around the stage, "like life was happening everywhere." That's what New York's streets are like. That's why we enjoy them.

Tommy's partner in setting the show whirling was Andy Blankenbuehler. At the time, he had a string of Broadway credits as a dancer but hadn't yet made a name for himself as a choreographer. Andy recalls an early meeting—a job interview, essentially—with Lin, Tommy, and Lac. In retrospect, this was a historic moment: the first-ever meeting of the "Cabinet," the quartet of collaborators who would one day make *Hamilton*. It did not feel historic at the time.

"All they did was talk about *The West Wing*," Andy recalls. He sat there drinking his Starbucks and thinking, *I've never seen* The West Wing. *This is not going to go well for me.*

It didn't. They picked somebody else. But when that didn't work out, they called him.

You might recall from stories about *Hamilton* that Andy was a driven, relentless force of creation, bursting with ideas, exacting in the expectations he placed on the cast.

"YOU LOOK FOR THE ADULT IN THE ROOM, AND YOU REALIZE IT'S YOU."

That Andy is the mellow, easy-to-please version of the Andy who choreographed *Heights*.

"It was like working with a mad scientist," says Stephanie Klemons, who collaborated with him on both shows. "He was legit twenty times more intense."

Consider the circumstances: He had to prove himself as a choreographer, he had to catch up with Voltron (the shorthand, the in-jokes), he had to recover from knee surgery (bad for anyone, worse for dancers), he had to get by without much money, and on top of everything else, he had to manage his concern for his wife during a very difficult pregnancy (a month of bed rest at the hospital, his nightly visit after tech).

So yes, Andy was in a focused frame of mind. But some of his intensity had nothing to do with his circumstances and everything to do with how he thinks about his craft: that it really is "life or death."

"It's not just a show. I mean, it's a show. But if we're telling a good story, it really has to change people's lives. The audience should not have a hard time suspending their disbelief. We have to figure out how to transport them. When I drive myself so hard, it's because I know when we're only at an eighty-five or a ninety-two."

He also knew what he didn't know. He asked Luis Salgado to assist him on choreographing the Latin dances in the show. (Luis began his dancing life in Vega Alta, Puerto Rico—the Miranda hometown. He used to buy his pencils from Lin's aunt.) A storytelling vocabulary began to emerge. Reinterpreted forms of hip-hop dance would pervade the show, but the Latin dances would be reserved for situations where characters might really dance salsa or bomba or plena.

For Andy, much like the characters in the show, fitting into a new space didn't always come easily. He didn't immediately see how he could situate his expansive dances within the tight quarters of Anna's set.

"It taught me a huge, great lesson. You have to put parameters in your way to make honest choices," he says now.

"There is no open football field in Manhattan. There are subway entrances and street corners and rushing taxis. Things like the subway pole to go down the steps—that's real life. A doorway to go into a bodega is real life. And so

that made me stop choreographing dance steps and made me start choreographing honest ideas for those characters."

It's another way of recognizing an underappreciated fact of life: We exert ourselves and shape the spaces around us, but all the while they are shaping us right back. Tommy and the team had created something sufficiently like a city to make people behave the way they do in a city: the dodging and weaving, the steady improvisation. Andy didn't have the reference in mind, but the adjustment he described sounds like a paraphrase of one of the great celebrations ever offered of city living.

To the legendary urbanist Jane Jacobs, the intricacy of a crowded city sidewalk was its own art form, a special kind of dance: not "a simple-minded precision dance with everyone kicking up at the same time, twirling in unison and bowing off en masse, [but] an intricate ballet in which the individual dancers and ensembles all have distinctive parts which miraculously reinforce each other and compose an orderly whole."

We came to work and to live and we got a lot in common . . .

WITH THE DESIGNERS, the actors, and Voltron—a sextet now that Andy had joined them—all doing their parts, the stage started to look like a functional distillation of an actual corner in the Heights. But in one case, the realism turned out to be a little too real.

In Act One, the news that somebody has bought a winning lottery ticket brings almost all the characters onstage to fantasize about that unimaginable windfall: $96,000. At 37 Arts, the song faded at the end, and the characters turned and walked offstage. Which is usually what happens when people wrap up a conversation.

To the producers, the song cried out for a big finish, a "button" that would thrill the audience. The creative team didn't disagree. "It undersold itself," Quiara says. "It underplayed its hand." They just couldn't figure out how to fix it, not in the days left until the first paying customers arrived, not with so many other things they were still learning how to do.

For his opening night gift, Tommy would give Lin a bag of buttons. "Because it felt like none of our numbers ended," he says.

96,000

1. Why $96,000? It's not enough money to permanently change someone's life . . . it's just enough to get a little breathing room. Which is all any of us really wants, at the end of the day.

I also think the number ninety-six represents a socioeconomic divide in my head: I went to school on Ninety-fourth Street, and Ninety-sixth Street was the dividing line between the Upper East Side and East Harlem. The same McDonald's cheeseburger was more expensive on Eighty-sixth Street than it was on 106th Street. I crossed that line from uptown every day to go to school. So I think, subconsciously, the number ninety-six has a wealth-line connotation for me.

2. The first verse of this song is probably the one most influenced by our hip-hop improv group, Freestyle Love Supreme. I really wanted this to feel like the characters are making up lyrics impromptu. There are few places in musicals where you're really aware that the characters themselves are lyricists: Sweeney and Mrs. Lovett singing "A Little Priest" comes to mind.

3. The original lyric in the stage version referred to D-nald T—p, back when he was a cartoon version of a rich man for the working class. He had a board game, books, and his name on a bunch of New York buildings. Now his name connotes some of the most shameful/saddest chapters of our country's young history, so in the movie version, we swapped him out.

4. Another note on these pop culture references: Being firmly aware that pop culture references date really quickly (I remember reading the libretto to *Godspell* in high school and not understanding literally two-thirds of the jokes), I gave myself a hundred-year rule: Don't reference it if we won't still be talking about it in a hundred years. Frodo. Pinocchio. Big Pun. Y'know, forever sh—.

5. The joke here being that Graffiti Pete is flipping a hacky/racial old joke ("more chins than Chinatown"—I think I first heard this in a Weird Al lyric) and using it *wrong*—Ho isn't a popular Japanese last name at all; Pete can't even racism right. Anyway, I wanted a really *wrong* punch line here so Usnavi would react quickly and efficiently to shut him up. It doesn't age well. In the movie, we swapped it out for "I got more flows than Obi-Wan Kenobi, yo," which I like better, because it feels like he's riffing off Benny's Frodo reference but got the wrong sci-fi/fantasy franchise.

6. This is a very Pharcyde-influenced punch line. I also like hanging a lantern on the fact that it *isn't that much money*, but it's enough to dream.

USNAVI: Ninety-six thousand . . . ①

SONNY, BENNY: Damn . . . ②

USNAVI: Ninety-six thousand . . .

(Holding a Slurpee, GRAFFITI PETE pokes his head in.)

SONNY: Dollars? Holler.

USNAVI: Ninety-six thousand . . .

GRAFFITI PETE: Yo, somebody won!

USNAVI: Ninety-six thousand . . .

BENNY: Yo.
If I won the Lotto tomorrow
Well I know I wouldn't bother goin'
    on no
Spendin' spree.
I'd pick a business school and pay the
    entrance fee!
Then maybe if you're lucky, you'll stay
    friends with me!
I'll be a businessman, richer than
    Nina's daddy!
Tiger Woods ③
And I on the links and he's my caddie!
My money's makin' money, I'm goin'
    from po' to mo' dough!
Keep the bling, I want the brass ring
    like Frodo!

USNAVI: Oh no, there goes Mr.
    Braggadocio.
Next thing you know, he's lying like
    Pinocchio— ④

BENNY: Well, if you're scared of the bull, stay out the rodeo!

GRAFFITI PETE: Yo, I got more hos than a phone book in Tokyo! ⑤

USNAVI: Ooh, you better stop rappin', you're not ready.
It's gonna get hot and heavy, and you're already sweaty—

GRAFFITI PETE: Y-y-yo-yo

USNAVI: I'm sorry, is that an answer?
Shut up, go home, and pull ya damn
    pants up!
As for you, Mr. Frodo of the Shire—
Ninety-six g's ain't enough to retire.

BENNY: I'll have enough to knock your
    ass off its axis!

USNAVI: You'll have a knapsack full of
    jack after taxes! ⑥

(SONNY runs to ABUELA CLAUDIA.)

SONNY: Ninety-six thousand!

ABUELA CLAUDIA (CROSSES HERSELF): *¡Ay,
    alabanza!*

(ABUELA CLAUDIA disappears into her
apartment. SONNY runs to the salon.)

SONNY: Ninety-six thousand!

DANIELA: *¡No me diga!*

SONNY: Ninety-six thousand!

VANESSA: *I never win shit!*

SONNY: Ninety-six thousand!

(CARLA and DANIELA come out to the street.)

BENNY: For real, though, imagine how it
    would feel goin' real slow,
Down the highway of life with no
    regrets
And no breakin' your neck for respect
    or a paycheck.
For real, though, ⑦
I'll take a break from the wheel and
    we'll
Throw
The biggest block party, everybody
    here.
It's a weekend when we can breathe,
    take it easy . . .

WOMEN, MAN: Yo! Ma, it's me, check my
    tickets!

7. In my own personal journey of Writing to
Chris Jackson's Voice, I think this refrain
is probably my biggest breakthrough. "For
real, though . . ." is something Chris just
naturally says (alongside "That's what's
up"), and building on that to create a whole
picture was great fun.

CARLA: Check one two three ⑧
What would you do with ninety-six g's—

DANIELA: Who, me?

CARLA: I mean if it's just between you and me—

DANIELA: ¡Esa pregunta es tricky!

CARLA: I know—

DANIELA: With ninety-six g's
I'd start my life with a brand-new lease,
Atlantic City with a Malibu Breeze—

CARLA: And a brand-new weave—

DANIELA: Or maybe just bleach.

VANESSA: *Y'all are freaks.*

USNAVI: Yo, I'm just saying it's silly when we get into these crazy hypotheticals.
You really want some bread, then go ahead, create a set of goals
And cross them off the list as you pursue 'em,
And with those ninety-six I know precisely what I'm doin'. ⑨

VANESSA: What you doin'?

USNAVI: What'm I doin'? What'm I doin'?
It takes most of that cash just to save my ass from financial ruin.
Sonny can keep the coffee brewin', and I'll spend a few on you
Cuz the only room with a view's a room with you in it.
And I could give Abuela Claudia the rest of it.
Just fly me down to Puerta Plata, I'll make the best of it.
You really love this business?

SONNY: No.

USNAVI: Tough, Merry Christmas.
You're now the youngest tycoon in Washington Hiznits.

SONNY: *Yo!*
With ninety-six thousand, I'd finally fix housin',
Give the barrio computers and wireless web browsin'.
Your kids are livin' without a good edumacation,
Change the station, teach 'em about gentrification.
The rent is escalatin' ⑩

GRAFFITI PETE: What?

SONNY: The rich are penetratin'

GRAFFITI PETE: What?

SONNY: We pay our corporations when we should be demonstratin'

GRAFFITI PETE: What?

SONNY: What about immigration?

GRAFFITI PETE: What?

SONNY: Politicians be hatin'

GRAFFITI PETE: What?

SONNY: Racism in this nation's gone from latent to blatant!

GRAFFITI PETE, MEN: Oooooh!

SONNY: I'll cash my ticket and picket, invest in protest,
Never lose my focus till the city takes notice.
And you know this, man! ⑪
I'll never sleep
Because the ghetto has a million promises for me to keep!

(A stunned silence. VANESSA kisses SONNY on the cheek.)

VANESSA: *You are so cute!*

SONNY: *I was just thinking off the top of my head.*

USNAVI: *Ninety-six K. Go.*

VANESSA: If I win the lottery, you'll never see me again.

USNAVI: Damn, we're only jokin', stay broke then.

VANESSA: I'll be downtown,
Get a nice studio, get out of the barrio.

VANESSA:	BENNY:
If I win the lottery,	For real, though, imagine how it would feel
You'll wonder where I've been.	Goin' real slow, Down the highway of life With no regrets And no breakin' your neck For respect or a paycheck—

8. I tried to trace the origins of "check one two three," a hip-hop trope, but I fell so far down the rabbit hole. It's been memorably done by the Fugees, Black Star, KRS-One (probably the earliest), and many others.

9. It's fun to change Usnavi's flow. He's so *methodical* when he's just talking to his friends—rat-a-tat, every sixteenth note. Then Vanessa comes in, and he's all over the place, as syncopated as possible.

10. Something I always point out with school groups is that Sonny, the youngest character, is the only one who immediately thinks about others in his fantasy. Not just a better life for himself, but a better world. I shudder at how relevant his immigration lyrics have become in recent years, but I still think that's true. The youngest among us will save us.

11. "And you know this, man," is a signature Snoop lyric.

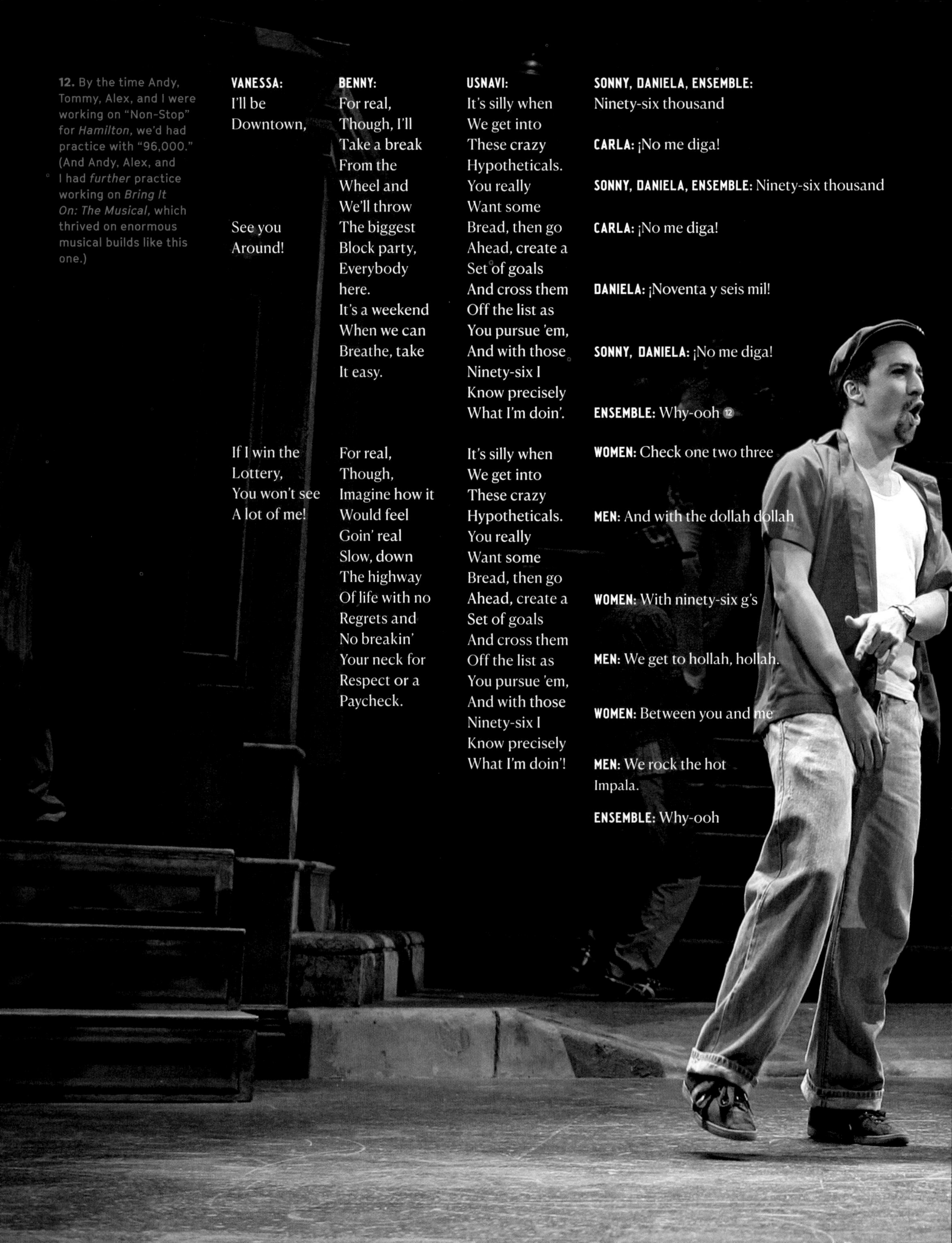

12. By the time Andy, Tommy, Alex, and I were working on "Non-Stop" for *Hamilton*, we'd had practice with "96,000." (And Andy, Alex, and I had *further* practice working on *Bring It On: The Musical*, which thrived on enormous musical builds like this one.)

VANESSA:
I'll be
Downtown,

See you
Around!

If I win the
Lottery,
You won't see
A lot of me!

BENNY:
For real,
Though, I'll
Take a break
From the
Wheel and
We'll throw
The biggest
Block party,
Everybody
here.
It's a weekend
When we can
Breathe, take
It easy.

For real,
Though,
Imagine how it
Would feel
Goin' real
Slow, down
The highway
Of life with no
Regrets and
No breakin'
Your neck for
Respect or a
Paycheck.

USNAVI:
It's silly when
We get into
These crazy
Hypotheticals.
You really
Want some
Bread, then go
Ahead, create a
Set of goals
And cross them
Off the list as
You pursue 'em,
And with those
Ninety-six I
Know precisely
What I'm doin'.

It's silly when
We get into
These crazy
Hypotheticals.
You really
Want some
Bread, then go
Ahead, create a
Set of goals
And cross them
Off the list as
You pursue 'em,
And with those
Ninety-six I
Know precisely
What I'm doin'!

SONNY, DANIELA, ENSEMBLE:
Ninety-six thousand

CARLA: ¡No me diga!

SONNY, DANIELA, ENSEMBLE: Ninety-six thousand

CARLA: ¡No me diga!

DANIELA: ¡Noventa y seis mil!

SONNY, DANIELA: ¡No me diga!

ENSEMBLE: Why-ooh ⑫

WOMEN: Check one two three

MEN: And with the dollah dollah

WOMEN: With ninety-six g's

MEN: We get to hollah, hollah.

WOMEN: Between you and me

MEN: We rock the hot Impala.

ENSEMBLE: Why-ooh

VANESSA:	BENNY:	USNAVI:	WOMEN, MEN:
I'll be Downtown,	For real, Though,	It's silly when We get into These crazy Hypotheticals.	With ninety-six g's
	I'll take a Break from The wheel		MEN: We movin' on Tomorrah.
		You really Want some Bread, Then go ahead, Create a set of Goals	
	And we'll Throw		WOMEN: A brand-new lease
			MEN: We rock beyond Mañana.
See you Around!	The biggest Block party, Everybody Here.	And cross them Off the list as You pursue 'em,	WOMEN: A Malibu Breeze
			MEN: We drop the mama Drama. We stop at the Bahamas!
	It's a weekend When we can Breathe,	And with those Ninety-six	
		I know precisely What I'm doin'!	WOMEN: Why-oh!
Around!	Take it easy. Ooh, whoa, ho!	And with those Ninety-six I Know precisely What I'm doin'!	MEN: We drink piña Coladas! Poppin' lockin'
			WOMEN: Who-oh!
			MEN: Drop it like it's Hot!

WOMEN, MEN: Who-oaa!
Who-oaa!

VANESSA: I'll be downtown!

USNAVI, BENNY, SONNY:	WOMEN, MEN:
We could pay off the debts	Who-oaa!
We owe.	Who-oaa!

VANESSA, CARLA, DANIELA:

We could tell everyone	
We know.	Who-oaa!

USNAVI:

I could get on a plane and	
Go.	Who-oaa!

USNAVI, BENNY, SONNY:
We be swimmin' in
dough,
Yo!

USNAVI, BENNY, SONNY, VANESSA, GRAFFITI PETE, MEN:

No tiptoein'	Who-oaa!
We'll get the dough 'n'	

COMPANY: Once we get goin'
We never gonna
Stop tiptoein'
We'll get the dough 'n'
Once we get goin'
We're never gonna—

PIRAGUA GUY, MAN, BENNY, DANIELA, CARLA, VANESSA:	WOMEN, MEN:	USNAVI, SONNY, GRAFFITI PETE:
Ninety-six thousand	We'll get the dough	Wha'?
Ninety-six thousand	'N'	Wha'? Wha'?
Ninety-six thousand	Once we get goin'	Wha'?
		Wha'?

COMPANY: We'll get the dough 'n'
Once we get goin'
We're never gonna stop!

13. Jon Chu's cinematic translation of the "whisper section" is transcendent to me.

CHAPTER *Nine*

THAT WAS AMAZING

IT TOOK ONLY ONE preview performance for Andréa Burns to feel better. After worrying whether the salon ladies could become more than just comic relief, and generate actual sympathy, she was delighted to find that the audience was right there with them.

"It was really beautiful. I remember people laughing, but they were also so caring," she says of the first performance Off-Broadway. "I got how beloved the salon was."

She wasn't the only one learning lessons. All through the preview period, Voltron watched the audience watch the show. Day after day they fired a volley of changes at the cast and the seven-member band, trying to make the best possible version of what they had created in time for the critics to arrive.

Nobody at 37 Arts was learning more than the audience. It's not easy to convey the sensation now, after more than a decade in which musical theater has gotten more adventurous in both style and subject matter, but *In the Heights* represented a genuine breakthrough in 2007. A couple of them, in fact.

For decades, musical theater had resisted almost every attempt to diversify its sonic palette. Consider Latin

music. Since *West Side Story* in 1957, the salsa wave of the '70s had crested and the Latin explosion of the '90s had remade mainstream pop, but all the Broadway musical had to show for it was sixty-eight performances of Paul Simon's Latin-inflected score for *The Capeman* in 1998. Hip-hop had long since proven to be a powerful, dexterous way of telling stories and had become the shared culture of young people everywhere, but only flickers of it had reached Broadway. No show had integrated rap this completely into its score, or tapped so fully into its storytelling potential, returning theater (if you view it from the right angle) to its ancient roots as verse drama.

Lin's score would have represented a new frontier for musical theater if it had drawn on either of these traditions. It drew on *both*.

Then there was the story that Lin and Quiara were telling. Unlike *West Side Story, Guys and Dolls, My Fair Lady, Oklahoma!, South Pacific, The Phantom of the Opera, Spring Awakening, Rent, Les Misérables,* and *The Who's Tommy,* to cite a few ready examples, *Heights* wasn't an adaptation of an existing book, play, opera, or album. Unlike *Evita, Gypsy,* and *Hamilton,* it wasn't based on a real person's life. Even

Cats was something else before it was *Cats*. *In the Heights* asked its audience to take seriously a completely original story depicting life as it was really lived, right here in the present day, in a neighborhood a couple miles north of where they were sitting.

The show's fusion of new sounds (new for musical theater, anyway) with traditional craft can be heard to best effect in "Paciencia y Fe," the showcase number for the community's matriarch, Abuela Claudia. Musically, the song is a mambo, a form of dance music from Cuba; lyrically, it's an evocative trip back through her memories, all the way to her youth in Havana.

"One of the things I've always been curious about is: Where did that song come from?" asks Jeffrey, more than a decade later. "I did not understand. How can a twenty-four-year-old man write a song about a seventy-five-year-old woman with such heart? You can have that big of a heart at twenty-four, but how do you know so many details about her life that make the song feel so powerful, deep, organic, whole? 'Scrubbing the whole of the Upper East Side'—you know what I mean?"

Lin's answers to Jeffrey's questions can be found in his annotations on pages 88–90. But to appreciate the total effect on audiences at 37 Arts, you have to know about two vital collaborators, both of whom share Abuela Claudia's roots in Cuba.

"BEING CUBAN IS a difficult thing," says Olga Merediz, who played Abuela Claudia at 37 Arts. "It means having to leave everyone behind. Everything you know. Your home, you know?"

She was born in Guantánamo. In 1961, in the aftermath of the revolution, her family was living in Havana. Her parents told their friends that they were taking five-year-old Olga and her brothers on a trip to Jamaica. She brought a suitcase of clothes, but not any toys. They told everybody they'd be gone for the weekend. She didn't see Cuba again for fifty-four years.

"SINGING THAT SONG COSTS ME. I HAVE TO GO THERE."

▲ Alex Lacamoire and Olga Merediz

From Jamaica they went to Miami, from Miami to San Juan. That's where Olga grew up, among other exiles. After college she moved to New York to start a new life as an actor—or at least to try.

"All of that is in 'Paciencia y Fe,'" she says.

The song is long enough, and demanding enough, to challenge anybody who tries to sing it. Finding an actor who had the wherewithal to perform it eight times a week, and was the right age for the role, proved to be a challenge of its own. (Olga wasn't the right age. She needed a gray wig and stooped shoulders to *seem* like she was.) But that doesn't mean it came easily to her.

To prepare to sing the song each night, she had to get into a kind of trance, attaching a memory to each of the lines, all of the sweet and bitter memories. She needed to take the audience on a journey through Claudia's life: the story of losing one home and trying to find another—an experience that Olga knew intimately.

"It's deep for me, and it's painful," she says. "Singing that song costs me. I have to go there. I have to *go there*."

Today she lives in a Midtown apartment: a high floor, lots of sun. She keeps mementos of home. She also has the poster from the show's Off-Broadway run, the one with a foot-high picture of Lin's face. Sometimes she gives him a kiss when she walks by.

ALFREDO AND MARIA came from Cuba, but they didn't meet there. They met in Los Angeles, where they welcomed a son, a boy with curly hair and an intense, even spooky, facility with music. When he was nine, the family moved to Miami. His musicianship impressed people there, too—so much so that when two of his high school acquaintances, Janet Dacal and Henry Gainza, heard that Lin, Tommy, and Bill were looking for a musical collaborator, they mentioned his name: Alex Lacamoire.

The way Lac tells the story, he was originally supposed to be a kind of outside consultant to the project: tabulating his hours, sending invoices to Jill Furman. Jill

has no memory of this, which makes sense, considering Lac had so much fun that he never sent anything.

"I don't remember a handshake, like a 'Hey you're in the band' kind of thing," he says, laughing. "They just kept calling me."

Lac had been working steadily in New York theater since his collaborators were in college. When he joined *Heights* in 2004, he was the associate conductor and pianist on *Wicked*. Lin and Bill would meet him backstage at the Gershwin Theatre. On the way in and out, they got to see how a band comes together, what happens in a Broadway pit. "We learned fundamental 101 shit just by going to meet him at work," Lin says.

Lac brought more than his professionalism to *Heights*: He brought his memories—his roots. "Every Christmas party, every Thanksgiving party, people would be blasting salsa music in Miami," he recalls. Once he started working on the show's Latin music, "all of that stuff started to pop off the page," Bill says. Especially "Paciencia y Fe."

"The fact that it's about a Cuban woman, that my family came from this island, that they started someplace else and had to make a new life—I'm sure all of that history tapped into something for me," says Lac.

He first encountered the song when Lin presented Voltron with an immensely long version of it, tracing Abuela Claudia's whole life in its lyrics. A second, shorter draft brought the song closer to its final length. As Lin talked through what he imagined for the number, Lac played pieces of it, neither of them going all out. A few days later, Lin, Lac, and Bill got together at a rehearsal studio to record a demo version. This was standard procedure for them in 2004. But according to Lac, what happened that day was "total magic."

They decided not to rehearse—Lac was due back at *Wicked* too soon for that. So they just hit record and began.

Listening to the demo now, you know it was just one guy at the piano, and that he had the same ten fingers as most of the rest of us, but what Lac did was virtuosic enough to sound orchestral: a fully realized mambo. Lin

WHAT HAPPENED THAT DAY WAS
"TOTAL MAGIC."

(to borrow Lac's technical term) "sang his ass off." There were plenty of melancholy moments in Abuela Claudia's story, but Lin sounds joyous all the way through.

To Lac, music is a conversation: When Lin left some open space after a lyric, he played a fill—something "salsatastic," Lac says. But even when Lin was singing, Lac pivoted with the changes. On the line that starts, "Sharing double beds," Lin unexpectedly began to sing softly. Lac immediately dropped his volume to keep up with him.

The further they went like this, each feeding the other, the more excited they both got. "It sounds silly, but it felt like playing a videogame," Lac recalls. "You only have one life left, and you're about to save the princess, so your heart starts beating: *Am I going to make it to the end of this in one piece?*"

At the end of four and a half unbroken minutes, Lin belted his last note and sustained it, Lac ran a flourish all the way down the keys, and Bill laughed like crazy. There's no way to know which one of them was clapping in disbelief.

It's not just that Lac had brought Lin's song so vividly to life. And it's not just that each of them was recognizing a kindred creative spirit in the other. They were astonished because Lin hadn't brought fully notated sheet music to the studio that day, just a lyric sheet with the chord symbols written above the lines. All the horn breaks and licks, all the grace notes, every mambo flourish: Lac had made those up on the spot, pulling the ideas from his imagination and a lifetime of absorbing Latin songs.

If you want to hear what excited them all so much, just listen to the song on the cast album: A lot of what the band is playing comes from what Lac improvised that day.

Paciencia y Fe [1]

1. I don't know where "Paciencia y Fe" came from, as a phrase. It's not a catchphrase of my abuela's. But it felt like those words together had their own rhythm. Even the brass sections of this song echo the rhythm of the phrase when you say it aloud. That rhythm guided the writing of this song, which traces Abuela Claudia's life, and those two words, a legacy from her own mother, guide her through this moment. This "Calor, calor, calor" section is an inversion of something my abuela used to sing, but the words to her song were "Amor, Amor, Amor . . ."

2. I've never been to Cuba. I wanted to get some details right, so I called our Cuban family friend John Gutierrez and just asked him a bunch of questions, beginning with, "Which neighborhood in Havana would be the equivalent of Washington Heights—diverse, working class, lots of small businesses?" Almost all his answers from that day are in the song.

3. Why Cassiopeia? Just like the song's title, I like the rhythm of the word. Also, it's the only constellation I know.

ABUELA CLAUDIA: Calor . . . Calor . . . Calor . . .
Calor . . . Calor . . . Calor . . .
¡Ay Mamá!
The summer's hottest day!
¡Paciencia y fe! ¡Paciencia y fe!
Ay, carajo, it's hot!

(She makes the sign of the cross.)

But that's okay!
Mamá would say, "¡Paciencia y fe!"
It was hotter at home in La Víbora,
The Washington Heights of Havana!
A crowded city of faces the same as mine!
Back as a child in La Víbora,
I chased the birds in the plaza [2]
Praying, Mamá, you would find work,
Combing the stars in the sky for some sort of
     sign!
Ay Mamá, so many stars in Cuba . . .
En Nueva York we can't see beyond our
     streetlights . . .
To reach the roof you gotta bribe the supa . . .
Ain't no Cassiopeia [3]
In Washington Heights . . .
But ain't no food in La Víbora . . .

I remember nights, anger in the streets, hunger
     at the windows,
Women folding clothes, playing with my
     friends in the summer rain . . .
Mamá needs a job, Mamá says we're poor, one
     day you say
"Vamos a Nueva York . . ."
And Nueva York was far, but Nueva York had
     work, and so we came . . .

And now, I'm wide awake
A million years too late.
I talk to you, imagining what you'd do,
Remembering what we went through.

(The music swells into a mambo groove. Passersby
on the sidewalk come to life, waving hello to ABUELA
CLAUDIA as they pass.)

¡Nueva York! ¡Ay Mamá!

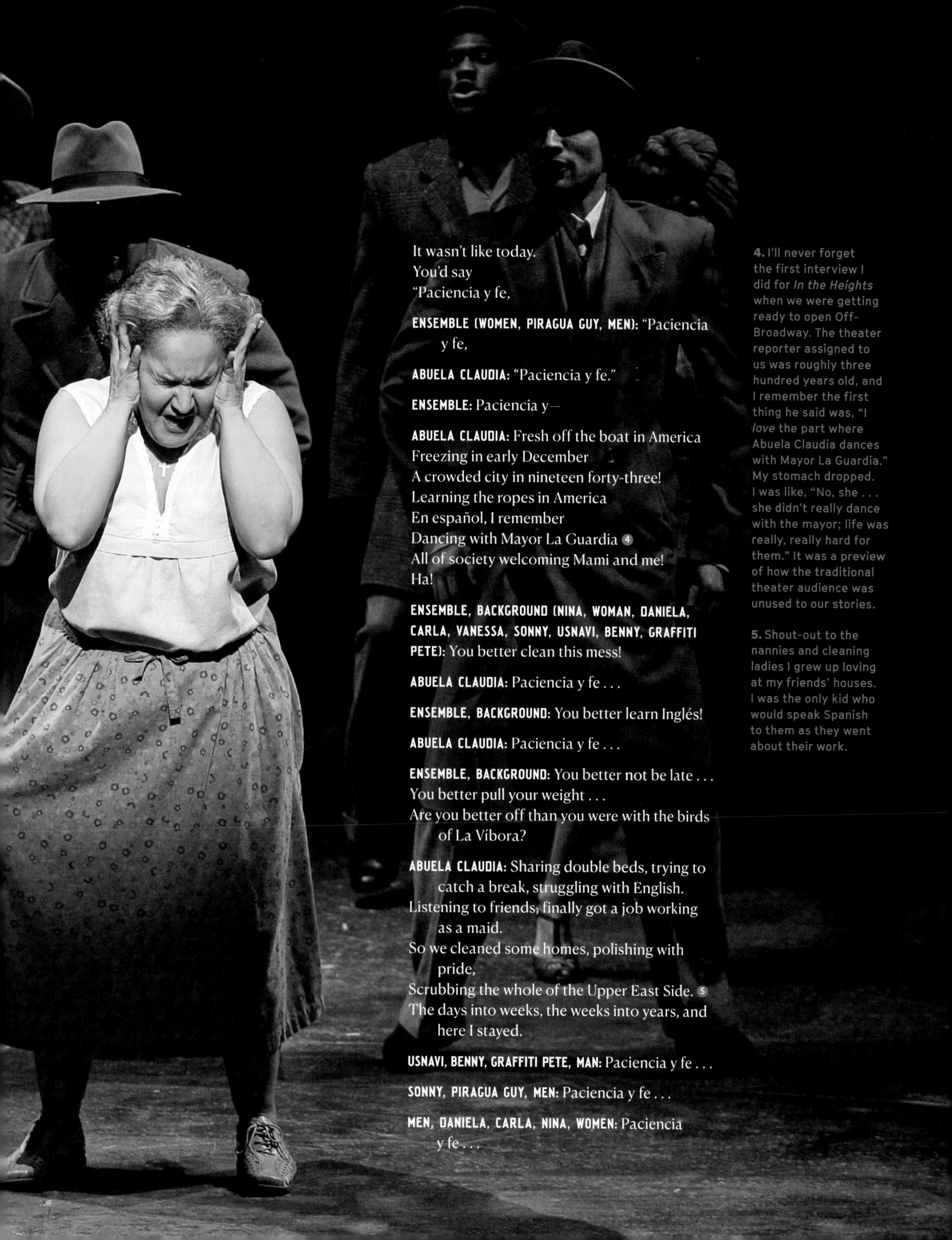

It wasn't like today.
You'd say
"Paciencia y fe,

ENSEMBLE (WOMEN, PIRAGUA GUY, MEN): "Paciencia
    y fe,

ABUELA CLAUDIA: "Paciencia y fe."

ENSEMBLE: Paciencia y—

ABUELA CLAUDIA: Fresh off the boat in America
Freezing in early December
A crowded city in nineteen forty-three!
Learning the ropes in America
En español, I remember
Dancing with Mayor La Guardia ④
All of society welcoming Mami and me!
Ha!

**ENSEMBLE, BACKGROUND (NINA, WOMAN, DANIELA,
CARLA, VANESSA, SONNY, USNAVI, BENNY, GRAFFITI
PETE):** You better clean this mess!

ABUELA CLAUDIA: Paciencia y fe . . .

ENSEMBLE, BACKGROUND: You better learn Inglés!

ABUELA CLAUDIA: Paciencia y fe . . .

ENSEMBLE, BACKGROUND: You better not be late . . .
You better pull your weight . . .
Are you better off than you were with the birds
    of La Víbora?

ABUELA CLAUDIA: Sharing double beds, trying to
    catch a break, struggling with English.
Listening to friends, finally got a job working
    as a maid.
So we cleaned some homes, polishing with
    pride,
Scrubbing the whole of the Upper East Side. ⑤
The days into weeks, the weeks into years, and
    here I stayed.

USNAVI, BENNY, GRAFFITI PETE, MAN: Paciencia y fe . . .

SONNY, PIRAGUA GUY, MEN: Paciencia y fe . . .

MEN, DANIELA, CARLA, NINA, WOMEN: Paciencia
    y fe . . .

4. I'll never forget
the first interview I
did for *In the Heights*
when we were getting
ready to open Off-
Broadway. The theater
reporter assigned to
us was roughly three
hundred years old, and
I remember the first
thing he said was, "I
love the part where
Abuela Claudia dances
with Mayor La Guardia."
My stomach dropped.
I was like, "No, she . . .
she didn't really dance
with the mayor; life was
really, really hard for
them." It was a preview
of how the traditional
theater audience was
unused to our stories.

5. Shout-out to the
nannies and cleaning
ladies I grew up loving
at my friends' houses.
I was the only kid who
would speak Spanish
to them as they went
about their work.

6. Everything comes full circle eventually. The first draft I ever wrote of this song, which took most of the summer of 2004, was Abuela's whole life flashing before her eyes. Fast-forward to the *Heights* film: I'll never forget getting a call from Quiara, who was on set in the 191st Street tunnel, saying, "Lin, watching Olga sing in this tunnel, it really feels like her deathbed song." She was prescient: Months later in the editing room, Jon and Myron Kerstein found that "Paciencia y Fe" worked infinitely better *as* her deathbed song in the film version, which was not how Quiara had initially scripted it. So we're back to where we started in 2004: Her life *is* flashing before her eyes. And these lyrics now read:

> *I made it through, I*
> *survived, I did it.*
> *Now do I leave or*
> *stay?*

7. As you've read in this chapter, this song was much longer in its first draft. I love that it ends with a question on the variation of home—do these birds I feed go home, am I meant to go home? How is La Víbora home after a lifetime here? Do I join them?

ABUELA CLAUDIA: And as I feed these birds
My hands begin to shake.

ABUELA CLAUDIA:
And as I say these
    words
My heart's about
    to break.
And ay Mamá,
What do you do
    when your
Dreams come true?
I've spent my life
Inheriting
Dreams from you.

DANIELA, CARLA, NINA, WOMAN, SONNY, MAN, BENNY, GRAFFITI PETE, USNAVI (OFFSTAGE: WOMEN, PIRAGUA GUY, MAN):
Ooh,

Ooh, ooh,

And ay Mamá!

And ay Mamá
Aah, ah!

(ABUELA CLAUDIA holds up a lottery ticket.)

ABUELA CLAUDIA: What do I do
    with this winning ticket?
What can I do but pray? ⑥

I buy my loaf of bread
Continue with my day.
And see you in my head,
Imagining what you'd say.
The birds, they fly away
Do they fly to La Víbora? ⑦

(She stops and laughs.)

All right, Mamá. Okay!
¡Paciencia y fe!

CARLA, NINA, CAMILA, DANIELA, WOMAN, SONNY, USNAVI, BENNY, GRAFFITI PETE (OFFSTAGE: WOMEN, PIRAGUA GUY, MEN): ¡Calor, calor, calor!

Recuerdo

NÚMERO DOS

OLGA MEREDIZ

ABUELA CLAUDIA IN THE ORIGINAL
OFF-BROADWAY AND BROADWAY CASTS
AND THE FILM VERSION

Singing is so personal. It comes from your soul or you're not doing it correctly, I think. That's why I don't sing that often. [*Laughs*] Because I can't just phone it in. Maybe I should try that! It would be so much easier!

You could never do that with "Paciencia y Fe." The song has so many layers. I tried to give every line a memory of Abuela Claudia's. Because she's an older lady, and when people are old, all they have is memories. I would see my mother daydream at almost ninety-five, moving in and out of the present, going back to Cuba when she was vibrant and young. Abuela Claudia has those memories, too.

When I visited Cuba for the first time, fifty-four years after we fled, I was hoping memories would come back. I had the address of our old house, but the taxi driver didn't understand it—all the names had changed. We asked an old person, who pointed us in the right direction. It looked exactly like the picture I'd brought with me. They'd done no work on it. I knocked on the door, and it opened, and I said, "I used to live here. Would you mind if I looked around?" But no memories came back. You know when you're traumatized, you block things out? I think that's what happened to me. I was so traumatized when my parents and brothers and I had to leave so abruptly that it's just one big black hole for me now.

When I played Abuela onstage, I kept some special things pinned to my bra strap. Like little saints and virgins from my Cuban family. And I wore my father's chain of the Virgin Mary, just to ground that whole Cuban story for myself. I did it for the movie, too. It's under my costume, so you can't see it. But it's there. I know it's there.

CHAPTER Ten

I FELL IN LOVE ON A SATURDAY

QUIARA MET HER HUSBAND, Ray Beauchamp, for dinner at a place around the corner from 37 Arts. She was eager to celebrate having crossed the finish line. Also, being eight months pregnant, she was eager to eat.

A few minutes earlier, the creative team had frozen the show. It meant that after more than three years of revising the script every day, up to literally the last minute (she and Lin lobbing a few final rewrites to Chris Jackson and Mandy Gonzalez for one of the Benny-and-Nina scenes; the stage managers telling them they really, *really* needed to stop), she had no choice but to close her laptop. She had done all she could before the critics arrived, which was going to happen that night. It was January 31, 2007.

After dinner, Ray said goodnight and headed home. Quiara returned to the theater, curious to see if the last-minute changes were going to help. It was cold in New York that night, but Quiara noticed she was beginning to feel warm. She also noticed, looking down at her jeans, that her water had broken.

By now she was nearly back to 37 Arts. Chris Jackson was standing outside.

"Chris," said Quiara.

Chris looked at her legs.

"*Q,*" said Chris.

He ran inside to find Tommy.

"Well," said Quiara a few seconds later, when Tommy emerged, "I guess I'm going to go home."

"Okay," said Tommy. "I'm going to go with you."

She tried to wave him off, but Tommy said—"in his very Tommy way," she recalls—"Quiara, *I'm going to go with you.*"

Later she would reflect that her body "literally unclenched after freezing the show—my body was ready to move on with life." But she did not have that calm perspective as the taxi zoomed up Tenth Avenue.

"Whoa!" Quiara said, feeling some strange new sensation.

"What's happening!" Tommy said.

"A lot's happening!" she replied.

Tommy walked her into her apartment. She and Ray left soon afterward for the hospital. "I knew after that, Quiara and I were going to be siblings," Tommy says.

A few hours later, after the critics had come and gone, the actors were taking off their makeup when they got the news: Quiara's daughter, Cecilia, had joined the family.

PEOPLE IN SHOW BUSINESS love to talk about family. They say things like, "We really became a family on this play" (or movie, or series, or whatever). Custom demands it, the way it demands that a doctor, syringe in hand, say, "You'll feel a slight pinch," or that you, smiling your best smile, tell a friend the new haircut looks great. A more honest answer might be bad form.

In some respects, there's no avoiding the language of family when describing *In the Heights:* With such a young company, in which almost everybody was of child-bearing age, it's not surprising they bore their share of children. (Another example from the *same month:* Elly Blankenbuehler, Andy's wife, was released from bed rest in time to attend the final dress rehearsal. The baby kicked like crazy during the show—an auspicious sign for a choreographer's son. Luca made his debut the next day.)

But when people in *Heights* talk about family, they are talking about something beyond its rolling baby boom. Even if you grade what company members are saying on a curve, aware of the tendencies of show folk to reach for family metaphors, you are left with a sincere and widespread belief that they shared a powerful bonding experience. They felt they were part of something rare or even unprecedented in their lives.

"*Somos familia,*" they say. The question is—*why?*

ONE FACTOR IS TIME and its adhesive properties. Most theater jobs last a few months. By the time this company started performing at 37 Arts, Lin had worked with Bill for seven years, Tommy for five, Quiara and Lac for nearly three, and the actors for various lengths of months or years. Almost all of them were in their twenties: It's not just a figure of speech to say that they grew up together.

"SOMOS FAMILIA," THEY SAY.

Janet Dacal, who had been there from nearly the beginning, recalls the nights on the beach at the O'Neill, when they'd watch the shooting stars. It felt like they were having too much fun for it to be a job. She called the whole experience "a party *con* pay."

As always, space plays a role. 37 Arts was located on West Thirty-seventh Street—heavy emphasis on *West*. In 2007, the far west side of Manhattan between Ninth Avenue and the Hudson River wasn't as developed as it is now. Once you got all the way over there, you weren't readily going back. (A company nickname for 37 Arts: "New Jersey.") And in early 2007, nobody had the option of disappearing into a smartphone screen. Which meant that the cast was discovering the truth of Benny's lyrics in "When You're Home": A place feels different, and *is* different, depending on who's in it.

When most of those company members looked around 37 Arts, they found a rare sight indeed: a room full of people who looked like them.

"I never had this experience before," says Eliseo Román, who played Piragua Guy. "I'm usually *the one.*"

To be a Latino actor in 2007 meant competing against other Latino actors for a handful of roles. If you managed to get cast, it usually meant you would be the only Latino person in the room: *the one.* "Unless you did *West Side Story,* which was half," Eliseo adds. "But sometimes the Sharks were white."

On two-show days, when the cast had hours to fill between their matinee and evening performances, the show's celebration of Latino culture would continue after the last note was sung. Javier Muñoz liked to organize potlucks. "That's important in our culture. It's how we can share love," he says. People would tell stories about their families, their lives, their childhoods. In Javier's case, he opened up about his parents and how he was helping them both fight cancer. "When you start to combine your actual identity with your work, that's something different, something richer," he says. "It's blurring lines, which is beautiful."

The *Heights* company wasn't entirely Latino. Much like Washington Heights itself, it comprised an amalgam of races. Joshua Henry, now a Broadway star who had an ensemble role in *Heights,* says the friendly warmth of the room reminded him of how he grew up in Miami, in a Jamaican family among people from many corners of Latin America. Chris Jackson recalls the feeling of solidarity among the Black and Latino company members, the feeling that "we were all in this together."

"The world doesn't know us, doesn't know how brilliant this collection of Black and brown folks could be," he recalls feeling. "We were shouting into the darkness: 'There's joy here. We are a joyous people.'"

This feeling of solidarity got an enormous if unintended boost from the layout of 37 Arts. There were only two dressing rooms: one for all eleven men, and one for all eleven women. Seasoned veterans like John Herrera sat elbow-to-elbow with rookies. The place gave you no choice but to share music, conversation, and the smell of what your castmates brought for lunch.

Even the stage dimensions conspired to bring people together. During "Paciencia y Fe," Janet, Eliseo, Lin, and Robin De Jesús sang backup vocals for Olga Merediz. But because they had only a few feet to maneuver in the stage-left wing, they had to form a circle, with their arms around their neighbors' shoulders, like a team huddle.

Stephanie Klemons learned about this when she went on for an absent ensemble member one night: Lin had to grab her while singing and pull her in.

"Oh my God," she says, "we were so freaking close."

"OH MY GOD," SHE SAYS, "WE WERE SO FREAKING CLOSE."

97

THEN THERE'S *In the Heights* itself.

Unlike most musicals—unlike most *anything*—the show has no villains. That's what Quiara meant about this being the story of a community rising or falling together: The forces that pressure the characters are bigger than all of them. In a famous bit of Broadway lore, Jerome Robbins kept the Jets and Sharks separate during rehearsals of *West Side Story* to breed hostility between them. *Heights* didn't give Tommy a chance to do that even if he'd wanted to. (He didn't want to.)

"It's such a loving piece," says Quiara. "I can just hear the critics in my head, but it's about merit and integrity and good deeds. I'm sorry, you know? And that infuses the spirit of working on it."

To Lac, some of this camaraderie is encoded in the score.

"I truly believe that there is something about Lin's music where you feel the love inside of it," he says. "You feel a heartbeat behind it that is very warm and approachable. And I contend that there are other shows where you might love the music and think it's great, but there's a distance behind it—something not quite as penetrable. Maybe that writer is holding something closer to their chest. The grip's a little tighter, or they're afraid of being vulnerable. But Lin

is a bleeding heart. He'll cry about something and not be ashamed of it. Anyway, that's just my theory."

For some members of the company, the communal spirit doesn't come from the story or the score alone, but from both together—the way they add up to depict a familiar world. Nobody caught her reflection more clearly than Karen Olivo.

She remembers being startled by her first exposure to the show, a recording of the O'Neill presentation. The characters were like her family; their struggle was one she knew all too well. It seemed as though Lin was talking to her.

"I was like, *Who's this f---ing person? And how did he know how I felt?*"

Vanessa, the hard-edged salon girl, the object of Usnavi's hopeless devotion, "is who I actually was when I was younger," she says. She grew up in a tough family situation, first in New York, then in Florida—the daughter of two immigrants who never had much. She always dreamed of performing on Broadway and got some early opportunities, but she made things hard for herself.

"I was a bit of a knucklehead," she says now. "I always wanted to do the job, but I didn't have a support system that would help me facilitate a certain level of work." That changed at 37 Arts. She was "surrounded by mentors," she says. The advice and encouragement from people like Andréa opened up new possibilities for how she could play Vanessa—and all her roles since then.

"Being in a room with people who look like my cousins and my sisters and my grandmothers, it changes you. Immediately you're at home and you're accepted—you don't have to be anything other than what you are," she says.

Company members express this sentiment with such striking frequency—*even accounting for the way show folk like to talk*—that it's worth considering a possibility. The sense of community that pervades *In the Heights* isn't an accidental by-product of Lin's conception: It was *the whole point*.

Lin dreamed up the show while seeking a place where all the parts of himself would make sense: New York and Vega Alta, Hunter and Inwood, Juan Luis Guerra and Big Pun, *Les Mis* and *Rent*. Eight years later, at 37 Arts, that space of Lin's dreams was rendered literal. With so little happening in the area around the building, and so few people inside it, the *Heights* company made the space their own. It echoed with their music, it ran on their rhythms: rooftop picnics on sunny days, onstage dance parties on rainy ones, group naps in the theater aisles.

If Lin's only connection to the show had been writing it, he could have felt as out of place at 37 Arts as he often did on Dyckman Street—"like a reporter on my neighborhood," he says. But when he signed in at the stage door six days a week, it wasn't as The Author, a figure set apart from everyone else: He was playing Usnavi. He was just one of the show's twenty-plus performers. It meant everything

to him to be part of "a group of like-minded people, a company of fellow actors who treated me as a fellow actor."

"The fact that the show that's about a community created its own community, and those people became such a family for me—that was the most amazing thing," he says.

HERE'S ONE LAST THEORY for why this show felt different.

Looking back on his first experience as a production stage manager, Jason Bassett thinks that company members were accommodating so much of the time (though not *all* of the time—"It's a family, so you're going to have things," he says wryly) because the show's future always seemed precarious. (Tommy, asked if he was certain that the Off-Broadway run would lead to a Broadway transfer, replies: "No! Jesus, no.") The feeling that emanated from the company was: *Let's love it as long as we can.*

The reviews for the Off-Broadway production, when they arrived, suggested they might get to love it a little longer: Critics embraced the novelty of the show and the charisma of the performers, even as they found reasons to complain about aspects of the story. Tommy remembers reading a review on Kevin's BlackBerry, then walking outside to sit down: "It was like my lungs were in chicken wire and someone cut it. I hadn't realized they had been held so tight."

Now Jill, Kevin, and Jeffrey faced a decision.

The reviews were good, but they weren't wall-to-wall raves. The box office was healthy, but the show wasn't selling out. Were they prepared to bet millions of dollars on a Broadway transfer for a new musical, by unknown creators, with no stars and a salsa-and-hip-hop score? No one was forcing them to close the show and gamble on reopening it in a bigger, more expensive theater. It would have been reasonable to let the show keep running Off-Broadway until interest dwindled, then end the story there.

In May, they assembled everyone in the seats of 37 Arts to announce their decision.

There are worse ways for New Yorkers to hear that it's time to move out.

LET'S LOVE IT AS LONG AS WE CAN.

When You're Home [1]

1. 2005. I have an *amazing* first date with this young woman named Vanessa Nadal. We went to the same high school, grew up twenty blocks apart uptown, but didn't really connect till *this* date. I take her to the Washington Heights spots that are important to me; she takes me to hers. I call Tommy Kail and say, "I met this girl," and begin describing the date. Tommy cuts me off: "Stop talking to me and write the *Benny and Nina love song right f—ing now.*" Here it is.

2. When collaboration leads to a joke: I was (am) so proud of the lyric "And the 1 slash 9 climbed a dotted line to my place."

Tommy: "But they stopped running the 9 line."

Me: "But I'm . . . not taking that line out."

Tommy: "But it makes no sense."

Compromise: Benny's response.

3. Everything Nina sings at the top of this song is true. I remember gazing at the subway map on our long A train rides as a child, experiencing the A to the top, and the Bronx hovered above us. Or as Priscilla Lopez's character Diana Morales says in *A Chorus Line*, "It's uptown and to the right." (I also used to imagine the arrow in the lower corner as Pac-Man eating the subway dots, but that doesn't really serve the lyric.)

4. There were so many versions of Nina's first song where Benny is giving her a tour, and I'm so glad we waited till this song/moment—it's a progression of their relationship, not the first step.

5. I remember my sister's first neighborhood boyfriend came over to our house to ask for a wrench to open the hydrant on the corner. Still admiring the chutzpah on that kid, I gave the trait to Benny.

6. Love Benny's uncertainty here . . . and INTO SOME FAST LYRICS I LOVE YOU HAHAHA NEVERMIND KEEP MOVING.

7. This is based on the private garden in Castle Village, near where my wife grew up. It was part of her tour for me.

8. Love the "Bennett *Park and* **/** When it *darkened*" rhyme.

NINA: I used to think we lived at the top of the world
When the world was just a subway map
And the 1 slash 9 climbed a dotted line to my place.

BENNY: There's no 9 train now. [2]

NINA: Right.
I used to think the Bronx was a place in the sky
When the world was just a subway map
And my thoughts took shape [3]

NINA, BENNY: On that fire escape . . .

NINA: Can you remind me of what it was like
At the top of the world?

BENNY: Come with me. [4]
We begin July
With a stop at my corner fire hydrant.

NINA: You would open it every summer!

BENNY: I would bust it with a wrench [5]
Till my face got drenched
Till I heard the sirens,
Then I ran like hell!

NINA: You ran like hell!

BENNY: Yeah, I ran like hell!

NINA: I remember well!

BENNY: To your father's dispatch window,

(He bangs on the window.)

"Hey, let me in, yo!
They're coming to get me!"

NINA: You were always in constant trouble—

BENNY: Then your dad would act all snide, but he let me hide
You'd be there inside—

NINA: Life was easier then.

BENNY: Nina, everything is easier
When you're home . . .
The street's a little kinder when you're home.
Can't you see
That the day seems clearer
Now that you are here or
Is it me? . . .
Maybe it's just me . . . [6]

We gotta go, I wanna show you all I know.
The sun is setting and the light is getting low.

NINA: Are we going to Castle Garden? [7]

BENNY: Maybe, maybe not, but way to take a shot, when the day is hot
I got a perfect shady spot a little ways away that oughta
Cool us down.

NINA: Cool us down—

BENNY: Welcome back to town . . .

NINA: Now back in high school when it darkened
You'd hang out in Bennett Park and [8]

BENNY: Usnavi would bring his radio . . .

NINA: As I walked home from senior studies
I'd see you rapping with your buddies.

BENNY: With the volume high

NINA: I walked on by.

BENNY: You walked on by—

(A cluster of guys enter, listening to a boom box.)

USNAVI, GRAFFITI PETE, MEN, SONNY:

¡No pare, sigue, sigue!
¡No pare, sigue, sigue!
¡No pare, sigue, sigue!
¡No pare, sigue, sigue!
¡No pare, sigue, sigue!
¡No pare, sigue, sigue!
¡No pare, sigue, sigue!
¡No pare, sigue! ⑨

DANIELA, CARLA, WOMEN:

Whoaa
Oh!
Whoaa
Oh!
Whoaa
Oh!
Whoaa
Oh!

BENNY, ENSEMBLE (BOTH GROUPS): When you're home

BENNY: Oh, the summer nights are cooler

BENNY, ENSEMBLE: When you're home.

NINA: Now that you're here with me . . .

BENNY:
And that song you're
Hearing is the
Neighborhood just cheering
You along—

ENSEMBLE:
Ooh
Ooh
Ooh

Ooh

NINA: Don't say that.

BENNY: What's wrong?

NINA: Don't say that!
When I was younger, I'd imagine what would happen
If my parents had stayed in Puerto Rico.
Who would I be if I had never seen Manhattan,
If I lived in Puerto Rico with my people.
My people . . . ⑩
I feel like all my life I've tried to find the answer,

Working harder, learning Spanish, learning all I can.
I thought I might find the answers out at Stanford
But I'd stare out at the sea
Thinking, where'm I supposed to be?
So please don't say you're proud of me, when I've lost my way . . . ⑪

BENNY: Then can I say:
I couldn't get my mind off you all day.
Now listen to me!
That may be how you perceive it
But Nina, please believe
That when you find your way again
You're gonna change the world and then
We're all gonna brag and say we knew her when . . .
This was your home. ⑫

NINA: I'm home—

BENNY: Welcome home—

NINA: When you're here with me—

BENNY: Welcome home—

NINA: I used to think we lived at the top of the world.

BENNY: Welcome home—

NINA: I'm home—

BENNY:
You're finally home.
You're home!

NINA:
I'm home—
I'm home!

(Sun sets on the neighborhood.)

9. Just to mention that our ensemble members had dance solos here, and they were debated/changed/improvised/argued about more fiercely than any other moment in the show. But from the vantage point of me and Nina Lafarga, who watched that moment from the bodega, they were never less than thrilling.

10. I've said it before, and I'll say it again: This feels like the most autobiographical lyric in the show. The feeling of an alternate life if your parents had stayed on the island where they're from. The sense of permanent displacement—not quite at home here or there—longing for a sense of peace in an alternate life that never existed. And wondering if you'd recognize yourself and your passions and the things you've come to know if you hadn't grown up where you did. Hey, we've found the moment where these annotations become my therapy session, cheers!

11. I will never forget the day we first rehearsed this scene for the movie in J. Hood Wright Park, a park on 175th Street that is walking distance from where we live now and central to our lives. I called Vanessa and said, "I know you're working from home today, but get over here." As we watched Benny and Nina dance past the building where Vanessa's grandmother once lived, she turned to me saying, "Is my grandmother's building gonna be in the *movie*?" Waterworks. Vanessa brought our kids to set every day we filmed that sequence.

12. I cried when Benny came up with this response and told me to write it down. That's genuinely how it felt to write it.

GAME OF ★★★ CHESS

"THAT WILL never work. It's not even a success *Off*-Broadway."

This is how Jeffrey remembers the conventional wisdom about the show's chances in the summer of 2007. The decision to gamble on a Broadway run committed him, Kevin, and Jill to filling the Richard Rodgers Theatre, a space triple the size of 37 Arts, eight times a week—*for years*.

That's why, one sunny day in July, the actors, the creative team, and a film crew took over a block in Washington Heights to make a TV commercial for *In the Heights*. "We wanted to capture the spirit of the show," Jill says, "how much energy it had, the kind of music it had, that it was fun and joyous." She remembers how much they enjoyed the day, in spite of the stakes.

"We pinned everything on that commercial," Jeffrey says.

In retrospect, the shoot was its own sort of first preview: a glimpse of what it would be like to observe the characters of *In the Heights* in their natural habitat, dancing across the sidewalks with cameras rolling. Mandy, Karen, Robin, and other cast members watched real-life counterparts of their characters stroll by.

The TV commercial was a conventional way to reach the conventional Broadway audience, but the producers also saw the opportunity—and the necessity—of tapping into the Latino audience. Here they had a secret weapon to deploy.

"I called everyone I knew," says Luis Miranda. He worked his connections around the city, particularly in Spanish-language radio and TV.

His first pitch was a personal appeal: "My son wrote the show, and it's *fantastic*. You've gotta come see it."

His second pitch leaned on ethnic solidarity: "They're not going to let us on Broadway again! We have to make this a hit, just as Jews did with *Fiddler on the Roof*!"

If the show ran long enough, and if Tony voters blessed it with a Best Musical award, the producers knew their chances of attracting traditional Broadway patrons would rise. But Luis knew it wouldn't matter to the people he was trying to reach. "It's like, *Who's that?*" he imagined someone saying. "*Tony's the cousin of who?*" So it was now or never.

The producers had lined up a handful of major investors for the show's Broadway transfer, backers whose names would appear above the show's title in the opening-night *Playbill*: Sander Jacobs, Robyn Goodman, Walter Grossman, Peter Fine, Sonny Everett, and Mike Skipper. Still, in case anyone was tempted to take it easy, they had a fresh memory to keep them hustling. Another Seller/McCollum show that Lin considered a "big sibling" had ascended to Broadway a few months earlier. It had bigger names and stronger buzz than *In the Heights*. It seemed like an easier sell.

It lasted a month.

THE ACTORS DID ANYTHING and everything they could to pay their bills between the Off-Broadway closing and the first Broadway preview. Stephanie wore a Quiznos cup and handed out coupons on Thirty-fourth Street. Karen made a pilot for a kids' show "that will haunt me for the rest of my life."

The start of pre-Broadway rehearsals brought relief, steady paychecks, and new friends. Carlos Gómez began playing Kevin Rosario. Tony Chiroldes, Afra Hines, Krysta Rodriguez, and Shaun Taylor-Corbett rounded out the ensemble. Blanca Camacho and Rogelio Douglas, Jr., joined Michael Balderrama and Stephanie Klemons as swings, ready to step into the ensemble as needed. They allowed Andy to make his dances bigger and more sophisticated—if he could figure out how to do it with even less space than he'd had at 37 Arts. (The essential trade-off of New York real estate: better location, less room.)

The universe provided Andy with one solution—and just in time. On the morning that Voltron was supposed to work out an ending for "96,000," he listened to the song while riding an exercise bike at the gym. The video for "Thriller" happened to come on the TV—and the beats of the two songs happened to match. A little fireworks show began in his brain.

When he got to the rehearsal studio, he proposed a new combination at the end of the song. It would start with the whole cast clapping over their heads, as Michael Jackson had in the video. Now everybody in the meeting had fireworks in their brains. With Lac playing, they decided that the dancers should drop into slow motion for a phrase, everybody whispering. Then they should burst into a final chorus, culminating in an explosion that Bill designed.

"And that," Andy says, "is how it ends."

As rehearsals shifted into the Richard Rodgers Theatre for the final round of tech, everybody felt that new material had made the storytelling clearer and the emotions deeper than they had been Off-Broadway, particularly a trio of new songs toward the end of the show. But with the first performance drawing nigh, an unpleasant by-product of those changes emerged. Act Two had become really, really glum. Andy dubbed a stretch of its songs "the suite of sadness."

They couldn't undo all the new work they had just done. But they were also running out of time to do much more. On one of the final nights of tech, while the company took a ten-minute break and most of the actors drifted out of the theater, Voltron stuck around and mused about their Act Two problem.

In broad strokes, all six of them agree on what happened next, even though no two accounts exactly match. It's like a major-key reprise of the unhappy meeting at the O'Neill picnic table three years earlier.

THE **UNIVERSE** PROVIDED ANDY WITH ONE SOLUTION— AND JUST IN TIME.

GAME OF CHESS

Somebody wondered aloud if the solution might be to give the audience a little breather—not by taking something out, but by adding something new.

Well, which character do people like? Somebody else mentioned the Piragua Guy—a neighborhood fixture Lin had introduced in Act One, in a song he'd written in circumstances that he describes on page 108.

Suddenly the conversation wasn't so aimless.

Lac sat down at his piano (which was, at that point in tech, in the audience, in front of the stage). He started playing "Piragua." Lin, joining him, started improvising new lyrics. Bill and Quiara tossed him ideas. Tommy began thinking about how to work the song into the tech schedule; Andy calculated which dancers he would need to stage it.

The stakes were so high, and their shorthand was so short, that before the ten minutes were up, the "Piragua" reprise was done.

Somebody returning to the theater asked Tommy how his break had gone.

"I think we just wrote a song," he said. "I don't know what you did on *your* break."

THAT FIRST BROADWAY PREVIEW, on February 14, 2008, felt different for the actors than the shows at 37 Arts had, and not just because of all the new songs. *Heights* had always demanded their full commitment, but the extra pressure, extra money, and extra attention of Broadway asked for something new: "We weren't used to having to be *serious*," Robin says.

He gives an example. While at 37 Arts, the company took part in the 2007 gala of one of New York's big nonprofit theaters. Afterward, Kevin took a bunch of the actors to Tao for a long night—"an amazing freaking night," Robin says—of drinking and food.

During the Broadway run, the company took part in the same theater's 2008 gala. Afterward, somebody proposed that they all go out again. This time, Kevin said no—at least not with him picking up the tab.

"My job was to prepare them for the road ahead as much as possible," Kevin says. From producing *Rent* and the shows that followed it, he had a visceral knowledge of

Broadway's demands that the young actors didn't. There was no leeway for missing a performance, or even for missing a *step*. Tony voters might be in the audience any night.

It wasn't just the actors: Lin and Quiara were coping with new pressures, too, not always successfully.

"A lot of people were asking at the time, 'Is this your dream come true?'" she recalls. "And it was a weird question to be asked, because I felt like if I answered honestly, it would seem really ungrateful. And I didn't feel ungrateful about it—but it just wasn't my dream."

She respected the traditions of Broadway, but the place didn't have the mystique for her that it had for Lin. Which didn't lower the stakes one bit.

"It was huge. The pressure was huge. If my script is good or not will make a difference in people getting all of that money back or not," she recalls. "And then someone told me, *Whatever you do, don't read the chat rooms.*"

In 2008, Broadway gossip and opinion circulated in a handful of online chat rooms. The comments, often pseudonymous, could be vicious. Quiara discovered that only when she looked for herself.

"They're all like, *Her book's the worst thing ever,* and *It's awful,* and *She's a total liability.*"

Quiara had already dealt with criticism Off-Broadway, when the reviews tended to blame her libretto for the show's story problems. It had hurt at the time, but this sensation—of what she calls "personal evisceration"—was totally new and much, much worse.

Alone in the mezzanine one day, feeling stressed out and confused, she called her mentor, the playwright and educator Paula Vogel.

"She told me, just hold on a second," Quiara recalls. Paula put the phone down, returned a moment later, and began to read some of the most vicious and demeaning things Quiara had ever heard. They were a few of the criticisms that Paula had absorbed in her long and celebrated playwriting career.

Hearing her mentor say those things, understanding what it can cost to be part of the community of playwrights, Quiara gained the perspective she had lacked.

"I get it," she told Paula. Then she went back to work.

Lin had gone through his own discomfort, some of it physical. What he'd thought was a heart attack was

Recuerdo

NÚMERO TRES

ELISEO ROMÁN

PIRAGUA GUY IN THE ORIGINAL OFF-BROADWAY AND BROADWAY CASTS

1/9/11 IN THE HEIGHTS BROADWAY WEPA!

I was very fortunate when I got the offer for *In the Heights*. I was so happy. I didn't even have an agent when I auditioned. And then Piragua Guy went on to become more than I thought it would be—and more than I think *they* thought it would be.

What I most remember about playing him is the joy that I felt the character brought to the piece. He brought the authenticity of the Latin worker. Everyone knows him. Kids know him, adults know him. They see him every day.

One night on Broadway, I came out the stage door, and a young guy, nineteen or twenty, was waiting for me. He was crying. He told me that his father sold piraguas in Puerto Rico. When he saw me onstage, all of these memories came flooding back. His father was the breadwinner in the family—the one who made it possible for him to go to school and all of these things.

I think about him when I look at my ice scraper. I kept it from the show. I wrote our closing date on it.

To this day, whenever I see a piragua guy and I see a Mister Softee, I never go to Mister Softee. It's ingrained. If anybody wants ice cream, they better leave me and go around the block before they do. Because I am supporting my people.

---

actually severe heartburn, brought on by the wave of anxiety that had been sloshing around inside him since 37 Arts.

He had gone into therapy between the Off-Broadway and Broadway runs, for the first time since he was nineteen. With two psychologists for parents, Lin doesn't attach any stigma to psychotherapy. Like Quiara, he knew he needed an outside voice to help him reckon with the issues kicked up by his changed reality. He was beginning to enjoy some things he'd wanted for his whole life but wasn't always deriving the pleasure he expected to derive from them. Plus, there were flare-ups of his superstitions and the morbidity that has dogged him since a childhood friend died in an accident. "The stuff that is my stuff," he calls it.

Talking with his therapist helped. "It was like, 'Okay, good, the things that were taking up outsize real estate in my head, I spoke them into being, and now they're smaller.'" But it couldn't entirely remove the ache of the rite of passage he was going through in those early weeks at the Rodgers.

On one hand, he had become a Broadway writer and performer—an extraordinary ascent at a very young age. On the other, he was feeling "a bit of mourning," similar to what he has heard mothers describe after giving birth—missing the sensation of pregnancy, in spite of its pain.

"I missed not having to write *In the Heights* anymore," he realizes now. "I had spent my twenties doing it."

Piragua

1. I had to write "Inútil" for the show. I wasn't ready. I wrote this song to procrastinate on that song.

2. My go-to piragua flavor is tamarind. My kids like lemon and coconut.

3. Again, I wrote this to procrastinate, but embedded in the song is a metaphor for the whole neighborhood: scraping by in the face of daunting external and economic forces—in Piragua Guy's case, Mister Softee.

4. I think, from beginning to end, I wrote this song in half an hour? Fastest song I ever wrote—until the reprise.

PIRAGUA GUY: ¡Ay, qué calor, qué calor, qué calor, qué calo-o-or!

Piragua, piragua
New block of ice, piragua
Piragua, piragua
So sweet and nice, piragua

¡Tengo de mango, tengo de parcha,
De piña y de fresa!
¡Tengo de china, de limón,
De peso y de peseta, ay! ❷
Piragua, piragua
New block of ice, piragua
Piragua, piragua
So sweet and nice, piragua

It's hotter than the islands are tonight.
And Mister Softee's trying to
    shut me down.
But I keep scraping by the
    fading light.
Mi 'pana, this is my town.

Piragua, piragua
Keep scraping by, piragua ❸

Piragua, piragua
Keep scraping by, piragua

Keep scraping by, keep scraping by . . .
Lai lo le lo lai, lai lo le lo lai

Keep scraping by, keep scraping by . . .
Lai lo le lo lai!

Keep scraping by . . .

¡Qué calor, qué calor, qué calor, qué
calo-o-or! ❹

The DINNER SCENE

By QUIARA ALEGRÍA HUDES

GROWING UP, food was everywhere. Modest, belly-warming bowlfuls. Abuela had rice and beans on her stove no matter when you came through. Mom and Pop had a restaurant called El Viejo San Juan, at Third and Girard in Philly, en el barrio. (It's not a particularly Latino area anymore; gentrification has been nipping at the heels of many historically Latino neighborhoods in Philly since before my birth. So coming to Philly from Puerto Rico was not the final migration—it continued as my relatives got pushed farther and farther out from Center City.) At my folks' restaurant, local artists displayed their works on the wall, and the mofongo was delicious and garlicky, with a rich red sauce. When

writing, I love making an audience's mouth water, throwing in food mentions to give that sense of culture. In a migrant lineage (Abuela from Lares, Mom from Arecibo, me from Philly), traditional meals were a way to create consistency among generations. Food is home that travels with you.

So a dinner gathering is a natural dramatic centerpiece for me—a scene that can encompass all the dizzy joy and celebration of breaking bread (or rice) with a tight-knit community, along with the fights and disputes that bubble up in close family quarters.

For this pivotal moment in the plot— a halfway point—I started with dance. There was no family gathering growing up without nalguitas shaking. Not everyone was a great dancer, but everyone dove right in, and it was all about the freedom to let go and shake off life's frustrations. I

loved having Vanessa and Abuela Claudia dance in opposite styles. Vanessa's all about big moves, whereas Abuela is old-school: "Pretend you're dancing on a tiny brick." There's a Cachao song where he sings, "Pon este pasillo en un ladrillo." For elders like Abuela, subtle restraint can be very hot on the dance floor! The record scratch is another little detail to engage the generational differences. Abuela is so used to the scratch, it's become central to how she hears the song.

For me growing up, there were many skin tones eating and dancing at Abuela's. White Latinos and Afro Latinos and every shade in between. Same with hair texture and body shape. There was also class diversity, and I tried to put some of that in the script. We have college kids (Nina), business owners (Kevin and Camila), and the working class (Vanessa, Benny). Vanessa's over these hierarchies and unapologetic about defending herself. She can feel Kevin's eyes when he tells Nina to avoid becoming "just another girl stuck in el barrio." Vanessa shoots back: "Why you gotta look at me when you say

FOR ME GROWING UP, THERE WERE MANY SKIN TONES EATING AND DANCING AT ABUELA'S.

that?" On Broadway, we got a consistent laugh there. Because it rang true, it struck a chord. That pecking order can hurt.

The other tension I played with is how Kevin, a very loving patriarch, pulls a machismo power play. He sells the business to cover Nina's tuition after she loses her scholarship. But he does this on his own, an executive decision, then gets enraged when his wife calls him on it. "This is our business!" Camila says, baffled by his choice. "It was in my name!" Kevin fires back defensively, in breach of their vow to be equal partners. We have already seen Camila, earlier in Act One, doing the business's heavy lifting—paying the bills, keeping the paperwork in order. But in the end, the man calls the shots. It's a betrayal.

111

For the movie, I knew we could take Dinner Scene 2.0 to a whole 'nother level. Jon Chu and I got in the room and started trading stories. His parents moved to California from Taiwan and Hong Kong (his father has roots in Sichuan as well) and opened up a Bay Area restaurant that's thriving fifty years later. In the restaurant business, that's tremendous success. Jon and I grew up in kitchens, tasting new and classic dishes, seeing the world through a food lens. So he said to me, "This is an opportunity to really win points with the audience and be authentic and detailed." He asked, what do we need? I was like, we gotta have pasteles; we gotta have bacalao; let's put some guava paste, queso, y Ritz on a tray. We made a mouthwatering menu. Beyond the basics like arroz con gandules, B-side dishes for special occasions. Even the pique, the hot sauce, was chosen with care. I said, we need a label hot sauce like El Yucateco but also an unlabeled pique from a local source. The pots and serving spoons were vetted, too! I had my mom send us images of her new and old pots to show the kind of patina a traditional caldero and olla gain over time.

For the dancing, Alice Brooks, the cinematographer, and Jon got the camera to eye level, hip level, so you're in the booty traffic. It feels affectionate and fun to be inside the dancing like that. Angles that

FOR THE MOVIE, I KNEW WE COULD TAKE DINNER SCENE 2.0 TO A WHOLE 'NOTHER LEVEL.

create immediacy and familiarity. Olga, who played the role on Broadway and in the movie, stuck with Abuela's refined subtle style. And this time, Cuca's the family member who's like, "Shake it, Abuela, let loose, come on!"

One way the camera helped was by clocking everyone's reaction as the tension escalates. When Kevin announces he's sold the business, we see Daniela's face—agreement and admiration. We see Nina coil with anger. Even Usnavi's ambivalence reads on the screen. Onstage, you need dialogue for these reactions to land. But onscreen, we can wordlessly do a lot. Jimmy Smits, our film's Kevin, breaks the news about selling Rosario's with an understated softness. And we watch his "good news" snowball into an argument with Nina. Beneath the stoicism and geniality we've come to know, both father and daughter are revealed to be strong fighters.

The dinner scene was shot over a few days. One day, Jon was sitting on the Rosario couch and called me over. "Quiara . . ." His warm, nervous tone of voice signaling something big. I sat beside him, and he said: "I want to ask your blessing for something. My baby's due in a few weeks, and I can't imagine a better name for him than 'Heights.'" The ask was quite formal, and I almost felt like a madrina in that moment. A naming madrina. Soon, Heights was born: Jonathan Heights Chu.

When we wrapped the dinner scene, a chapter in my career had finally been completed. I had been writing and rewriting that beast of a scene for fifteen years. Many actors had been a part of its development. Many drafts had come and gone. Various characters had been in it, then cut. It was, at last, complete.

NINA
The payment deadline passed.

KEVIN
Hey, enough lying. I called them.
Stop trying to protect me!

NINA
Finances were part of the issue.
Did you not hear the other stuff I
said?

KEVIN
About ignorant idiotas? Same
stuff I saw when I first came
here.

NINA
When you came there was a Puerto
Rican community to welcome you.
Lawyers, teachers, abuelas,
babies, first-generation, fifth-
generation... who had each other's
backs, who weren't invisible, who
had dignity. There's no community
at Stanford. They searched me,
Dad. I got searched.
        (getting heated)
On moving day, my roommate lost
her diamond necklace. Her parents
and the R.A. emptied my drawers,
turned over my purse. Eventually,
they found it in her bag. ~~Talk
about humiliating.~~

KEVIN
You're the best we got, Nina. If
you can't stay in the ring, what
does that say about us?

NINA
You can't put your life's work on
my shoulders.

KEVIN
        (to the guests)
Isn't she the best we got?

~~VANESSA~~
~~Whatever. Some of us can't afford~~
~~one class at FDC.~~

CHAPTER Twelve

ALMOST HOME

THE PRODUCERS ROLLED OUT an actual red carpet for Broadway opening night. It stretched along West Forty-sixth Street beneath the Richard Rodgers marquee. Many of the theatergoers who walked across it were there because of a family member: a spouse, parent, sibling, or, most frequently, child.

The actors, the band, the creative team: They were there because of Lin and his determination at age nineteen that if no one else was going to tell this story, he would have to do it. And he did it so well that at some point in the intervening eight and a half years, each of them decided to join him.

But Lin felt they were all there because of her.

PLENTY OF CAST MEMBERS were making their Broadway debuts that night and a few others had racked up multiple credits, but only one had legend status. In 1975, Priscilla Lopez was part of the original company of *A Chorus Line.* The show about the lives of Broadway dancers was one of the most sensational hits of its era. When she was the same age as most members of the *Heights* company, she and her castmates caught a full blast of fame: magazine covers, celebrity encounters, TV.

Doors opened for her. But like many Latina actresses of her generation, she faced pressure to remake herself in order to walk through them.

Would you be willing to change your name? they asked her. She would not.

"How could I betray my family, my parents, who worked so hard and sacrificed so much for me, by changing my name?" she says.

She won a Tony Award anyway, for a different musical a few years later. She also took jobs in shows about Latino characters written by non-Latino writers. "They don't know what the experience is," she says. "They imagine they know and write a play about it, but they don't know."

Priscilla hadn't done a musical in years when she met Jill Furman at a party in 2006. She wasn't sure what to make of the songs on the CD that Jill sent her. But her teenage daughter, Gabriella, heard them in the car, and told her she *had* to do it. So Priscilla accepted the offer and became Camila Rosario, Nina's mother, for the Off-Broadway run.

Amid the other factors that forged the cast into a community at 37 Arts, a major one is that the most famous actor in those crowded dressing rooms approached work this way: "I learned a long time ago, in one of my very early years as an apprentice in summer stock—every week I had to do something different: box office, wardrobe, paint sets, do props, clean toilets—I realized, 'Ahhh, it takes a village. It takes a cast. It takes a *company* to put on a show. So no one is more important than any other person. Without that spotlight operator, you're not going to be lit. I am a cog, sometimes a more important cog or a featured cog, but I am a cog.'"

Yet in her long and distinguished career, there was a gap in what Priscilla had experienced—a void that she couldn't see.

Her initial inkling of it came on her first day of rehearsal. She remembers that Mandy Gonzalez ran across the room, jumping over seats ("like a puppy dog," Priscilla says) to hug her and say how happy she was to be working with her.

"I didn't know her!" Priscilla says.

Curtain call on Broadway opening night: March 9, 2008

Once their onstage mother/daughter relationship had led to an offstage friendship, Mandy told her, "When I saw that 'z' at the end of your name, I knew I could make it."

Priscilla was stunned. She grew more stunned as other members of that young company found chances to tell her how much it meant to them to see her play Diana Morales in *A Chorus Line*—a Puerto Rican actress playing a fully realized Puerto Rican character at the very peak of the profession.

"I had no idea," Priscilla says. "When I did *A Chorus Line* or anything after that, or even before that, I was just doing my job."

For P. Lo (as her young castmates called her), *Heights* "filled a part of my soul that was missing," she says. "It gave me my family, my music, my history. It gave me that. And it gave me the knowledge that I had made a difference in the community that I didn't realize I was such a big part of."

On Broadway opening night, she found a moment alone with Lin. "You are throwing a rock in a pond," she told him, "and you have no idea the ripples that are going to come back to you."

FIVE MINUTES BEFORE the curtain that night, just like five minutes before the curtain *every* night, Chris Jackson gathered the company together under the stage, invited them to join hands, and began to pray.

"We didn't know how the world was going to receive it, but if it didn't work out, it wasn't going to be because we didn't give it our all," Chris says now. "We knew we were speaking for a whole part of the world that didn't have a voice."

Jason Bassett called places.

Seth Stewart, playing Graffiti Pete, leapt onto the stage, spray cans in hand.

As in most opening night performances, the laughs were louder than usual, the applause went longer. It was particularly potent for actors making their Broadway debuts. "It was all in technicolor," Janet recalls.

Lin ran into trouble as soon as he opened his mouth. "Yo, that's my wall!" he shouted as he chased Seth offstage. He listened for the clave beat, his cue to begin rapping the opening number. Except that everybody was cheering so loudly, he couldn't hear it. And since he was facing upstage, he couldn't make eye contact with Lac, who was conducting from downstage center, to get a cue. Panic set in. He knew the audience thought he was milking his big Broadway moment; actually, he was silently pleading for them to stop shouting so he could get on with it.

Lac spent the next two and a half hours gauging when to interrupt the cheering audience and start the next song. The fireworks effect that capped Act One, the result of continual experimentation by Nevin and lighting designer Howell Binkley, sent the cast and the audience to intermission. But after the break, as Lac steered the company toward the ending, he reached the limits of the professionalism that everybody had depended on since the bookstore basement.

BUT **LIN** FELT THEY WERE ALL THERE **BECAUSE** OF HER.

In the show's closing number, Usnavi realizes that he has found the place and the people he has long been seeking. Lin sang, "I found my island, I've been on it this whole time. I'm *home*!"

"He was so impassioned—he was singing it with tears in his eyes," Lac says. "I looked up at him and saw that, and I just started bawling. Here I am conducting and choking back tears! In that moment, it all hit me: *Oh my God, we made it.*"

A CHORUS LINE IS more than just a story about the sacrifices that dancers make for their art. Priscilla and her co-stars asked us to recognize that even a long row of people who look alike and move alike harbor an enormous variety of individual histories, dreams, and desires.

As the opening night crowd roared, the *Heights* cast formed a similar line, taking bow after bow.

Robin De Jesús was feeling grateful to have his whole family there. They didn't share his affection for Broadway: *In the Heights* was his first chance to share his love of musical theater with them. "It was like introducing my boyfriend to my best friend and hoping they get along," he says.

Joshua Henry was noticing that his face hurt. A fight scene during a performance a few nights earlier had led to stitches, a lip the size of a golf ball, and a directive not to sing. He had sung anyway. He was marveling at what Lin had done, the new home he had created for all of these artists on Broadway. He was hearing a lyric from *West Side Story* run through his mind: *There's a place for us.* He was realizing—at that very instant, he says—that he could rethink his whole songbook. "I don't have to sing some of these songs I thought I had to sing. I don't have to sing 'Ol' Man River' or 'Run and Tell That' to say who I am," he says. "I'm more than one type of thing."

Recuerdo

NÚMERO CUATRO

LUIS SALGADO

LATIN ASSISTANT CHOREOGRAPHER AND ENSEMBLE MEMBER IN THE ORIGINAL OFF-BROADWAY AND BROADWAY CASTS

I have so many things from the show. I just recently started letting some of them go. I had a hat that Janet gave to us on opening night, with spray-painted letters on the front. A young dancer I'd been working with on a musical saw the hat in the PBS documentary about *Heights* and told me how cool it was. So at our next rehearsal, I gave it to him.

Giving it to him was really two sides of the same story. One, the idea of letting go. *In the Heights* will live in my soul for the rest of my life. No matter how many shows I'm in, it shaped everything I want to do. So letting go of something physical gave me a deeper hold on something spiritual. The second is: I have so many people who believed in me, shaped me, mentored me, all the way back to growing up in Puerto Rico. So I need to do that for other people. He, at that moment, was hungry for more in life—for more adventures. The hat was a way of validating the fact that he's on the right path.

But I've kept my *Heights* softball team T-shirt. I think my son will inherit it at some point. Why not? It's part of his history. How cool would it be if there's a thirty-year reunion of the show? He can carry the Puerto Rican flag and sing "arriba esa bandera" and wear the shirt.

Eliseo Román was thinking of the talented actors who never got the chance to celebrate a Broadway opening night. He was trying to represent them. His life, he says, was "the happiest it had ever been."

Javier Muñoz was thinking he could have been one of those people who didn't get a chance: Four years earlier, he had been diagnosed with HIV. "I remember all of us singing together, I remember where I was looking in the mezzanine, I remember the walls, because I was alive," he says. "It was the dream come true, and nothing had stopped it. I was still here." His parents were there, too.

Priscilla, crying, was feeling that the cast had finished the work they had started. She was thinking, *We did it, we did it, thank you God.*

Eventually somebody handed Lin a microphone, and he began inviting members of the creative team onstage one at a time to share in the celebration.

Strange as it sounds, Quiara has no memory of being cheered by 1,300 people at the conclusion of a show she co-wrote. (Her chief memory of the day is from that morning, when she had come to the still-empty theater to leave gifts for the cast. Cecilia, who had recently turned one, had always wanted to run around the theater. On this day, Quiara let her do it, with Ray chasing her. "It was so calm," Quiara says. "That was such a nice memory.")

Kevin McCollum was thinking of Jonathan Larson, who didn't get to have a night like this.

Lin came right out and told everybody what he was thinking. After he introduced the final member of the creative team, he quoted "Paciencia y Fe": "Ay Mamá, what do you do when your dreams come true?"

The question sounded genuine.

BROADWAY OPENING NIGHTS are strange in a way that almost no other social function is strange. The big show, the performance itself, causes great anxiety for those involved, but the stakes are pretty low: Almost everybody has come to offer love and support, no matter what they see onstage. The show that really counts isn't big—it's *tiny*. After the bows and the cheering, the producers wait for a phone to ping, and the words that dance across that little screen—the adjectives, in particular—will settle the fate of the whole gigantic enterprise. It's as if your wedding toasts determine if you get to stay married.

Nobody knew what to expect. "It could have been a hit, or it could have been another show that gets closed because it's full of Latinos," recalls Luis Salgado.

Tommy felt that they had made the show better, deeper, and truer since the critics had reviewed it Off-Broadway.

"HE WAS SO IMPASSIONED— HE WAS SINGING IT WITH TEARS IN HIS EYES."

erupts in one of its expressions of collective joy, the energy it gives off could light up the George Washington Bridge for a year or two.")

So it was a good party.

At Chelsea Piers, along the Hudson River, more than a thousand people ate, drank, and danced. If you're impressed by how Broadway performers dance onstage while pretending to be other people—as they do in "The Club" sequence of *Heights*—you should see how they dance on a night like this, when it had rarely felt so good to be themselves.

Mandy had invited her parents to make the trip from Southern California to be there. She needed them to see this story that reflected their lives. "My dad even got up and danced with me—which never happened at another Broadway party," she recalls.

The celebration went on and on. "The party was lit. We lived our lives," says Robin. Sometime in the early hours, Lin absorbed one last round of congratulations and headed for home.

The trip was shorter than it used to be. During the Off-Broadway run, he had moved out of his old neighborhood to a new place on the Upper West Side.

Whatever the reviews said this time, he felt, "We did the best we could." For years he had imagined the moment when he would learn the verdict, standing there arm in arm with his comrades.

In fact, he was in the men's room when a stranger let him know the reviews were good. Tommy says he was glad to hear it—"and I was like, 'Wait, what's your name?'"

(The adjectives in the *New York Times* review, which mattered more to the show's future than all the others combined, included "spirited," "ebullient," "zesty," and "ear-tickling." The crucial line was: "When this musical

The Club [1]

1. Something interesting: There's *always* been a club number in *Heights*, even in the Wesleyan version. Something about taking the conflicts we've been building and having permission to truly let them play out on a dance floor is so liberating and theatrical.

2. And again, I love applying Usnavi's nervous flow to this salsa groove—it's where we begin to differentiate themes and see how they crash together and on top of one another.

3. The joy of approaching lines of dialogue as if they're trumpet breaks—that's what I'm going for here. It's *so* syncopated.

4. Again, Benny and Nina in their first real conflict, fueled by alcohol and a dance floor. They sing, Usnavi raps, and it lends the club all this great variety.

CLUB PEOPLE: Vanessa!

(USNAVI tries to keep up with her.)

USNAVI: Damn, this is nice.
I really like what they've done with the lights.
So the hot club in Washington Heights.
You might be right, this music's tight.
Yo, did I mention that you look great tonight?
Because you do, you really— [2]

VANESSA: Usnavi, relax!

USNAVI: Relax. ¿Qué relaxed? I'm relaxed.

(A couple dances by.)

MAN, WOMAN: Wepa! Vanessa!

USNAVI: So you've been here before.
I don't go out, I get so busy with the store
Y cada día it's a brand-new chore.
My arms are sore, no time for the dance floor.
But maybe you and me should hang out some
    more.
I'm such a dork, but I—

VANESSA: Let's go get a drink.

USNAVI: Something sweet.

VANESSA: You know me. A little bit of cinnamon.

COMPANY: Wepa! Vanessa!

(USNAVI joins BENNY at the bar. BENNY is doing shots.)

BENNY: Here's to getting fired!

USNAVI: To killing the mood!

USNAVI, BENNY: ¡Salud!

(They do a shot.)

BENNY: Without so much as a thank you!

USNAVI: Five long years.

USNAVI, BENNY: Cheers!

(They do another shot.)

BENNY: To finally getting Vanessa,
Man, fix your collar—

(He fixes USNAVI'S collar.)

USNAVI, BENNY: Holler!

BENNY: To doing shots on a weekend!

USNAVI: As long as you buy 'em, l'chaim!

(Another shot. JOSÉ approaches VANESSA.)

JOSÉ: Hey you!

VANESSA: Who?

JOSÉ: You!

VANESSA: Who, me?

JOSÉ: You wanna dance? [3]

VANESSA: Naw, man . . .

JOSÉ: Okay, I took my chance . . .

USNAVI: It's cool, it's cool, hey, if you want to . . .

VANESSA: You don't mind?

USNAVI: I'm fine! I'm fine!

BENNY: Yo!

USNAVI: Yo!

BENNY: *Who's Vanessa talkin' to?*

USNAVI: *Some dude!*

BENNY: *Some dude?!*
That's messed up, she's tryin' to make you
    jealous!

USNAVI: Jealous, I ain't jealous, I can take all
    these fellas, whatever!

(USNAVI grabs VANESSA from JOSÉ and dances with her. JOSÉ is pissed. NINA enters.)

NINA: Benny, can we take a walk outside?

BENNY: And there she is.

NINA: I'm so sorry, I didn't know. [4]

BENNY: Who let you in? Yo, this is the girl who
    cost us our jobs today!

NINA: I'm gonna make it right!

(He raises his glass to her.)

BENNY: A toast to the end of all I know!

This is one of those miracle sections that always worked—"amaretto *sour*/ghetto *flower*" and the extra rhyming kicker "*How are.*"

6. It's a little "Dance at the Gym" from *West Side Story*, it's a little *Rent*, it's entirely *Heights.* Shoutout to Oscar Hernández, who did the first pass at these dance arrangements.

NINA: You've had enough.

BENNY: Says the girl who has it all.

NINA: That's not fair.

BENNY: Well, why don't you run home to Daddy? He loves to remind me that I'll never be good enough for your
Family . . . for you . . .

NINA: You don't know me.

BENNY: Poor you.

NINA: I thought you were different.

(He shoves his drink in NINA's hand and pulls a random woman to the dance floor.)

BENNY: Salud.

(A chorus of boys swoops in on VANESSA, stealing her from USNAVI, alternating as they swing her around the floor.)

PIRAGUA GUY, GRAFFITI PETE, MEN: Vanessa, let me get the next one
Vanessa, let me interject some
The way you sweat, the way you flex on the floor,
It makes me want you more!

Vanessa, let me get the next one
Vanessa, let me interject some
The way you sweat, the way you flex on the floor,
It makes me want you more!

Vanessa, let me get the next one
Vanessa, let me interject some
The way you sweat, the way you flex on the floor,
It makes me want you more!

(USNAVI approaches YOLANDA at the bar.)

USNAVI: Bartender!
Let me get an amaretto sour for this ghetto flower.
How are you so pretty? **⑤**
You complete me.
You had me at hello, you know you need me
Truly, madly, deeply, let's get freaky.
Oh, I get it you're the strong and silent type.
Well, I'm the Caribbean island type
And I can drive you wild all night.
But I digress
Say something so I don't stress.

YOLANDA: No hablo Inglés.

USNAVI: Yes!

(USNAVI takes her out on the floor. Everyone is dancing. VANESSA and JOSÉ. USNAVI and YOLANDA. BENNY and CLUB GIRL. NINA finds another guy to dance with and spins by BENNY. BENNY is pissed. USNAVI swoops in and takes VANESSA out of JOSÉ's hands and dances with her. JOSÉ, without missing a beat, glides back in and takes VANESSA back, mid-turn. To add insult to injury, he grabs YOLANDA and is now dipping and spinning them both on the dance floor. During this impressive display, USNAVI and a very drunk BENNY slide in and each grab a girl, leaving JOSÉ dancing alone. JOSÉ, angry, starts to tap USNAVI on the shoulder. Without missing a beat, BENNY hauls and punches JOSÉ across the face. More and more instruments add to the mix. The dancing gets intense, crazy. It is a whirlwind of movement, a release of stress, when suddenly: ❻

THE POWER GOES OUT IN WASHINGTON HEIGHTS. ❼

Complete darkness. A cellphone light appears, illuminating a face. More and more cellphones light up, creating a blue glow in the club.)

7. I wrote this blackout based on a summer blackout that happened in 1991. It really only affected uptown, while downtown remained unaffected. I remember how much flak Con Edison caught for the fact that the blackout hit Black and Latino neighborhoods the hardest. Then in 2003, a massive blackout took out most of the Eastern Seaboard. But our blackout in the show already existed.

Blackout

(A flashlight comes on in the dispatch booth.)

PIRAGUA GUY: ¿Oye, qué pasó?

USNAVI: Blackout, blackout!

PIRAGUA GUY: ¡Vino el apagón ay dios!	**GRAFFITI PETE, MEN:** Oh no!

PIRAGUA GUY, MEN: ¿Oye, qué pasó?	**USNAVI:** Blackout, Blackout!	**GRAFFITI PETE, MEN, DANIELA, CARLA, NINA, WOMEN, VANESSA:** Oh no!
¡Vino el apagón Ay dios!	**BENNY:** Hold up, wait, Hold up, wait!	**ENSEMBLE:** Oh no!

USNAVI:
Yo! I! Can't see!
Quit shovin' you
Son of a—
It's an oven
And we gotta
Back out,
This is a blackout!
Chill, for real,
Or we're gonna
Get killed!
	BENNY:
	Nina, where'd you
	   go, I can't find
	   you—
	
	Nina, take it slow,
	I'm behind you—
		ENSEMBLE:
		Oh no!
		
		Oh no!
		
		Oh no!
		
		Oh no!

(A flashlight at the bodega. SONNY appears outside, holding a baseball bat, protecting the storefront.)

KEVIN: Calling all taxis!	**SONNY:** What's going on?	**MEN:**
KEVIN, USNAVI: Everyone relax Please.	What's going on? Suddenly I find The electricity is Gone. ②	Oh no! Oh no!
KEVIN: Calling all taxis!	What's going on? What's going on?	Oh no! Oh no!
KEVIN, USNAVI: Everyone relax Please.	I gotta guard The store, make Sure that Nothing's going Wrong!	

BENNY:
Somebody better
Open these
    goddamn
Doors!

VANESSA:
Somebody better
Open these
    goddamn
Doors!

BENNY:
Somebody better
Open these
    goddamn
Doors!

VANESSA:
And I can't find
Usnavi . . .

BENNY:
Nina, where'd
You go?
Nina, where'd
You go?
Nina, where'd
You go?
I can't find
You!

Nina, where'd
You go?
Nina, where'd
You go?
Nina, where'd
You go?
I can't find
You!

SONNY:
What's going on?
What's going on?

Gotta find Usnavi,
Tell him what is

Going on.

Nothing is on!
Nothing is on!

And I can't find
Usnavi . . .

USNAVI:
Vanessa,

Vanessa,

Vanessa,

I gotta go . . .

Vanessa,

Vanessa,

Vanessa,

I gotta go . . .

ENSEMBLE:
Oh no!

Oh no!

Oh no!

No! No!
No!

NINA:
Has anyone
    seen Benny?

Benny . . .

Has anyone
    seen Benny?

Benny . . .

VANESSA:

Usnavi,
Help me!

Usnavi,
Help me!

1. "Blackout," like our opening number, has changed a lot as our plot has changed. In fact, in my demo, you can hear the varying microphone qualities over the years as I changed the plotlines in this song. But the opening and the initial rush out the club doors were always there. I was so happy when "Look at the fireworks" and "We are powerless" turned up. I remember this cut section for Kevin and Camila Rosario, sadly always relevant: "We've got the batteries and candles, look how ready we are/We used to have these blackouts every other night in P.R. . . ."

2. So much fun figuring out the puzzle of this and using the different sections to zoom all over the neighborhood.

KEVIN:
Please find Nina!
Find Camila!
If you see my family, bring
Them home!

VANESSA:

Find my way home

Usnavi, help me!

SONNY:
We are powerless
We are powerless!

You left me alone!

SONNY, WOMEN, CAMILA, PIRAGUA GUY, MAN: We are
    powerless
We are powerless!

GRAFFITI PETE: Yo! Yo! They throwin' bottles in
    the street!
People lootin' and shootin'.
Sonny, they wanna see a robbery
We gotta keep movin'!

SONNY: Naw, man, I can't leave, we gotta guard
    the store!

GRAFFITI PETE: They gonna bombard the store
    until you ain't got a store no more!

SONNY: I got a baseball bat on a rack in the back.

GRAFFITI PETE (OPENING A BOOK BAG): I got a
    couple Roman candles, we can distract the
    vandals!

SONNY: Hey yo, I see some thugs comin', man, we
    gonna get jacked up!

(GRAFFITI PETE rushes out of the store holding a Roman
candle, SONNY behind him wielding a bat.)

GRAFFITI PETE: Gimme a light, I'll be right back.
    Back up—

GRAFFITI PETE, SONNY: Back up, back up!

(We hear an explosion.)

**CAMILA, NINA, CARLA, ABUELA
CLAUDIA, WOMEN, USNAVI, BENNY,
SONNY, KEVIN, GRAFFITI PETE, MEN:**
Look at the fireworks . . .

Light up the night sky . . .

Look at the fireworks . . .

Light up the night sky . . .

**VANESSA, DANIELA, WOMEN,
PIRAGUA GUY, MEN:**
Look at the fireworks . . .
Look at the fireworks fly!

Light up the night sky!

Look at the fireworks fly!

Light up the night sky! ❸

SONNY:
It's late and this grate won't come down!
Come down!

SONNY:
It's late and
This grate
Won't come
Down!

We are
Powerless,
We are
Powerless.

We are
Powerless,

We are
Powerless!
Powerless!

CARLA:
Oh God, so much
Panic
The crowd was
Manic with
Everybody
Screaming and
Shoving
And shouting
And slapping
And everyone's
Frantic, what's
Happening with
You?
We are
Powerless!

We are
Powerless!

DANIELA:

Mira mi amor
Hazme un favor
Despiértale
Abuela
Y a lo mejor
Ella tiene una
Vela.

¡Estuve
Bailando
Cuando vino el
Apagón.
Aquí hay gente
Pero no sé
Quienes son! ❹

MEN:

We are
Powerless!
We are
Powerless!

+PIRAGUA GUY, MEN:
Powerless.

+VANESSA, WOMEN:
We are powerless,
We are powerless!

(More explosions. USNAVI enters his apartment.)

ENSEMBLE: Look at the fireworks . . .

USNAVI: Abuela, are you all right?

ENSEMBLE: Light up the night sky . . .

ABUELA CLAUDIA: The stars are out tonight!

ENSEMBLE: Look at the fireworks . . .

USNAVI: You're not alone tonight . . .

ENSEMBLE: Light up the night sky . . .

USNAVI, ABUELA CLAUDIA: You're/I'm not alone
    tonight . . .

ABUELA CLAUDIA: Usnavi, please promise me
    you'll guard this with your life.

(She hands USNAVI a brown paper bag. He looks inside.)

USNAVI: Abuela, I've never seen— ❺

USNAVI, ABUELA CLAUDIA: This much money in my
    life!

(BENNY finds NINA on the street.)

BENNY: Nina, there you are!

NINA: I've gotta go!

BENNY: I'll get you out of here tonight!

3. Our final incarnation of "Blackout" was written for the movie. Instead of Nina and Benny fighting this time, it's Usnavi and Vanessa, with Benny going to help out at the dispatch. It was fun going in one more time.

4. Andréa Burns and I always called her section in this "The Hair on Lady Liberty's Head." I remember hearing that Frédéric Auguste Bartholdi, the sculptor who designed the Statue of Liberty, filled out the hair on the top of her head even though planes did not yet exist and there was no way to see it from overhead. This lyric is *so* detailed, but is totally buried in counterpoint and other melodies going on. There's no way to clearly see it—YET. Hence the nickname.

5. Obviously, the movie omits this section of the song in favor of a much bigger moment with Abuela. I think Quiara's decision to withhold the identity of the Lotto winner until later in the movie pays enormous dividends. And it was only in post-production of the movie that we discovered that putting "Paciencia y Fe" *after* "Blackout" made for an incredible storytelling moment and amplified Abuela's life story.

6. Vanessa—my wife, not the salon lady—always used to cry at this part, which is wild to me. I asked her why, and she said, "Because they're both stubborn, and they love each other."

7. Off-Broadway, we had to institute a $1 fine for anyone who sang the "En Washington Heights!" ahead of Alex's cue. It happened a lot.

NINA: I don't need anything!
Tonight, I can find my way home—

BENNY: Then find your way home! ⑥

(She stops.)

NINA: Without you—

NINA, BENNY: Without you—

(She runs away from him.)

GROUP 1 (USNAVI, KEVIN, SONNY, GRAFFITI PETE, MEN, VANESSA, CAMILA, ABUELA CLAUDIA, WOMEN): Look at the fireworks . . .

GROUP 2 (PIRAGUA GUY, MEN, DANIELA, CARLA, WOMEN): Look at the fireworks . . .

GROUP 1: Look at the fireworks . . .

GROUP 2: Look at the fireworks . . .

COMPANY: Light up the night sky . . .

CARLA, DANIELA, PIRAGUA GUY, MEN: Light up the night sky . . .

COMPANY: En Washington . . .
Look at the fireworks . . .
Look at the fireworks . . .

VANESSA, CAMILA, CARLA, WOMEN, ABUELA CLAUDIA, DANIELA, SONNY, PIRAGUA GUY, MEN, USNAVI, KEVIN: Light up the night sky . . .

WOMEN, GRAFFITI PETE, MEN: Light up the night sky . . .

(BENNY finds NINA, grabs her. They kiss, illuminated by fireworks.)

COMPANY: En Washington Heights! ⑦

End of Act One

Recuerdo

NÚMERO CINCO

ROBIN DE JESÚS

SONNY IN THE ORIGINAL OFF-BROADWAY AND BROADWAY CASTS

When I met everyone, I was only twenty years old. I'd been invited to play Sonny at the O'Neill. The whole time we were there, I spent my breaks on the phone or online, trying to get loans to go to college. I had already gotten accepted and thought that *In the Heights* would be the last thing I did before school.

Finally, Janet and Doreen pulled me aside. They said, "Baby, what are you doing?" I told them I was trying to get loans, since school started in a month and a half. They said, "You know this show's going to happen, right?" They spent thirty minutes convincing me to stay with it and not go to school.

A couple months later, I got cast in my first Broadway show, *Rent.* So I was able to do the workshop of *Heights,* then go to 37 Arts, and on to Broadway. Somehow I knew I was going to get nominated for a Tony Award, and I did. I found out when I was standing right outside Bubba Gump Shrimp Co., which is where I'd worked and been miserable when I tried to earn money for school. When I heard the news, what came out of my mouth was primal: I literally began to moan as if delivering a baby. I formed a sort of horseshoe shape with my body. The sound came from my ancestors, out of my intestines. The only other time I reacted like that was when I came out of the closet to my mother.

But once I got that nomination, I unraveled. I didn't understand how to handle success at that age. At first I felt grateful to be nominated. Then I developed imposter syndrome and started feeling really guilty. Why did I have this luck, when so many from my community didn't?

By the week of the ceremony, you want that shit. You want it so bad. When my category came, I felt my community wrap me in love. I felt like I could reach out and touch it. When my name wasn't called, I felt my shoulders drop—not from disappointment, but from an immense sense of relief. Because I had been so mean to myself.

Right after my category, it was our turn to perform. My castmates didn't know what to say to me. I said, "No, guys—I'm so happy, I'm so grateful, let's go kill this shit." And we did.

All these years later, I've kept my opening night gift from the producers: a charcoal drawing of the show [by Todd DiCiurcio]. It's so beautiful, and it brings back so much. I feel like, cheesy as it sounds, we really did grow so much in that period. We learned what family means to us, and friendship, and love, and artistry.

I remember on my first couple jobs after the show closed, I would compare it to *Heights*. It took a while to get rid of that. It wasn't serving anyone. Now I don't feel the need to compare any present job to that one. But I do feel the need to be grateful for it. If it's the best thing that ever happened for me workwise, then I'm just grateful that it happened at all.

In 2008, *In the Heights* received thirteen Tony Award nominations, more than any other show that year. One of them was for the all-important Best Musical award, though *Heights* wasn't expected to win it.

Early in the ceremony, which was televised live from Radio City Music Hall, Andy won the award for Best Choreography and Lac and Bill won for Best Orchestrations. None of them had been nominated before.

Neither had Lin, who won for Best Original Score. When he walked onstage, he accepted his trophy, turned to the mic, and started rapping this speech:

1. I thought a lot about what I might say if I was lucky enough to win, but I was too superstitious to write anything down. I'll never forget seeing a documentary wherein a theater producer showed his acceptance speech to the cameras before tucking it into his tuxedo jacket—where it *stayed*, because his show didn't win. So I had "Bill Sherman/Jill Furman" in my head, and I had "Andy Blank/Buzzetti for every spank," and I had "Back, son/ Chris Jackson." I'd recite those few lines in the shower or when I was alone in the week leading up to the Tonys.

2. Here's where the audience started applauding, and all the little index cards that only existed in my brain kinda fell on the floor. From here on out, I'm truly improvising.

3. You can see me looking around for how to proceed. Just before my segment, there was an honorary award for Sondheim, so that's where my brain went first.

Then I spotted my row, where my parents, sister, and Vanessa were beaming. So I made up lines about them next.

4. Then I remembered the flag in my pocket (which I'd intended to pull out whether I won or lost). I had just enough time to see my Titi Yamilla practically falling out of the mezzanine screaming before they whisked me away.

I used to dream about this moment, now I'm in it.
Tell the conductor to hold the baton a minute. ❶
I'll start with Alex Lacamoire and Bill Sherman,
Kevin McCollum, Jeffrey Seller, and Jill Furman,
Quiara, for keeping the pages turnin'.
Tommy Kail, for keeping the engine burnin',
For being so discernin' through every all-nighter.
Dr. Herbert for telling me, "You're a writer."

I have to thank Andy Blank for every spank.
Matter of fact, thank John Buzzetti for every
    drink.
Thank the cast and crew for having each other's
    backs, son.
I don't know about God but I believe in
    Chris Jackson. ❷
I don't know what else I got, I'm off the dome. ❸
I know I wrote a little show about home.
Mr. Sondheim—look, I made a hat!
Where there never was a hat!
It's a Latin hat at that!
Mom, Dad, and Cita, I wrote a play!
Y'all came to every play.
Thanks for being here today.
Vanessa, who still leaves me breathless,
Thanks for loving me when I was broke and
    making breakfast.

And with that, I want to thank all my Latino
    people. ❹
This is for Abuelo Guisin and Puerto Rico!

The last prize of the night was Best Musical. The winner was *In the Heights*. The entire company rushed onstage. Kevin and Jeffrey lifted Lin to their shoulders.

"We won the Tony [for Best Musical], and we're all standing on the stage of Radio City, and they said, 'All right, good night, and see you next year.' The lights came on, and every single person ran offstage. And everybody in the audience ran to the bathroom. I stood there by myself for a while and realized a truth: We just won the big prize, it was not three minutes ago, and people are already talking about next year and all they're thinking about is: *Where are we going to eat?*

"So it can't be about that. It has to be about the experience of making it." —TOMMY KAIL

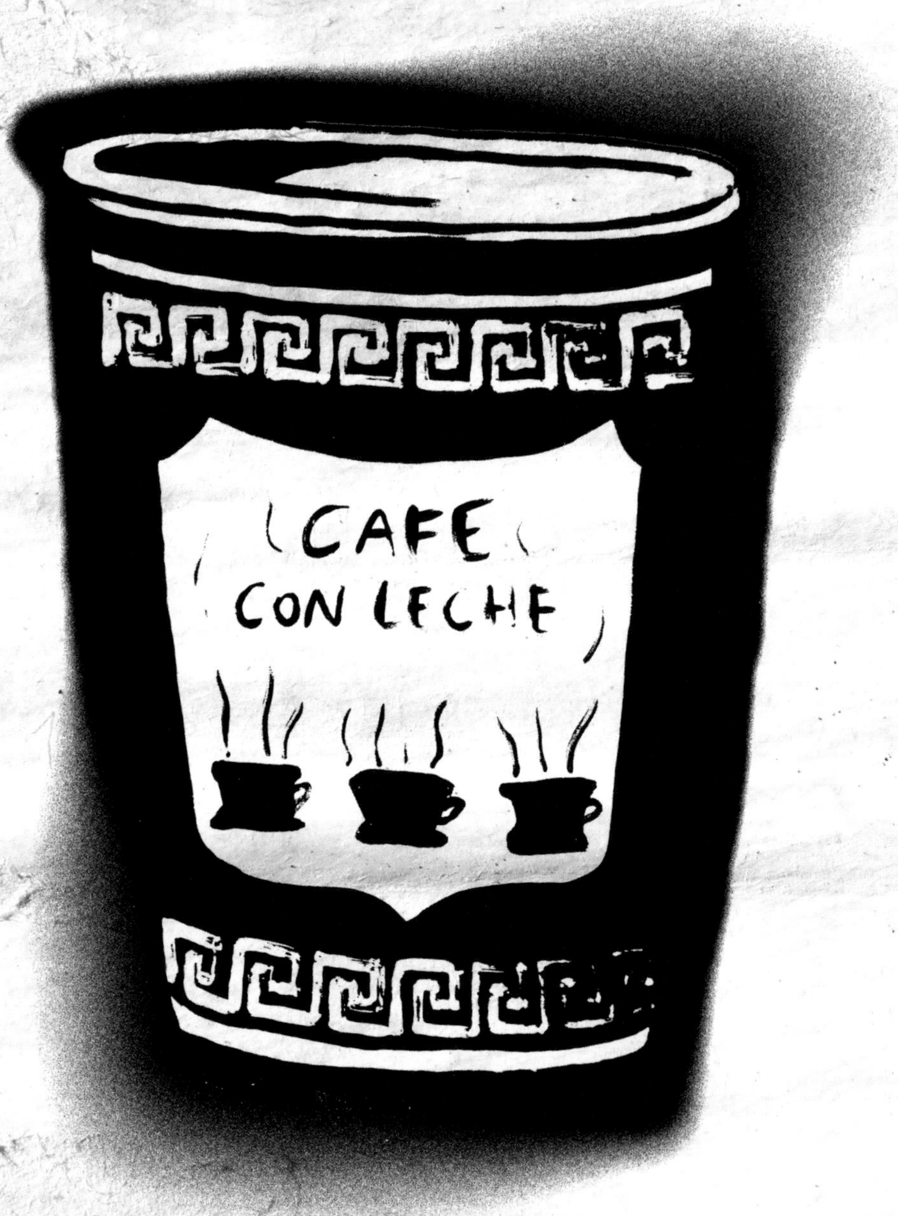
CAFE
CON LECHE

CHAPTER *Thirteen*

GOODBYE

37 ARTS WAS THE first to go. It had opened with high hopes of becoming a fixture on the Off-Broadway scene, but it ceased presenting theater shortly after *In the Heights* left. The building changed owners and dropped its old name before the show collected its Tony Awards in 2008.

Next to go were the little stores where Paul Tazewell had shopped for costumes. A few closed early in 2008. More closed when the Great Recession hit that fall. Still more closed in the recovery that followed, the years when New York was more and more becoming a city, as Usnavi puts it, of "rich folks and hipsters."

A burst pipe and flooded inventory couldn't shut down the Drama Book Shop. But a rent hike in 2018 told the owners that it was once again time to go. Its old location on West Fortieth Street, with its storied basement, sells "brand name ladies' clothing and shoes." As of this writing, anyway.

It's the nature of this propulsive city, more than most cities, to transform. A subtle aspect of the show's realism is acknowledging that Washington Heights has changed, is changing, and will change: The dilemma for the people who live there is how to respond.

As with places, so with people. The community that formed around the Broadway company of *Heights* went through the same experience as the one they depicted

onstage. The delirious party on Tony night marked the culmination of one phase of the show's life and the beginning of another.

"Once *In the Heights* was a success, that was the big bang that blew it all up," says Bill. "We scattered in our different directions."

KAREN OLIVO WAS THE first to go. A few months after opening night, she was offered the role of Anita in a Broadway revival of *West Side Story*. It's one of the iconic roles in all of musical theater—an easy call, right?

"It was the worst. The absolute worst," she recalls. "I didn't want to leave. How could you want to leave your favorite place?"

But this was not any old Broadway revival of *West Side Story*. It would be directed by the show's librettist, Arthur Laurents. It would feature Spanish translations of Stephen Sondheim's lyrics, by none other than Lin.

The prospect scared Karen. Which is how she knew she had to do it.

"I wept like a baby," she says. "Oh, I cried night after night." She doesn't remember telling her castmates that she was leaving, only that it happened fast. She got the offer on a Thursday; that Sunday, she played Vanessa for the last time.

Karen would win a Tony Award for playing Anita, but other members of the *Heights* company wouldn't have the same immediate good fortune. Joshua Henry left for a different gig even before Karen did, but soon returned. His run of acclaimed star turns on Broadway would begin a little later.

Regardless of what came next, some actors had trouble moving on, particularly the young ones. Robin says he's not the only cast member who felt "ruined" after leaving the show. "Real talk: There's a world where the best job we could ever have is now in our past, and we have to move forward anyway," he says. "Being twenty-one and feeling that way—that'll f--- you up."

It wasn't just the actors. "After *Heights*, it's really hard to do other collaborations," Andy says. "It's *really* hard."

He credits the show with having started his career as a choreographer. Not just because people offered him so many jobs afterward and not even because it won him a Tony Award, but because his Voltron collaborators changed him in some deeper and more meaningful way.

"They made me my best self," he says.

WHEN NEW ARTISTS JOINED *Heights,* the old-timers would fold them into their customs and traditions. Andréa Burns invited other Jewish members of the company to her dressing room to celebrate Passover. They would use the paper inserts from their wig caps to cover their heads, break bread together, and pray. "I think we did it because the show is so much about honoring family and culture and tradition," she says.

Her young son, Hudson, became a kind of "company mascot," she says: You'd see him at the parties; he'd be dancing around. When he turned five, everybody gathered on the big staircase in the lobby to sing "Happy Birthday." They did it again when he turned six. When he turned seven, Andréa remembers how bittersweet it was, knowing this was his last *Heights* birthday.

By then, December 2010, the producers had announced that the show would close. It would ultimately run 1,184 performances. It was a success by all the standard metrics, both financial, since it recouped its investment, and creative—all the awards, all the careers that were launched. But its most powerful effects are less tangible.

People around Broadway called *Heights* a breakthrough. It was, but not because the show invented something. Salsa and hip-hop existed long before Lin started writing. The breakthrough was combining those old forms in new ways for an audience that might not be familiar with either—or the cultures that nurtured them. *Heights* does on a macro level what its characters do again and again on a micro level in "Breathe," "No Me Diga," and, most explicitly, "Sunrise": *translation*. (There will be term papers about this, if there haven't been already.)

> " THE SHOW IS SO MUCH ABOUT **HONORING FAMILY** AND **CULTURE** AND **TRADITION**."

You could identify this or that show that followed *Heights* to Broadway, settling in the richer musical terrain that Lin and Quiara had opened. A more significant shift occurred between the ears of the people who develop new work. Every producer draws a mental line that separates the ideas worth supporting from the ones that are too crazy to try. *Heights* moved that line in a lot of brains. *Hey, if the salsa-and-hip-hop show made by nobodies in a bookstore basement can make it, why not this?*

The show's most lasting impact is the least tangible: its influence on the artists coming next. Creative inspiration can be hard to spot and slow to appear. Did anybody at the Nederlander Theatre on a winter night in 1997 know what *Rent* was doing to the mind and heart of the seventeen-year-old in the balcony's last row? Or what, years later, it would lead Lin to do?

With that timetable in mind, it's too soon to gauge the show's full impact. But we know a *few* people who came to *In the Heights,* and we know one or two things that it has led them to do.

A couple of acting students, Melissa Barrera and Corey Hawkins, were inspired to see people who looked like them, and stories familiar to their experience, on a Broadway stage. Another student, Anthony Ramos, was so galvanized by the sight that he decided not to give up on acting.

Two film-industry professionals, production designer Nelson Coates and costume designer Mitchell Travers, were thrilled by the music and the story and the lovingly exact way their Broadway counterparts had rendered a New York neighborhood onstage. They both saw it more than once.

Jon M. Chu, who went to the show without knowing what to expect, was surprised to be sobbing at the end: Usnavi's realization that he had found his home in Washington Heights dredged up powerful memories from his youth, before he was a movie director, when he was still a first-generation Asian American kid in California.

THE SHOW HAD A RAUCOUS VIBE THAT NIGHT.

If any of them attended the same performance, they didn't realize it. None of them had met. But give it time. Before long they would be working together every day, trying to recapture the astonishment they had felt at the Rodgers while making their movie version of *In the Heights.*

ON CLOSING NIGHT, LIN'S trip to the Rodgers took longer than it used to take. He didn't mind.

Living in the West Sixties had been good for his commute but terrible for his soul. When his one-year contract playing Usnavi had ended, he'd left the show and immediately moved back to his old neighborhood. He traveled to the theater on January 9, 2011, from the uptown apartment he shared with Vanessa Nadal. They had gotten married a few months earlier; Rubén Blades had sung at the reception.

The show had a raucous vibe that night. It helped that so many *Heights* alumni were in the audience. They were easy to spot: At the end of "Carnaval del Barrio," they were the ones waving flags of Latin American nations over their heads. It was an expression of pride in where they'd come from and a celebration of the show they'd spent months or years making.

They were also cheering for Lin, who had returned to play Usnavi for the show's final weeks. After the curtain call, he once again invited the producers and creative team to join the cast onstage. With everybody lined up behind him, Lin freestyled one last rap. You have to imagine it heavily punctuated by cheers:

I know how upset some of y'all are getting,
But listen, *In the Heights* ain't closing, this is
    spreading.
And, yeah, I'm up here on this lectern,
But one day you'll be somewhere midwestern,
Somewhere chillin' in some outer theater lobby,
Some little high schooler is gonna be playing
    Usnavi!
So I want all of y'all to grab this:
That little white kid is gonna know what a Puerto
    Rican flag is!
And wherever you all roam,
Remember for a time this Broadway was home.

Sunrise [1]

1. As painful as it was to lose "Sunrise" for the movie—losing Abuela in the blackout meant there was no time for this moment in its aftermath—I didn't *really* lose it. Listen carefully to the dance [illegible] in "When the Sun [illegible] Down" and you'll hear the opening theme of "Sunrise," a moment that I think is incredibly powerful for fans of this song (for me, it's powerful for me).

2. Heaven hath no joy like a student matinee where two characters emerge from a fire escape, half-clothed, the morning after, and one says, "Are you ready to try again?" The *screams*! We had to add measures of music to accommodate the scandalized youth screams!

3. Originally, "Sunrise" didn't have a Spanish lesson within it—it was just a pretty good pop song wherein Benny and Nina grappled with their night and how they'd break their romance to Nina's dad/Benny's boss. When either Tommy or Quiara suggested the song could be a Spanish lesson, the thing just *burst* open. Sometimes the breakthrough is just one more good idea away.

4. More bilingual rhyming: calor/dolor, llámame/ámame, last night/that's right, blue/do. This is the best crossword puzzle work, finding the right words that work as a scene, a song, and a progression of their relationship.

NINA: Are you ready to try again? [2]

BENNY: I think I'm ready.

NINA: *Okay. Here we go.*
Esquina [3]

BENNY: Corner

NINA: Tienda

BENNY: Store

NINA: Bombilla

BENNY: Lightbulb—

NINA: *You're sure?*

BENNY: *I'm sure.*

NINA: Three out of three, you did all right!

BENNY: Teach me a little more . . .

NINA: Calor

BENNY: Heat

NINA: Anoche

BENNY: Last night

NINA: Dolor [4]

BENNY: Pain

NINA: That's right.
Llámame.

BENNY: Call me.

NINA: Azul

BENNY: Blue

NINA: Ámame.

BENNY: Love me.

NINA: Perhaps I do—

BENNY: Well, how do you say kiss me?

NINA: Bésame.

BENNY: And how do you say hold me?

NINA: Abrázame.
Al amanecer. At sunrise.

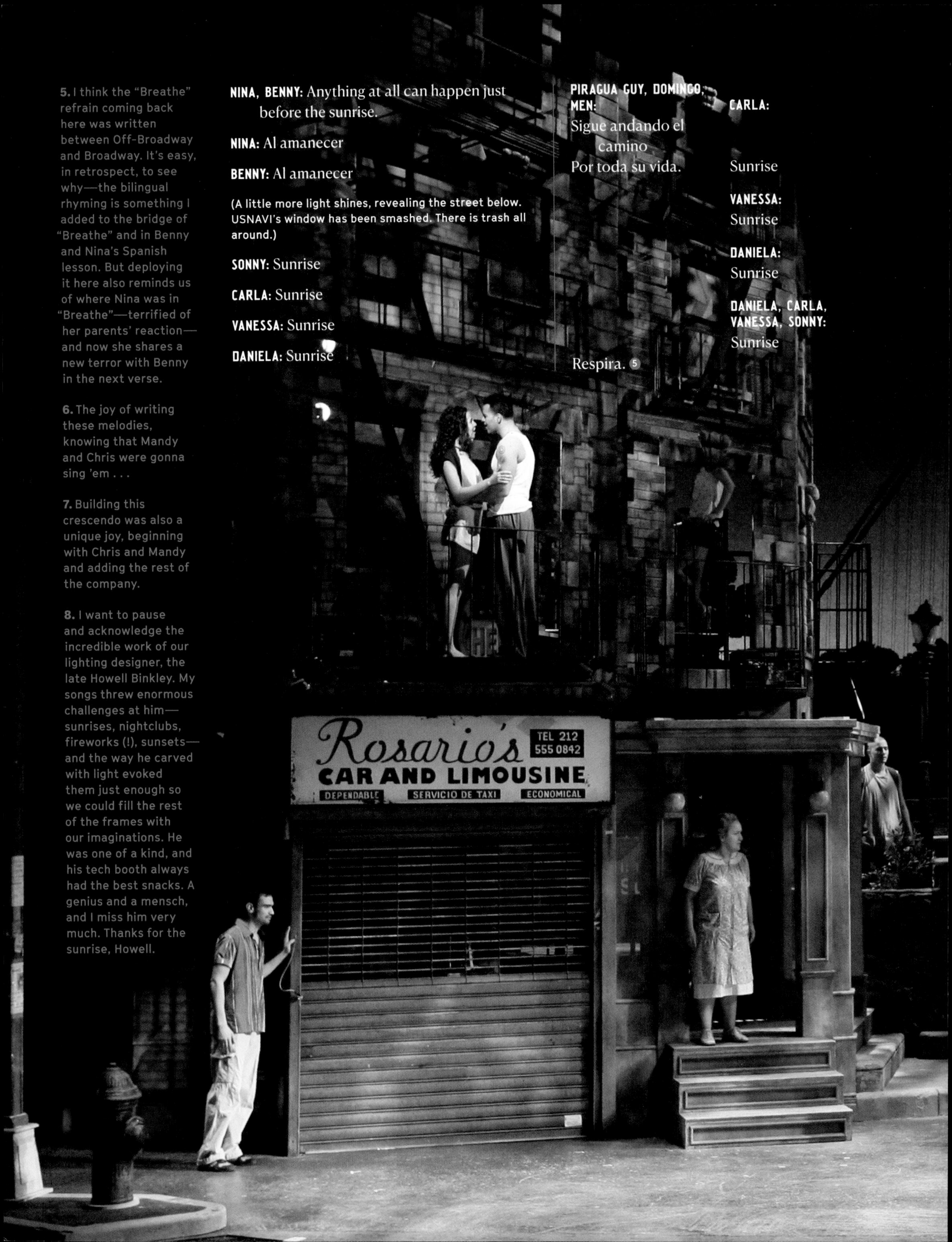

5. I think the "Breathe" refrain coming back here was written between Off-Broadway and Broadway. It's easy, in retrospect, to see why—the bilingual rhyming is something I added to the bridge of "Breathe" and in Benny and Nina's Spanish lesson. But deploying it here also reminds us of where Nina was in "Breathe"—terrified of her parents' reaction—and now she shares a new terror with Benny in the next verse.

6. The joy of writing these melodies, knowing that Mandy and Chris were gonna sing 'em . . .

7. Building this crescendo was also a unique joy, beginning with Chris and Mandy and adding the rest of the company.

8. I want to pause and acknowledge the incredible work of our lighting designer, the late Howell Binkley. My songs threw enormous challenges at him— sunrises, nightclubs, fireworks (!), sunsets— and the way he carved with light evoked them just enough so we could fill the rest of the frames with our imaginations. He was one of a kind, and his tech booth always had the best snacks. A genius and a mensch, and I miss him very much. Thanks for the sunrise, Howell.

NINA, BENNY: Anything at all can happen just before the sunrise.

NINA: Al amanecer

BENNY: Al amanecer

(A little more light shines, revealing the street below. USNAVI's window has been smashed. There is trash all around.)

SONNY: Sunrise

CARLA: Sunrise

VANESSA: Sunrise

DANIELA: Sunrise

PIRAGUA GUY, DOMINGO, MEN:
Sigue andando el camino
Por toda su vida.

Respira. 5

CARLA:

Sunrise

VANESSA:
Sunrise

DANIELA:
Sunrise

DANIELA, CARLA, VANESSA, SONNY:
Sunrise

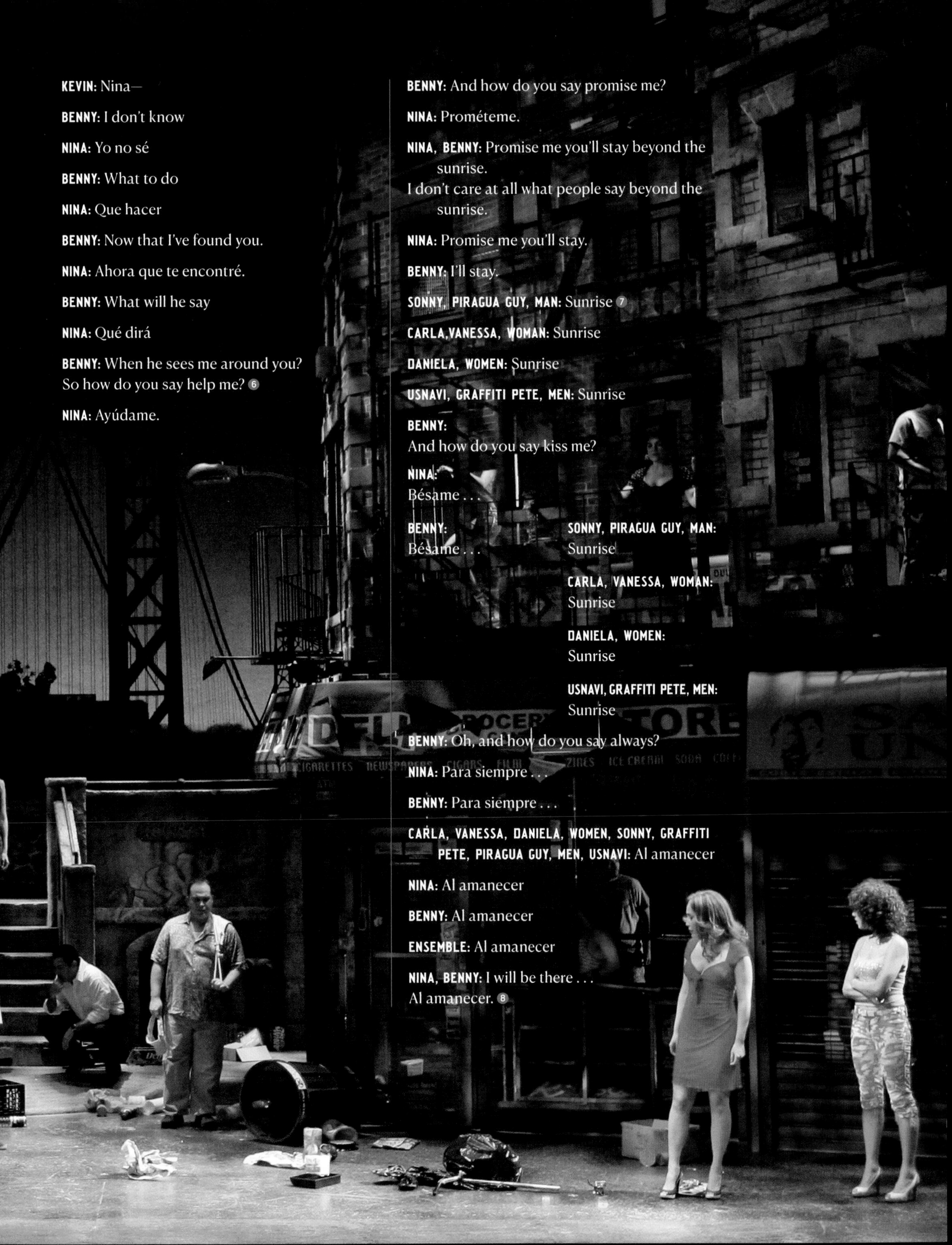

KEVIN: Nina—

BENNY: I don't know

NINA: Yo no sé

BENNY: What to do

NINA: Que hacer

BENNY: Now that I've found you.

NINA: Ahora que te encontré.

BENNY: What will he say

NINA: Qué dirá

BENNY: When he sees me around you?
So how do you say help me? [6]

NINA: Ayúdame.

BENNY: And how do you say promise me?

NINA: Prométeme.

NINA, BENNY: Promise me you'll stay beyond the
   sunrise.
I don't care at all what people say beyond the
   sunrise.

NINA: Promise me you'll stay.

BENNY: I'll stay.

SONNY, PIRAGUA GUY, MAN: Sunrise [7]

CARLA, VANESSA, WOMAN: Sunrise

DANIELA, WOMEN: Sunrise

USNAVI, GRAFFITI PETE, MEN: Sunrise

BENNY:
And how do you say kiss me?

NINA:
Bésame . . .

BENNY:	SONNY, PIRAGUA GUY, MAN:
Bésame . . .	Sunrise
	CARLA, VANESSA, WOMAN:
	Sunrise
	DANIELA, WOMEN:
	Sunrise
	USNAVI, GRAFFITI PETE, MEN:
	Sunrise

BENNY: Oh, and how do you say always?

NINA: Para siempre . . .

BENNY: Para siempre . . .

CARLA, VANESSA, DANIELA, WOMEN, SONNY, GRAFFITI
   PETE, PIRAGUA GUY, MEN, USNAVI: Al amanecer

NINA: Al amanecer

BENNY: Al amanecer

ENSEMBLE: Al amanecer

NINA, BENNY: I will be there . . .
Al amanecer. [8]

CHAPTER Fourteen

STAND ON MY SHOULDERS

DANIEL YEARWOOD WAS SURPRISED when the director began to sing along with his *Heights* audition. He was hoping to be cast as Benny, which meant performing "When You're Home." When he reached the song's bridge, she jumped right in, delivering a note-perfect rendition of Nina's lyrics about feeling lost. Then she kept going, harmonizing with him all the way to the end.

He was only seventeen and had seen just a couple of musicals, but he knew enough to be impressed.

The admiration was mutual. He got the part.

Once rehearsals started, she kept laughing at things Daniel did, or shaking her head. She'd say, "He's like a mini Chris."

After a couple of days of this, he said, "What do you mean?"

"Chris Jackson," she replied. "I'm married to him."

The director was Veronica Jackson, and the production was at the Kips Bay Boys & Girls Club in the Bronx. For more than a century, the club has provided activities and instruction to young people from the neighborhood: mostly Black or Latino, mostly the children of immigrants, and mostly from families below the poverty line. Veronica and the show's other director, Dominic Colón, had spent their formative years going there, learning what they

needed to know to make careers in entertainment. So did J. Lo. So did Kerry Washington (who had a brief stint as Nina before Hollywood called—and before Veronica proved to have such potent chemistry with Chris, onstage and off).

In 2012, the Kips Bay drama teacher who had meant so much to Veronica and Dominic passed away. They felt they should put on a show, something he might have done. There was no mystery about which show it ought to be.

That is how a few dozen teenagers in a little theater in the Bronx got to be among the first people in the world to perform *In the Heights*.

SUCCESSFUL MUSICALS, LIKE OTHER living creatures, proceed through phases as they grow. First come years of germination in studios and rehearsal rooms, then the sunshiny stretch of months or years on Broadway, then dispersal across the nation via one or several tours. As the members of the original creative team leave for other projects, they make the show available for licensing. That means professional, amateur, and student companies get to plant the seed in their own gardens and see what grows.

Since 2011, licensing for *In the Heights* has been handled by the Rodgers & Hammerstein Organization, a

146

division of Concord Theatricals. Ted Chapin, the president of R&H, always seeks out exciting new voices, so he had jumped at the chance to represent Lin and Quiara's show. But he admits to being concerned by the early response when R&H began pitching *Heights* to producers: It was "a little slow," he recalls. He briefly wondered if R&H might not recoup the advance it had paid for the rights.

"People would say, 'Oh, it's got some *rap music* in it, Michelle,'" recalls Michelle Yaroshko, the senior vice president of professional licensing at Concord. She tried to help producers identify the elements that were familiar. Wasn't a hip-hop number really a form of patter song? And wasn't *Heights* really, deep down, a show about family? Who can't relate to family?

The more theaters that did the show, Michelle was relieved to find, the more theaters wanted to do it. Its productions began to spread, largely along trails carved by earlier migrations: from New York to other cities, then out to the suburbs, then beyond. The show's career around the country began to seem like the vision Abuela Claudia offers to Usnavi: a legacy of "Hundreds of Stories," going on and on, each one a little different from the last.

And it wasn't just professional companies, either. *Heights* has become a staple of high school drama programs, exactly as Lin intended. His closing night prophecy—that white kids in the Midwest would learn what a Puerto Rican flag is—has come true many, many times.

MOST OF THOSE PRODUCTIONS happened without the involvement or even the knowledge of the original creative team. This, too, makes the Kips Bay production exceptional, because members of the *Heights* community were right there in the room. Carlos Salazar, who had performed in the national tour, choreographed the show. Veronica arranged for the cast to receive visits from Broadway company members Andréa Burns, Jon Rua, Seth Stewart, and an actor who was originally a little skeptical of the whole operation.

"I thought she was crazy," says Chris. "But that's where her heart is."

Staging *In the Heights* was hard for the Kips Bay cast in ways that it hadn't been for the original Broadway company. "There were some kids in foster homes, some who

HEIGHTS HAS BECOME A STAPLE OF HIGH SCHOOL DRAMA PROGRAMS, EXACTLY AS LIN INTENDED.

Esmeralda Castellon
and Lin-Manuel Miranda

were homeless and killing themselves just to get there," Veronica recalls. Rehearsals were "beautifully challenging," Dominic adds, "because if it wasn't one thing, it was another."

Figuring out the logistics of getting all those young actors to and from rehearsal was only part of the difficulty. "*Heights* is a story about home, and that's not necessarily an easy, pretty picture for a lot of young people," Dominic says. "That brings up a lot of stuff. So we knew we needed to create a space where people felt safe." He and Veronica designed the rehearsal process to allow a lot of time for talking about what was happening in everybody's lives.

Daniel was more fortunate than many of his castmates in how he grew up, but he felt the same deep connection to the material they did: "All of our childhoods, we were coming up with what Lin spoke about: 'In five years, when this whole city's rich folks and hipsters.'" He loved getting the chance to play such a big role in a musical, which he'd never done before. He loved getting to work with the cast, committed young artists of "all shapes, all sizes, all colors—all in a room learning '96,000.'"

And he loved spending time with Chris. As a kid, Daniel had liked to sing, but it was only after he heard Chris and the rest of the original *Heights* cast that he started to think he could make a career in musical theater. He soaked up the advice Chris offered—not just about playing Benny, but about how to carry himself, what to expect.

Chris, for his part, saw a lot of himself in Daniel: a young Black man with talent, trying to find his way. In fact,

to an uncanny degree, he saw a lot of his *Heights* castmates in the whole company at Kips Bay. "They're having roughly the same experiences we had when we were putting the show up. They're saying some of the same things, having some of the same breakthroughs in rehearsal," he says.

"The first time they sang 'Alabanza,' everybody was in tears—which is exactly what happened to us. I would just hug them and say, 'I understand, I understand.'"

IN APRIL 2013, the young cast shared their production of *In the Heights* with the world. They performed four sold-out shows to an audience comprising community members, *Heights* superfans, and members of the original company—including Lin, Lac, and Tommy, who came to see it in one intimidating clump.

Veronica and Dominic were stupendously proud of the actors. "Those young people were able to take their pain, or whatever it is, and turn it into light," Dominic says. They even made Tommy cry. ("A *lot*," Tommy says.)

Eight years later, the production goes on reverberating in their lives. Veronica says the actors came to form a community of their own, establishing unusually close ties. They still reach out to her.

For Daniel, being part of *In the Heights* wasn't just inspiring, it was useful. He drew on the lessons it had taught him very frequently in the job he would secure a few years later: playing John Laurens and Philip Hamilton in the Broadway cast of *Hamilton*.

Recuerdo

NÚMERO SEIS

ESMERALDA "EZZY" CASTELLON

DANIELA IN THE 2013
PRODUCTION AT KIPS BAY BOYS
& GIRLS CLUB IN THE BRONX

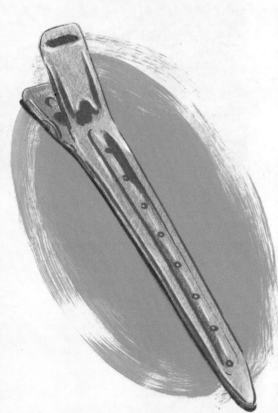

I first saw *In the Heights* a year after my dad passed. It became something my sister and I used to heal. I saw it, like, nine times. I did! And I fell in love with Daniela. I was like, "I am her, she is me, we are one." We were maniacs.

During closing week on Broadway, Lin came back, so of course we had to go. After the show that night— I believe in God—I prayed, "Lord, if you ever, *ever* bring this production back, I want to be Daniela, please let me be Daniela, I promise I will be the best Daniela ever." I really prayed this! I'm not even joking. But my sister just said, "The show's over, Ezzy. We can go."

So a couple of years later, my best friend, Joseph Dominick Martinez, was one of the producers of the show at Kips Bay Boys & Girls Club. I begged him to be in it, because I'm an actor and comedienne myself, but he said it was only for teenagers. Except then at the last minute, they needed somebody to play Daniela. He texted me, "Hey, would you consider it?" I was like, *"Hell motherf---ing yes."* I felt like I'd been cast on Broadway.

I met the other actors and started working with Dominic [Colón] and Veronica [Jackson]. And then who shows up at rehearsal one day but Andréa Burns. I was starstruck. I was like, *"It's the real Daniela—oh my God!"* She came up and said, "Are you Daniela?" I said yes. She was like, "All right, come on." And she went straight to work on me. So that was awesome. I had a little bit of a tough time executing one of the songs, but she just looked at me and said, "You can do this thing. That's why I'm pushing you." It was about believing in myself. And we got through it.

At the end of rehearsal, she told me, "You did amazing work, and this is for you." And she handed me a hair clip from the original show. She said, "I'm passing the torch to you. Now *you* become Daniela." Of course, I was a mess. "I'll do a good job! I promise!"

I personally felt like the show was overwhelming, in a good way. And I did use the clip onstage. Afterward, I put it in a plastic cup with the name of the show on it.

That musical is something else. It absolutely changed my life. It did. And it definitely turned the world upside down at Kips Bay. I grew up in that area. Now when I go up there, they're all like, "Daniela, *heeeey!*"

Hundreds of Stories [1]

1. This song is a joy in musically bouncing different characters off each other—the opening chords are the same as "Paciencia y Fe," but the chorus opens up to something much warmer that Abuela and Usnavi share. Then the rap section is *all* Usnavi . . . At a certain point, your characters tell you how they sound, and you become a stenographer.

2. I loved performing this rap because of the emotional whiplash—they've had this unbelievable good fortune, but even as he tries to imagine a better future, his darker memories just flood the frame.

3. Usnavi's a real name: We had a family friend who worked in immigration; she told me that she met an Usnavi, and I filed it away for future use. This musical moment was written between Off-Broadway and Broadway because I realized that half the audience still hadn't pieced together Usnavi's etymology. I always enjoyed the cascading laughs from Latino and non-Latino audiences—Latinos already laughing by "name the baby," and the quarter dropping for everyone else on "It really said 'U.S. Navy,' but hey." Sometimes Olga and I would sit in that laughter as an unintentional third wave of laughs would erupt, as everyone got on the same page.

4. Abuela taking on Usnavi's cadence here is such a lovely grace note.

USNAVI: Abuela.

ABUELA CLAUDIA: Are you okay?

USNAVI, ABUELA CLAUDIA: ¡Paciencia y fe! ¡Paciencia y fe!

USNAVI: Let me see it again!

(He looks in the bag.)

ABUELA CLAUDIA: We kept it safe.

USNAVI: So we survived the night
What happens today?

ABUELA CLAUDIA: A third for you.

USNAVI: Uh huh uh huh. Uh huh uh huh.

ABUELA CLAUDIA: A third for me!

USNAVI: ¡No pare, sigue, sigue!

ABUELA CLAUDIA: The rest for Sonny—
And with our share of the money
And with our share of the money—

Dream of the seaside air!
See me beside you there!
Think of the hundreds of stories we will share
You and I!

USNAVI, ABUELA CLAUDIA: Ayy . . .

ABUELA CLAUDIA: Now you can sell your store!
Open a bar by the shore!
I've told you hundreds of stories
About home. Make some more.

USNAVI, ABUELA CLAUDIA: More . . .

USNAVI: Yo! I know just where to go!
There's a little beach named Playa Rincón
With no roads, you need a rowboat or motorbike
To reach this beach and it's just a stone's throw
From home.
My folks' home.

Before I was born.
Before they passed on
And left me on my own, in New York, with the
    grocery store.
They would talk about home, I listened closely
    for
The way they whispered to each other
'Bout the warmer winter weather.
Inseparable, they even got sick together.
But they never got better . . . passed away that
    December
And left me with these memories like dyin'
    embers
From a dream I can't remember . . .
Ever since then it's like
Another day deeper in debt with different
    dilemmas.
The bodega's a mess, I'll be seeing less of
    Vanessa.
Abuela, I don't know how I can keep it
    together . . . ❷

ABUELA CLAUDIA: Remember the story of your
    name?
It was engraved on a passing ship on the day
    your family came.
Your father said, "Usnavi,
That's what we'll name the baby."

USNAVI: It really said "U.S. Navy," but hey . . . ❸
I worked with what they gave me, okay . . .

ABUELA CLAUDIA: They'd be so proud of you
    today . . .

USNAVI: Then by the end of July

ABUELA CLAUDIA: Uh huh uh huh. Uh huh
    uh huh. ❹

USNAVI: Out where the sea meets the sky

ABUELA CLAUDIA: ¡No pare, sigue, sigue!

USNAVI, ABUELA CLAUDIA: Think of the hundreds
    of stories
We'll create
You and I!
Ay . . .

ABUELA CLAUDIA: We'll find your island—

USNAVI: I'll find my island sky.

ABUELA CLAUDIA: Ay, find your island—

USNAVI: But whatever we do it's—

USNAVI, ABUELA CLAUDIA: You and I!

CHAPTER Fifteen

PLAN B

A FEW MONTHS AFTER Broadway opening night, a Hollywood studio announced plans to make a movie of *In the Heights*. By 2010, Lin was excited enough about its progress to crack jokes in TV interviews about who should be in the cast. (Betty White was a definite yes, he said.) In fact, the only actor officially attached at that point was Lin himself, as Usnavi. It would be his first film role. By the technical definition of the term, it would make him a movie star.

He also told interviewers about the many conversations he and Quiara were having about the best way to translate the story to the screen. They needed to make big changes to what they'd done before. Between *Heights* and his other pursuits, he wasn't finding much time for a new project, a hip-hop album.

Looking back on those interviews a decade later, Lin is struck not by his youthful enthusiasm or his industriousness, but by what he calls his "naïveté."

"I was thinking, *I have a studio, I have a director, what's the problem?*" he says. "I didn't realize all the extra hoops that still had to happen."

In early 2011, the project went into turnaround. That is Hollywood-speak for "not going to happen." In the span of a few months, he went from having two high-profile iterations of *In the Heights,* both of which starred him, to zero.

He packed some clothes, notebooks, and his disappointment and flew to Atlanta. He had been offered a role

in a Disney film, *The Odd Life of Timothy Green*. Because he was playing something vastly smaller than a movie-star role, he had plenty of free time on set. One day he spent it talking with one of the film's producers, Scott Sanders.

As it happened, Scott was a Broadway figure in his own right, having produced a musical version of Alice Walker's *The Color Purple* a few years earlier. He was also a friend of Jill, Kevin, and Jeffrey. He counted himself "a huge fan" of *Heights*. "Lin and Quiara were celebrating people in their lives, and in their community, but there was a universality to it," he says. "We all have an abuela, whether we call her that or not."

All of this meant that when Lin asked him—without expecting much to come of it—"Want to produce *In the Heights?*" Scott took the question seriously, and had an answer ready.

"F--- yes," he said.

As soon as he could arrange it, Scott and his producing partner Mara Jacobs pitched the project to a studio that he felt confident would want it. He was surprised when they passed. But he was prepared to keep trying. "Tenacity is my middle name," he says.

He got an offer to make the movie on a very tight budget. But he thought *In the Heights* needed more resources than that, so he turned it down and kept trying. And trying. By his recollection, he approached twelve studios, growing

Anthony Ramos ▶

152

THIS TIME
WASN'T GOING TO BE
ANYTHING
LIKE THE
OTHER TWO.

less surprised and more despondent with every no. He thought back to the offer he had rejected: "Have I made a terrible mistake?"

His options were nearly exhausted when he got the yes he needed. For the second time, *In the Heights* was on its way to becoming a major motion picture.

Until, for the second time, it wasn't—and for more fraught reasons than before.

The studio that had given Scott a yes was The Weinstein Company. The film was well into preproduction when, in October 2017, *The New York Times* published shocking allegations of sexual misconduct by Harvey Weinstein, the company's chief executive. Quiara released a statement via Twitter: She could no longer work with the company, and she and Lin hoped to extricate the project and give it "a fresh start" elsewhere.

That might not be easy, or even possible. If the company filed for bankruptcy, its assets might be divided among creditors, which meant the right to produce *In the Heights* could end up in a third party's control. It was "a dangerous moment" for the project, according to Anthony Bregman, the independent producer who had joined Scott and Mara on the film a few months earlier.

Scott recalls that people around him were saying, *This is never gonna happen.*

In March 2018, The Weinstein Company *did* file for bankruptcy. Many of its projects *did* get tied up. But not *In the Heights*. A few weeks before the bankruptcy filing,

the company's option to produce the movie had lapsed, which meant that control had reverted to Lin and Quiara just in time.

They were now a decade removed from Broadway opening night. Twice they had tried to get the movie made, and twice they had failed. They now faced the prospect of a third round of pitches all over Los Angeles, hoping somebody would help them realize their Hollywood dreams.

This time wasn't going to be anything like the other two. Enough years had passed since Lin's ill-fated first round of interviews that he'd managed to finish that hip-hop album. Only it wasn't an album anymore, it was a musical: *Hamilton*.

By 2018, the question wasn't whether a studio wanted to make *In the Heights*. The question was which studio wanted it the most.

"Lin's star had risen to the outer edges of the galaxy," Scott recalls.

The movie's director wasn't far behind.

LIN THOUGHT JON CHU seemed nervous; Jon thought Lin had other things on his mind. Both of them were right.

Lin says he was "jaded" with Hollywood when they sat down for the first time, in 2016. He was willing to meet the directors Scott proposed for the movie, but his focus was on *Hamilton*. It needed to be: He was due at the theater soon after their coffee date for one of his seven performances every week in the title role.

Jon seemed nervous because he really wanted to direct *In the Heights*. Also he was hoping not to get caught in a lie. He had told Lin that *Hamilton* was great, but he hadn't actually seen it. He didn't want to be That Guy and ask Lin for the hottest ticket in the universe. (He'd go on pretending for a full year. The first time Jon set eyes on Lin after actually seeing the show, he thought, *Oh f---, that's Lin-Manuel Miranda.*)

So neither of them was in the ideal frame of mind to recognize how much they shared.

Like Lin, Jon is the son of parents who were born someplace else: mainland China in his father's case and Taiwan for his mom. They settled in Northern California, where they had five kids in six and a half years. Because his grandmother and lots of aunts were around, family dinners regularly included a couple dozen people, some crowded around the table, some sitting on the stairs. That's one reason why the close-knit world of *Heights* felt so familiar to him, in spite of the difference in cultures. "I knew what this was, even if I didn't know," he says.

Jon also shared Lin's sensation of feeling out of place: "I'm not Asian enough for some, and too Asian for others," he says. He hoped to gain perspective on where he belonged by retracing his parents' steps, much as Lin did when he spent summers in Puerto Rico. He remembers a trip to Hong Kong during high school. "Everyone looks at you with their defenses down and treats you like they're your family. Or you go into a store or a restaurant and they're taking care of you. It was a very strange thing. I felt like, 'Oh, this is how it feels to be more connected with someone that you don't know. Well, maybe this is who I am, then.'"

The feeling didn't last. When Jon opened his mouth, the local kids called him "gweilo," which translates to "white devil."

Oh, Jon remembers feeling, *I'm not this at all.*

(In Puerto Rico, local kids sent Lin the same message by way of a different insult: "el gringuito.")

The two of them suffered extreme cases of a malady that most of us share: Who hasn't felt homesick at home?

▼ Jon Chu and Lin-Manuel Miranda at their first meeting

NEW YORK - 2016

But what's unusual—and surprising—is that both of them reached for the same treatment to feel better: that distinctive piece of '90s technology, the camcorder.

Lin says he spent high school videotaping his friends having fun, his friends rehearsing plays. "I *was* Mark," he says, referring to the scarf-wearing, emotionally blocked filmmaker in *Rent*. Late in the show, Mark's friend Roger calls him out for hiding behind his work, using a camera to avoid facing failure and loneliness: "For someone who longs for a community of his own/Who's with his camera, alone?" Lin, watching that scene at seventeen, took Roger's lines as "a personal indictment," he recalls. "It was easier for me to be a cameraman in my life than to participate in my life."

Jon took the camera thing even further than Lin. When he didn't have an actual camera, he would sometimes take a tissue box, stick an empty toilet paper roll on one end of it—so it had the general shape of a TV news camera—and use it to do fake interviews with other kids. "It allowed me to be friends with them without being friends with them," he says. "'Oh, that's the video guy, that's the weird video guy.'"

▲ Jon, his daughter Willow, and Christopher Scott

Eventually, Jon got his hands on a real camera as a student at USC film school. He was talent-spotted by Steven Spielberg and started making movies that were stylish and often dance-centric, like *Step Up 2: The Streets*. They had the energy of the musicals he had always loved—he uses the name "Jon M. Chu" because as a kid his grandfather took him to see *Yankee Doodle Dandy,* about the actor and composer George M. Cohan—even though they weren't really musicals. It took him until his mid-thirties to wonder why, if he loved musicals so much, he wasn't making them.

In fact, he was beginning to feel "creatively empty," he says. He enjoyed his work, but it didn't reflect his life or his deepest passions. He remembers thinking, *I need to find somewhere I can show people who I am.* He decided it was time to face his "cultural identity crisis."

That's when Lin and Quiara's musical about immigrant children trying to find a home crossed his desk.

You can see why he was nervous.

Over coffee, Jon told Lin about his experience being first-generation, about how the themes of the show resonated so powerfully with his life. Lin, already a fan of Jon's work, liked everything he heard. He would have been excited if he was capable of being excited about anything involving Hollywood at that point.

"I thought, *This guy understands the musical in his bones and will make a great movie if he gets the chance.* I just didn't know if he would get the chance."

They would all find out together in May 2018. That's when Lin, Quiara, Jon, and the producers started pitching the movie around Hollywood for the third time.

In a series of meetings with executives from a half dozen studios, they shared details of Jon's concept and Quiara's screenplay. She had come to feel a new responsibility in her writing partnership with Lin during the years he was absorbed in *Hamilton*. "This was on me, basically," she says. New elements of the story emerged; others disappeared. An entire character, Camila Rosario, went away, taking her song, "Enough," with her.

The response from the studios wasn't just gratifying—it was startling. Marketing staffers recorded funny videos set to the *Heights* opening number. They decorated back lots to look like Washington Heights. Of all the warm greetings that the *Heights* team received, one stood apart, and the reason owes a lot to the way Jon had begun to handle his cultural identity crisis. He had become attached to *Heights* at the same time he started work on a movie that addressed his experiences even more directly: *Crazy Rich Asians*. The movie hadn't been released by May 2018—all the magazine covers and think pieces and long lines at the box office were still a few months away. But execs at Warner Bros. knew what they were about to release. They believed that having Jon back, in a creative collaboration with Lin and Quiara, could yield a big event movie that was also a true cultural moment. "We desperately, desperately wanted the film," says Blair Rich, who was then the studio's global head of marketing.

"OH, THIS IS HOW IT FEELS TO BE MORE CONNECTED TO SOMEONE THAT YOU DON'T KNOW."

On the day of the pitch meeting, most of the Heights team went to Warner's headquarters in Los Angeles. Lin, the father of a new baby boy, stayed in New York, where he would join the meeting by videoconference from the studio's office at the Time Warner Center. Blair and her team seized the chance to show Lin why they were the right studio for the movie: Beyond having a global marketing reach, they had a unique commitment to the cultural specifics of Washington Heights.

So when Lin stepped off the elevator that day, he walked into a corporate lobby that had been transformed to look like the 181st Street subway station. A conference room, spanning half a floor, had been remade as a bodega, stocked with everything you'd find in one on Dyckman Street—right down to that morning's newspapers. The walls were lined with photos of Washington Heights residents, plus captions in which they said how excited they would be to see their neighborhood on the big screen.

Somebody handed Lin a piragua. He thought the guy looked familiar. It was an actual piragüero from uptown.

After his experience on *Crazy Rich Asians,* Jon could assure the team that Warner Bros. would back up this big show with real commitments: "I knew they said what they meant and meant what they said."

So when studio executives said that Jon could have the resources to film it the way he wanted to film it, when they said the movie would get a summer release, guaranteed to maximize the attention they could bring to bear, and when they gave final cut to Lin, he knew they would stand by all of it. (It's unusual, to say the least, for a composer/lyricist to get final cut. But Lin told Jon, "*You* have final cut.")

A few weeks later, Warner Bros. announced it was going to make *In the Heights*. Lin—as excited as he had been eight years earlier, but much, much wiser—tweeted a link to one of the news reports.

"I'll pop the champagne when cameras are rolling and @quiarahudes & I are walking to set, in our neighborhood," he wrote. "But still. So excited for Usnavi to finally find home."

157

Enough

1. Jeremy: What was it like for twenty-seven-year-old Lin to hear Priscilla Lopez sing one of his songs?

Lin: INTIMIDATING, JEREMY.

2. I think "Yapapapapa!" is an actual P. Lo-ism that I grabbed. She's such a delightful, larger-than-life presence that I just wanted to give her the ball and watch her dunk on her family.

3. I think in most marriages, one of the deadliest verbal blows one can land is, "You sound like your mother/father when you (insert behavior here)." The fact that she deploys it this early in the tune? Watch out.

4. I was so gratified when I found this line: "When you have a problem, you come home." It speaks so much to who Camila is, and it's wrapped around *her* idea of home, which is the loaded word around which our show hinges.

5. And again, the rhetorical gymnastics here: She's just made mincemeat out of Kevin's behavior; then if Nina for a second thinks she's in the right, she whips around to Nina and in three lines paints a picture of an eternally devoted father. To quote Willy Shakes: *All are punished.*

CAMILA: Oh my God, enough!
Now you listen to me . . .

NINA: *Mom . . .*

CAMILA: ¡Carajo, I said enough!
I'm sick of all this fighting!

KEVIN: *Cami . . .*

(CAMILA makes a yapping noise in his direction.)

CAMILA: Yapapapapa! ❷
I think you've said enough.
Now listen to what I say.
What I say goes.

Papi, you've pushed us all away!

KEVIN: *I'm trying to . . .*

CAMILA: I don't wanna hear it! We make
decisions as a family.
And throwing Benny out like that?
You sound just like your father! ❸
We both know what a sonofabitch he was!
You think it all comes down to you . . .

(KEVIN goes to embrace her.)

KEVIN: Cami, let's talk about it . . .

(CAMILA shoves him away.)

CAMILA: No no no no no!
No no no no no! No, you don't!
When you have a problem, you come home. ❹
You don't go off and make matters worse on
your own.
One day you're gonna come back home
And you're not gonna find me waiting anymore.

KEVIN: *I'm sorry . . .*

CAMILA: Huh. Damn right you're sorry.

(CAMILA turns her attention to NINA.)

So you stayed out all night.

NINA: *Mom . . .*

CAMILA: I'm talking now. ❺
You scared us half to death. You know that,
right?

NINA: *I'm sorry—*

CAMILA: Don't apologize to me. You save it for
your father.

NINA: *What?*

CAMILA: Look at your father.
He doesn't sleep when you're gone.
He's worked his whole life to help you go
farther.
And he can't admit when he's wrong.
Now who does that remind you of?
You two deserve each other!
For months you've lied to us.

What did we do . . .
To make you think we wouldn't do anything
    and everything for you? ⑥
When you have a problem, you come home.
You don't run off and hide from your family all
    alone!
You hear me?
When you have a problem, you come home.
As long as we're alive, you're never on your own.
Leave Benny,
Take Benny,
It doesn't make any difference, as long as you
    come home!

KEVIN: *Camila—*

CAMILA: No no no no no!
Enough lying
Enough screaming
I'm done trying
And I am leaving it up to you.
It's up to you.
I'll see you both back home. ⑦
Enough!

6. This song isn't autobiographical, but if anyone in my life were to sing it, it would be my dad over my mom any day. My father can turn anger on and off like a faucet, and he can remain hyperarticulate even at his angriest, a trait I share (though it's not a faucet for me; it's a day-ruiner and utterly draining). The times I have seen my parents the angriest were the various times when my sister and I put our safety on the line. Now? As a parent? I get it.

7. And *here*, the trumpets evoke the horns at the end of P. Lo's star-making tune "What I Did for Love" from *A Chorus Line.* God, I love P. Lo.

The BEACH

By QUIARA ALEGRÍA HUDES

WE HAVE TO SEE the beach. Hear the ocean. See footprints in the sand.

That was my first thought when tasked with turning the stage play into a screenplay. I didn't want to replicate the theater experience onscreen, to awkwardly cram a live experience into two dimensions. No, the movie had to retain all the spiritual DNA of the stage show but be filmic. Take us different places. Put us in landscapes that aren't possible onstage.

The beach. The beach.

I knew we needed it but wasn't sure how. Early screenplay drafts had snippets of the beach appear in the bodega—little

reminders of Usnavi's yearning for the D.R. Like, Usnavi's standing at the register and a shallow tide laps against his sneakers. Like, Usnavi's restocking cereal boxes and there's a pile of sand where the Cheerios should be. Like, a seagull perches on the Lotto machine. So that the audience feels plugged in to Usnavi's desire for escape, for home.

Symbolic images. They weren't integrated into the plot in a meaningful way. The beach setting, I felt, should be essential to the story line. So I scrapped all those snippets.

Meanwhile, something my Titi Ginny once said kept repeating on loop in my memory. She was telling the story of getting off an airplane from Puerto Rico, seeing big concrete buildings for the first

time. How impersonal and drab her new home looked, how foreign and intimidating the Bronx was on first glance. Titi Ginny said, "I felt like one tiny grain of sand from the beaches I left behind." I wrote my aunt's line down, missing her tremendously (she passed away in 2009). I put the note card beneath a bigger note card that said "ABUELA CLAUDIA." I like to outline and brainstorm this way, using note cards and paper scraps so I can shuffle ideas to new places as the piece evolves.

That Abuela Claudia line became a tentpole. A lot of note cards came and went, got added, removed, crossed out, thrown away, but that note card never changed.

The beaches I left behind . . .

That feeling of hearing Titi Ginny tell her old-head stories. I loved it so much. It fascinated me, being born and raised in Philly and not on an Arecibo farm. She was speaking of a faraway land, once upon a time . . .

Once upon a time. I realized an older Usnavi could capture that essence, telling his story to children. The storyteller on the beach. He found his island. *In the Heights*

had always been a generational piece, and the children on the beach added an entirely new generation. The next generation after Sonny, played in the movie by Olivia Perez, Analia Gomez, and Dean and Mason Vazquez.

One of the children is Older Usnavi's young daughter. I named her Iris after a kick-ass North Philly activist who helped launch the community gardening movement. Older Usnavi is telling his daughter about the strong women of Washington Heights. He's presenting her with role models. There's Nina, using proximity to power to go fight for her community's rights. There's Vanessa, choosing the path of a community artist, finding inspiration on the sidewalk. There's Daniela, reminding everyone to party through adversity and celebrate their roots. And there's Abuela Claudia, bien servicial, always of service, savoring life's small details and little acts of kindness.

What path will Older Usnavi's daughter choose? Will she emulate the role models her dad presents or perhaps forge a path

"I FELT LIKE ONE TINY GRAIN OF SAND FROM THE BEACHES I LEFT BEHIND."

```
                   GIRL (V.O.)
          What does sueñito mean?

                   MAN (V.O.)
          It means 'little dream.'


FADE IN:

EXT. BEACH (DOMINICAN REPUBLIC) - DAY

We find SEÑOR USNAVI, 40s, a jokester with a heart of
gold, on the sand.  An Igloo cooler is his chair.  KIDS
gather before him in bathing suits and beach gear.

                   KID #1
          That's it?  No story?

                   KID #2
          Can we go in the water?

                   SHY GIRL
          Let him explain.

We LINGER ON this Girl.  Eyes bright, full of curiosity.

                   OLDER USNAVI
          Bueno, it's the story of a block
          that disappeared.  Once upon a
          time in a faraway land called
          Nuevayol was un barrio called
          Washington Heights.  Say it, so it
          doesn't disappear.

                   KIDS
          Washington Heights.

                   OLDER USNAVI
          Oye... the streets were made of
          music.
```

all her own? He wants her to know: There are many ways to become a strong woman.

For the movie, we had to cut some numbers from the score. It wasn't easy, because Lin-Manuel writes exquisite songs, especially "Hundreds of Stories," which I love. In that song, Usnavi and Abuela Claudia dream of "the hundreds of stories we'll create" back on the island. We learn the origins of Usnavi's name. "It was engraved on a passing ship on the day your family came. Your father said, 'Usnavi, that's what we'll name the baby.'" "It really said 'U.S. Navy,' but hey . . ." It's an iconic moment in the stage musical. The song "Hundreds of Stories" became Older Usnavi's beach. I even found a way to get the story of Usnavi's name into the movie: the last rewrite I did. I was nervous that any scene I wrote couldn't live up to Lin's brilliant lyric. But a few days before we headed to the beach shoot, I realized: *Of course! He tells the kids the story of his name.* It felt natural. Then, I was done writing the movie.

THE BEACH.
I KNEW WE
NEEDED
IT BUT WASN'T
SURE HOW.

CHAPTER *Sixteen*

EVERYTHING IS MELTING

WASHINGTON HEIGHTS IS DENSE enough, and lively enough, to offer a distilled version of the New York paradox: Life is a nerve-fraying ordeal that you miss terribly as soon as it's gone. (According to local custom, people don't just double-park here, they *triple*-park.) Everybody knew that shooting a movie there would be difficult and expensive. But Jon couldn't imagine doing it any other way.

For all of its fantastical touches—what Jon calls its "sing-to-the-stars-y" energy—*Heights* has always drawn power from its realism, a depiction of life as it's actually lived. The sweet spot for the movie, Jon felt, would be offering "a very truthful take on living in Washington Heights, then upping it."

In other words: No matter how fraught the process might be, the cast, the crew, and all of their gear—up to and including their fake sun in the sky—were going to spend the summer of 2019 in Washington Heights.

"The essence of a movie dictates where you shoot it," explains Kevin McCormick, a Warner Bros. executive who was integral to *Heights*. "And there's no way you could not have made this in Washington Heights. To have a movie about this community and not film there would be such a lost opportunity."

The first thing they did there was listen. Members of the production team, particularly Samson Jacobson, the location manager (born and raised in the area—a definite plus), and Karla Sayles, the director of public affairs at Warner Bros., met with community leaders to field questions and respond to concerns. Once again, Luis Miranda was a vital resource, drawing on relationships he had built over decades to make introductions.

The producers vowed to do all they could to limit the physical footprint of the shoot. Cast members shared trailers that they might otherwise have kept to themselves. The production hired people from the neighborhood for roles onscreen and off. Instead of catering every meal, they encouraged actors and crew to buy lunch in area restaurants. They even funded a student production of the show at George Washington high school.

What you see onscreen is a two-hour-and-fourteen-minute record of movie professionals falling in love with a place and its people. They arrived uptown to discover that Washington Heights really *was* different from most places in New York. Locals opened the hydrants on hot afternoons and played dominoes on the sidewalks. The piragüeros really did park their carts on the sidewalk to hawk their flavors of the day. The fascination seemed to be mutual: Actors got used to seeing whole families—little kids and their abuelitas—watching from their stoops at any time of the day or night.

Which is not to say that it came easily.

To Alice Brooks, the director of photography, the weather problems were "insane." If a storm popped up on the radar anywhere nearby, they had to suspend production. This happened with schedule-wrecking regularity. They expected to be free of such interruptions when they went underground to shoot "Paciencia y Fe" on the subway. Instead, they experienced a torment familiar to every New Yorker but with a twist: They weren't waiting for the train to appear so they could ride it to work, they just needed the garbage train to pass by so they could go back to shooting their movie.

The need to solve the endless riddles of New York filmmaking had led the producers to add Anthony Bregman to the team. At this point, he reckons, he's filmed in just about every corner of his hometown, always looking for ways to capture the authentic look and feel of a place—even when the movie is surreal. (He produced *Eternal Sunshine of the Spotless Mind,* a valuable point of reference for the reality-bending frame of Quiara's screenplay.) So he wasn't especially rattled when, on the night they filmed "Alabanza," a nearby building caught fire, or when, on another night, gunshots rang out nearby.

"You want the life of the city?" Anthony asks. "The life of the city is complicated."

The production lost valuable shooting time on both of those nights. They found ways to make it up later. But other days offered no second chances. Anthony remembers looking at the calendar before summer began, getting a feel for what lay ahead. Some days seemed manageable; some days seemed tough. Then there was "Carnaval del Barrio."

"That day," he says, "was impossible."

WHAT TURNED OUT TO BE a defining episode in the whole long history of *In the Heights* almost didn't happen at all. Many a movie executive had suggested over the years that there wasn't enough plot in "Carnaval del Barrio" to justify a song that was very long and very crowded, which made

"THE LIFE OF THE CITY IS COMPLICATED."

it very expensive. But the song's power doesn't come from the plot, it comes from the theme. The characters rally one another's spirits amid a citywide blackout. They raise their flags and celebrate their heritage—and their humanity—in defiance of every force telling them not to.

That community-fortifying aspect of the song is "essentially the DNA of *In the Heights* for me," Quiara says. Beneath the joy, there's a legacy of struggle and resilience. "'Carnaval' unearths that history. All we have is our fight to be here together, the testimony to our spirit."

To help ensure that the number would remain in the movie, she hooked it into the plot more securely, situating it as a farewell number for the salon ladies, who have been priced out of the neighborhood. But the budget wasn't the only limiting factor. "Carnaval" is unique in requiring virtually every member of the cast to be present at the same time.

The actors' complicated schedules meant that Jon wouldn't get all the filming days he wanted. He would get only one.

Which meant it was time for the hard, slow, unglamorous legwork of moviemaking: planning, organizing, rehearsing, designing, equipping, and rehearsing some more—months of it, all to give themselves the best possible chance to "make the day," to film the whole gigantic number in the time available.

In the world of making movies, "day" is a flexible unit of time, especially for a scene that would be filmed outdoors—in this case, a courtyard between two apartment buildings around the corner from where Lin went to preschool. They scheduled the shoot for a Monday, when union rules would let them start the earliest. And they picked June 24, one of the longest days of the year.

They didn't realize it would also be one of the hottest.

THE SONG WOULD BE filmed more or less in order. Which meant that for the production, as for the characters, the salon ladies would lead the way.

Some of the movie's actors were new to musicals. Not Daphne Rubin-Vega, who plays Daniela. When *Rent* blew the mind of seventeen-year-old Lin-Manuel Miranda, she was onstage, playing Mimi. But when she arrived for hair and makeup on "Carnaval" day—at 4:30 in the morning—even *she* was feeling nerves. The uneven concrete floor of the courtyard wasn't like where they had rehearsed. The prospect of filming a seven-page song before nightfall seemed crazy.

She began to hear a voice of doubt in her brain, one that's encoded in a specific ugly memory. After wrapping her first film, she had gone to the airport to fly home to New York and mentioned to the woman at the ticket counter that she had just acted in a movie.

"That's funny," said the woman, who Daphne believes to have been Latina like herself. "You don't *look* like an actress."

Worries about how they looked, questions about what they were wearing, a general feeling of negativity—Dascha Polanco was feeling them, too. She always loved arriving on set to play Cuca, one of Daniela's fellow salon ladies, because it felt so much

like coming home. She was born in the Dominican Republic and while growing up in Brooklyn used to make frequent trips to the Heights with her friends. ("Washington Heights is a small Dominican Republic," she explains.) Now she, too, wondered if she belonged. *Am I capable of remembering the steps?* she asked herself.

She decided to stop those doubts—for herself and the other salon ladies. She grabbed the hands of Daphne and Stephanie Beatriz, who played Carla, and formed the women into a profane prayer circle.

"Shake that shit off," she told them. "I'm not going to let anyone or anything interfere with my performance today."

Daphne laughs as she tells the story. "She was so hilarious and said we were going to protect each other from that insecurity. That was such a beautiful thing—going in there with that determination to represent."

By 5:30 A.M., when the sun rose over Queens, sixty dancers had arrived. Christopher Scott, the film's choreographer, tried to prepare them for what was coming, backed by his full team of associate choreographers: Emilio Dosal, Ebony Williams, and Dana Wilson, as well as associate Latin choreographer Eddie Torres, Jr., and assistant Latin choreographer Princess Serrano. By six A.M., dozens of crew members had joined them, making the thousand careful adjustments needed to help a movie look spontaneous.

Recuerdo

DAPHNE RUBIN-VEGA

DANIELA IN THE FILM VERSION

Incredibly impactful experiences have this prism-like quality, where the meaning changes over time, for the better and the worse. *Rent* meant one thing, and then somebody wasn't there to experience the fruits of their labor, which meant the rest of us had to bear witness. And that was excruciating.

The thing doesn't change. *We* do, and that changes how we see the thing. I can't help but wonder: By the time *In the Heights* comes out, how different will we be, and how different will the world be, from right now [January 2020]? We're living in a time when shit can happen. When shit *will* happen. But I don't know what it will be.

I collect chairbacks from the projects I work on. I kept mine from *In the Heights*. It's special to me. It's my memento, and it makes me feel a kind of giddy anticipation. I can't wait to see what the world is going to do with the movie. I have a feeling things might be different, but I don't know what they'll be. Except for this one thing:

What's going to be different is there won't be as many people who grow up the way I did—who watch films and never see anybody who looks like them. It won't be like that. Whatever else might happen, it won't be like that ever again.

It was almost nine A.M. by the time Jon called "Action." The cameras started rolling, Daphne started singing, and the clock kept ticking.

ARRANGE THE ACTORS, POSITION the cameras, do a take, reset everybody, do it again. As the sun climbed higher that morning, the temperature rose to what one crew member estimated to be nine hundred degrees. Look closely—see the sweat on people's bodies? Most of it didn't come from the makeup department. But there wasn't time for extra breaks to cool off.

"Please be quiet," a voice on the loudspeaker boomed. "We gotta go."

At one point that morning, Jimmy Smits got his turn to shine. Playing Kevin Rosario wasn't his first *Heights* experience. He had seen the show Off-Broadway and been "blown away" by it, he says. He had offered to help in any way he could, eventually recording a radio ad for the show.

His devotion to *Heights* carried into rehearsals for the film. As they got underway, he told Chris Scott and the choreography team, "I know I'm playing the dad, but the last thing I want to see is myself in the background, just waving my hands. I want to go all in." They obliged him. He sometimes hobbled home from the dance studio to ice himself for hours.

His payoff came on "Carnaval" day. He had a featured moment in the song: an intricate, whirling combination. The cast and crew watched him do it again and again, cheering him on. He could feel "a lightning bolt of energy" around the set, something he'd experienced only rarely in his long career.

Over the applause after one take, a voice rang out, ricocheting off the walls: "That shit was crazy! For our ancestors!" It was Anthony Ramos. He, too, had a long history with *Heights,* but it wasn't as happy as Jimmy's.

Very early in his career, he had tried to get cast as Sonny on the show's national tour. It meant taking a bus into Manhattan from a gig he was doing in New Jersey, going through round after round of auditions. At last he made it to the big moment: a callback in front of Tommy Kail, Alex Lacamoire, and Lin himself.

He gave the song everything he had. He didn't get the part.

He thought he'd missed the one chance he would get to work with Lin, the writer who'd evoked Anthony's own world, Latino New York, so beautifully on a Broadway stage. He needn't have worried. A few years later, the same guys would hire him to originate the roles of John Laurens and Philip Hamilton, Alexander's son, in *Hamilton.*

When Anthony got to know Tommy and Lac well enough, he asked if they remembered not casting him as Sonny. They said they did.

"You weren't ready yet," Lac said.

Anthony knew he was right. "Only a homie would tell you that," he says.

But he needed one more break to make his way back to *Heights* and find himself sweating in the courtyard that morning.

In 2018, Stephanie Klemons, an original cast member of both *In the Heights* and *Hamilton,* directed a production of *Heights* at the Kennedy Center in Washington. The night before rehearsals were set to begin, she lost an actor to an injury. She reached out to Anthony: Could he step in with zero notice?

He didn't feel physically or mentally ready, and was about to pass, but decided to do it. That's how he got a second chance to show Lin what he could do in *Heights*—not as Sonny this time, as *Usnavi.* In a series of tweets, reproduced on this page, Lin commemorated how overwhelmed he was watching Anthony step into the role he once played. He, Quiara, and Jon all agreed that when the cameras started rolling, Anthony should be their Usnavi.

The bond between Anthony and Lin added to the drama of filming "Carnaval." Lin played Piragua Guy, so

Lin-Manuel Miranda ✔
@Lin_Manuel

Imagine you buy a pair of tap shoes.
They're snug, and you've never taken lessons, but you love them.
You love the music you make in them.

6:23 PM · Mar 16, 2018 · Twitter Web Client

1,769 Retweets   **642** Quote Tweets   **19.7K** Likes

Lin-Manuel Miranda ✔ @Lin_Manuel · Mar 16, 2018
Replying to @Lin_Manuel
Your tap phase ends.
You put the shoes in a box in the attic.
You grow up. You have a family. Years pass.
4   324   8.1K

Lin-Manuel Miranda ✔ @Lin_Manuel · Mar 16, 2018
One day, you hear tapping coming from a nearby room.
Your kid has found your tap shoes.
And he SOARS.
Oh, the music he makes.
The fit is not snug. It's perfect.
9   375   9.7K

Lin-Manuel Miranda ✔ @Lin_Manuel · Mar 16, 2018
And something inside you shifts and you realize,
oh, that's why you got the shoes, and that's why you saved them.
39   445   12.2K

Lin-Manuel Miranda ✔ @Lin_Manuel · Mar 16, 2018
Anyway.
That's the closest I can get to how it feels watching
@ARamosofficial play Usnavi.
326   1.1K   22.1K

he was in the courtyard, too—or, rather, directly above it, on a fire escape. It meant that the whole cast and crew had a clear view of the brief duet that he and Anthony sing in the middle of the number. To people who knew their history, the sight made time go all swirly. Anthony had originated the role of Lin's son in *Hamilton,* and now he was playing the role that Lin had originated, and somehow the two of them were singing a duet in Washington Heights.

A quirk of the production process made the moment even stranger and more potent. All day, the actors had been singing along to prerecorded versions of "Carnaval" piped over the loudspeakers. But somehow they hadn't gotten around to recording Anthony's side of his duet, so they had to fall back on the only other version on hand: the Broadway cast album. Which meant that Lin wasn't just singing with Anthony that day, he was harmonizing with himself at age twenty-eight, when every bit of what was happening around him would have seemed like a ludicrous dream. "It was like time travel," Lin says.

BY THREE P.M., WHEN everybody had returned from their lunch break—blood sugar bolstered by the ice cream truck that Stephanie Beatriz had hired—time was growing shorter, the day hotter. Now when choreographer Chris Scott talked to the dancers, many listened with hands on hips, hands on knees.

From his fire escape, Lin did his bit to keep up morale. He joined in the clapping that broke out between scenes; he made silly faces; he pulled up his shirt and did belly rolls. Guests watched from the edges of the shoot: Lin's dad and wife, Quiara's sister, Chris's mom, Anthony's sister and mom. Anna Wintour stopped by.

Jon is not the type to direct through a bullhorn, barking orders from the shade. When they'd filmed "96,000" earlier that month on a couple of unseasonably frigid days, he had jumped in the Highbridge Park pool with the cast.

On this day, he darted around the courtyard, giving notes to actors, framing shots, conferring with Alice. He is also not the type to speak in mystical terms, but when he thinks back on that day, he remembers "the sun shining down like a laser—it was like the sun was shining out of everybody."

By late afternoon, the boundary between the make-believe world of the movie and the real world of the shoot had all but melted away. They had reached the part of the song where Usnavi and Daniela try to call forth their neighbors' pride in where they come from. Anthony climbed onto a picnic table and faced the whole cast, rapping, "Can we sing so loud and raucous they can hear us across the bridge in East Secaucus?" Daphne stood near him, arms wide apart, raising them up, willing everybody to stand tall, to keep going.

Both of them were throwing all their skill and commitment into their performances, the stars of two of Broadway's epoch-making musicals doing what they had trained to do. But they also weren't acting.

"To raise the flag for your country, to dance and recognize that we're all here together, and belong here, we don't need to be forgiven for it, or ashamed for it," says Daphne of what she was feeling. "There's a pride in being here from Colombia, or Panama, the D.R., Puerto Rico, Cuba, wherever."

At eight o'clock, with the sun sinking toward New Jersey, the dancers were still dancing. Eleven hours had passed since Daphne had belted out "Hey!" to start the song. Now Jon was trying to get the right take of sixty-plus voices shouting "Hey!" to finish it. In the movie version of the scene, the blackout ends when the song does, so a voice on the loudspeaker would announce, "The power's on!" That's how the actors knew the right moment to cheer that it was over.

After one such cheer, it really was over. Not just the take—the song.

They had done it. They had made the day.

Jon jumped into a swarm of dancers. (Ever see a baseball player hit a walk-off home run, then leap onto home plate into the waiting arms of his cheering teammates? That's what this jump looked like.) People were clapping and shouting and hugging and crying. Alice thought the whole thing was a miracle.

"You know when you see people at a concert cry, and you're like, 'I would never do that'?" asks costume designer Mitchell Travers. "That's what I did." He thinks it's the most sheer human energy he has ever been close to.

Anthony Ramos, in the middle of the crowd, launched into a speech. He can't remember his exact words. He hadn't planned what he was going to say—he hadn't planned to speak at all. He just felt that something needed to be said.

"I might have said, today we made history," he recalls. "This was for our ancestors who didn't get the opportunity to do this—who were fighting to have a chance to do what we just did. It was for love of the culture. It was for our kids, who look like us, to be able to see themselves on the big screen, to see us singing about our pride. Some shit like that."

Somewhere in the crowd stood Dascha Polanco, cheering with the rest. She was sweaty, tired, tear-streaked—and beginning to feel the spirit move.

"I looked down and saw that concrete floor," she says, "and I saw those fire escapes up there, and I was like, 'New York.'"

She began a chant. It was slow and pitched low: "N-e-e-e-e-w York, N-e-e-e-e-w York." In seconds, the whole crowd took it up. "N-e-e-e-e-w York! N-e-e-e-e-w York!"

They were pointing to the sky. They were dancing.

"N-e-e-e-e-w York! N-e-e-e-e-w York!"

"It wasn't like chanting, 'Oh, I love New York,'" Anthony says later—meaning it wasn't a casual thing someone would casually say. "It was"—he drops his voice an octave and leans in—"I motherf---ing love New York. I'm proud to be from New York. I'm proud to be Latino from New York. That was the chant."

Lin, on his fire escape, was overwhelmed. Quiara, in the courtyard, guessed that people could hear them all chanting for blocks around. "It was the sound of joy and survival," she says. "And the sound of people who were really proud to be artists in community together—all our stories braided and interwoven at that one moment."

The long months of preparation had yielded the thing that movie people dream of creating: the burst of real emotion, the flash of genuine spontaneity. Some of it infuses what you see in the finished version of the song, but some of it can't be recovered now. It's an experience only for the people who got to be part of that impromptu celebration, the carnaval that followed "Carnaval."

That long day and its joyous finale capture, in miniature form, a lot of the *Heights* experience—what's powerful about it, what's rare. Instead of expecting little from the actors it featured, *Heights* demanded everything—not just what they could do, but who they were and where they came from. By fusing them with dozens of other artists making the same commitment, it gave them the feeling that Lin had wanted so badly for himself when he started writing the show: a sense of belonging, of being part of a group of people working toward a goal they all hold dear. That's why Anthony, looking back on filming "Carnaval," says, "That was one of the greatest days of my life. Period. If I never do another movie again, I did this."

"Something that arises in 'Carnaval' is a feeling of, 'There's a place for us,'" says Quiara. "But the place is not one that says, 'Oh, I definitely fit in' or 'I definitely don't.' It holds those questions. It allows those questions to exist."

Those questions, she has come to see, are universal.

"People are like, 'What is my place in the world?' That question is actually part of your place in the world," she says. "There's something about *In the Heights*. It takes such a burden off to hear, 'Yeah, there's a place for you. Here it is.'"

"IT TAKES SUCH A BURDEN OFF TO HEAR, 'YEAH, THERE'S A PLACE FOR YOU. HERE IT IS.'"

The spontaneous
chant after
"Carnaval del Barrio."

Carnaval del Barrio [1]

1. In the first version of "Carnaval," Camila began the song. The carnaval was an annual community event that she organized. The shift to Daniela happened somewhat organically. As the emphasis of the show shifted from the Rosarios to the neighborhood, it made sense to give the song's leadership to Daniela. First of all, we made the song impromptu, not a planned event. Second, when we decided that Daniela's salon was on the way out, the carnaval could become her last hurrah. And as the number developed, we realized this would be our Act Two "check-in" with all the characters. The opening number establishes them, "96,000" encapsulates all their dreams, "Blackout" finds them all in crisis, and "Carnaval" keeps all the story lines moving against the backdrop of the entire community.

2. My everlasting regret is that I spent summers in Puerto Rico and not that many winters: Maybe this is my subconscious aching for the holiday traditions we didn't get in New York. Vega Alta is my dad's hometown.

3. There are two types of Nuyoricans: those who have a family coquito recipe and those who have a hookup. My dad makes a pretty mean brew, but my hookup for the better part of a decade has been Javier Muñoz's parents, who make me five bottles every holiday season.

DANIELA: Hey . . . Hey . . .
What's this tontería that I'm seeing on
    the street?
I never thought I'd see the day . . .
Since when are Latin people scared of
    heat?
When I was a little girl
Growing up in the hills of Vega Alta
My favorite time of year was
    Christmastime! [2]
Ask me why!

CARLA: *Why?*

DANIELA: There wasn't an ounce of
    snow
But oh, the coquito would flow. [3]
As we sang the aguinaldo,
The carnaval would begin to grow!
Business is closed, and we're about to
    go . . .
Let's have a carnaval del barrio!

PIRAGUA GUY: *Wepa!*

(PIRAGUA GUY begins to scrape a slow beat.
DANIELA begins slowly.)

DANIELA: ¡Carnaval del barrio!
¡Carnaval del barrio!
Carnaval . . .

(SONNY joins her effort.)

PIRAGUA GUY: ¡Carnaval!

DANIELA: Del barrio . . .

PIRAGUA GUY: ¡Barrio!

DANIELA: Carnaval . . .

SONNY, PIRAGUA GUY: ¡Carnaval!

DANIELA: Del barrio . . .

SONNY, PIRAGUA GUY: ¡Barrio!

4. In many ways, this song is a mirror image of the opening number: We're not establishing characters anymore, but we are establishing where all the characters are against the backdrop of the neighborhood. So we really need to cement this chorus, because the verses are going to be all about story. Let's go!

5. Just like in "96,000," I'm chasing the feeling that these lyrics are being improvised in the moment. Which is how *all* musical theater lyrics should feel, like an honest moment that *happens* to be musical. But stating it explicitly never hurts!

DANIELA: We don't need electricidad!
Get off your butt, avanza!
Saca la maraca, bring your tambourine,
Come and join the parranda!

PIRAGUA GUY: Wepa!

(The community gets into it.)

DANIELA, MEN, WOMAN:	**SONNY, MAN, WOMAN:**
Carnaval . . .	
	¡Carnaval!
Del barrio . . .	
	¡Barrio! ❹

DANIELA, MEN, WOMEN, PIRAGUA GUY:	**SONNY, MEN, WOMEN:**
Carnaval . . .	
	¡Carnaval!
Del barrio . . .	
	¡Barrio!

SONNY, PIRAGUA GUY, MEN, DANIELA, CARLA, WOMEN:	**MEN, GRAFFITI PETE, WOMEN:**
Carnaval . . .	
	¡Carnaval!
Del barrio . . .	
	¡Barrio!
Carnaval . . .	
	¡Carnaval!
Del barrio . . .	
	¡Barrio!

CARLA: Ooh, me me me, Dani, I have a question.
I don't know what you're cantando.

DANIELA: Just make it up as you go
We are improvisando. ❺
Lai le lo lai lo le lo lai
You can sing anything.
Carla, whatever pops into your head
Just so long as you sing.

CARLA: My mom is Dominican-Cuban, my dad is from Chile and P.R., which means: I'm Chile-Domini-Curican, but I always say I'm from Queens! ❻

PIRAGUA GUY: Wepaaa!

SONNY, PIRAGUA GUY, MEN, DANIELA, CARLA, WOMEN:	**MEN, GRAFFITI PETE, WOMEN:**
Carnaval . . .	
	¡Carnaval!
Del barrio . . .	
	¡Barrio!
Carnaval . . .	
	¡Carnaval!
Del barrio . . .	
	¡Barrio!

(VANESSA takes center stage.)

VANESSA: Yo! Why is everyone so happy? ❼
We're sweating and we have no power!
I've gotta get out of here soon,
This block's getting worse by the hour!
You can't even go to a club with a friend
Without having somebody shove you!

DANIELA: Ay, por favor,
Vanessa, don't pretend that Usnavi's your
     friend, we all know
That he love you!

COMPANY: Ohhhh!!

CARLA: Wow, now that you mention that sexual
     tension, it's easy to see!

VANESSA: Yo, this is bogus . . . ❽

DANIELA: Haven't you noticed you get all your
     coffee for free?

6. This is a fun lyric with a snappy punch line, but it also contains the whole show: If we're from everywhere, as so many of us are, what do we claim as our central identities? So many of us contain so many hyphens.

7. It's nice to have characters who are not on board for this celebration: It keeps it from being all rah-rah-everyone's-happy and something closer to a raucous town hall.

8. "Bogus"—a Karen Olivo-ism that crept into the score.

9. In the stage version, the community didn't yet know the lottery winner; Usnavi's telling the neighborhood in the biggest way possible.

In the movie, Abuela has passed on, so Usnavi's rap is more personal: He's announcing that he's made plans to leave, just like Daniela and Carla. More reason to mourn, more reason to cherish the moment. Here are the movie lyrics:

Yo, yo, yo, y-y-yo-yo

Now, now, everyone gather 'round, sit

Down, listen, I got an announcement!

Wow, there's nothing here holdin' me down.

The word is out, tell the whole town I'm bouncin'.

Atención, I'm closin' shop

Sonny, grab everybody a soda pop

Twist off the bottle, kiss it up to God

And miss Abuela Claudia, it's time to fly, though.

Daniela, Carla, pack up the carro,

I'm bookin' a flight for D.R. tomorrow!

10. If I had more lyrical real estate, I'd list even more countries and flags, but alas! We tried to sneak as many in the movie as we could.

SONNY, PIRAGUA GUY, MEN, DANIELA, CARLA, WOMEN:	MEN, GRAFFITI PETE, WOMEN:
Carnaval . . .	
	¡Carnaval!
Del barrio . . .	
	¡Barrio!
Carnaval . . .	
	¡Carnaval!
Del barrio!	
	¡Barrio!

MAN: Here comes Usnavi!

(USNAVI enters from his apartment.) **9**

USNAVI: Yo, yo, yo, y-y-yo-yo
Now, now, everyone gather 'round, sit
Down, listen, I got an announcement!
Wow, it involves large amounts, it's
Somewhere in the range of ninety-six
    thousand.
Atención, I'm closin' shop!
Sonny, grab everybody a soda pop!
Yo, grab a bottle, kiss it up to God,
Cuz Abuela Claudia just won the
    Lotto!
Yeah, Abuela Claudia won the Lotto
And we're bookin' a flight for D.R.
    tomorrow!

COMPANY: Oh my gah!

(The company hoists USNAVI on their shoulders and begins marching flags around the street. SONNY exits into ABUELA CLAUDIA's place with a soda bottle.)

COMPANY: ¡Alza la bandera **10**
La bandera Dominicana!
¡Alza la bandera
La bandera Puertorriqueña!
¡Alza la bandera
La bandera Mexicana!
¡Alza la bandera
La bandera Cubana!

PIRAGUA GUY:	COMPANY:
¡Pa'rriba esa bandera!	Hey!
¡Álzala donde quiera!	Hey!
¡Recuerdo de mi tierra!	

11. These lyrics, in English:

Lift up that flag!

Lift it everywhere!

Reminder of my homeland!

I remember my homeland . . .

That beautiful flag!

Contains my whole soul!

And when I die,

Bury me in my homeland!

I remember being very proud of these lyrics: Remember, I'm pretty English dominant, so to write lyrics that really fly in Spanish takes much more effort.

   I'll also never forget my first time performing this song after my grandfather's funeral. The whole show, I was steeling myself to perform the eulogy in "Alabanza" later in the act. I was so focused on getting through that song that this reference to "when I die, bury me in my homeland" completely blindsided me, and I felt a sob rising in the happiest song in the show. Eliseo Román, our piragüero, saw it before I did: He squeezed my arm *so* hard on our dance here, he literally held me up when I felt like I couldn't keep singing. I'll always be grateful to him for it.

12. Flash forward to 2019, and I am playing Piragua Guy, and Anthony Ramos is playing Usnavi, and time has folded in on itself.

13. This gossip is more of a bombshell in the stage version than the movie version, but it survives both: I can't resist a hay/hey pun.

14. I love that this is the only non-rhyming lyric in the whole song: "She was my babysitter first." God bless Sonny.

15. I'll never forget our *last* performance of this on Broadway. Shaun Taylor-Corbett was playing Sonny, and his voice caught on "We close this bodega, the neighborhood is gone." It's as if the cast, crew, and audience simultaneously realized this was not only the last hurrah of the neighborhood but the last hurrah of the show at the Rodgers.

16. Again, the hook that keeps on giving, sung by the people most heartbroken over Usnavi leaving.

PIRAGUA GUY, USNAVI:

¡Me acuerdo de mi tierra . . .

Esa bonita bandera!

¡Contiene mi alma entera!

¡Y cuando yo me muera,

Entiérrame en mi tierra! ⑪

COMPANY:

Hey!

Hey!

(Dance break! USNAVI is in the center, gettin' love from the ladies, inverse of VANESSA's club number moment.) ⑫

DANIELA: Everything changes today

COMPANY: Hey!

DANIELA, CARLA: Usnavi's on his way

COMPANY: Hey!

DANIELA, CARLA: Off to a better place

COMPANY: Hey!

DANIELA, CARLA: Look at Vanessa's face!

BENNY: Everything changes today . . .

COMPANY: Hey!

BENNY: Goodbye, Mr. Rosario . . .

USNAVI: Okay!

BENNY: I'm taking over the barrio!

USNAVI: Yo!

USNAVI, DANIELA, CARLA: We're getting out of the barrio!

DANIELA: Hey, Mr. Benny, have you seen any horses today?

COMPANY: Hey!

BENNY: What do you mean?

DANIELA: I heard you and Nina went for a roll in the . . .

COMPANY: Hay! Hey! Ohhhhhh! ⑬

WOMEN:	MEN:
Benny and Nina	
	Benny and Nina
Sitting in a tree	
	Sitting in a tree
K-i-s-s-i-n-g!	
	K-i-s-s-i-n-g!
¡Qué bochinche!	
	¡Qué bochinche!
Nina and Benny!	
	Nina and Benny!
K-i-s-s-i-n-g!	K-i-s-s-i-n-g!

SONNY:
Hold up, wait a minute!
Usnavi's leavin' us
    for the
Dominican Republic?
And Benny went and
    stole
The girl
That I'm in love with?
She was my babysitter
    first! ⑭
Listen up, is this
What y'all want?
We close this bodega,
The neighborhood
    is gone! ⑮
They selling the dispatch,
And they're closing the salon,
And they'll never turn the
Lights back on cuz—

SONNY, VANESSA: We are powerless, we are powerless! ⑯

SONNY: And y'all keep dancin' and singin' and celebratin'
And it's gettin' late and this place is disintegratin' and—

GRAFFITI PETE, MAN: Wait a minute!

Hoo!

SONNY, VANESSA: We are powerless, we are powerless!

USNAVI: All right, we're powerless, we'll light up a candle!
There's nothing going on here that we can't handle!

SONNY: You don't understand, I'm not trying to be funny!

USNAVI: We're gonna give a third of the money to you, Sonny!

SONNY: What?

USNAVI: Yeah, yeah . . .

SONNY: For real?

USNAVI: Yes!
Maybe you're right, Sonny. Call in the coroners!
Maybe we're powerless, a corner full of foreigners.
Maybe this neighborhood's changing forever.
Maybe tonight is our last night together, however!
How do you wanna face it?
Do you wanna waste it, when the end is so close you can taste it?
You could cry with your head in the sand
I'mma fly this flag that I got in my hand!

PIRAGUA GUY:	COMPANY:
¡Pa'rriba esa bandera!	Hey!

PIRAGUA GUY, DANIELA:	
¡Álzala donde quiera!	Hey!

USNAVI: Can we raise our voice tonight?
Can we make a little noise tonight?

COMPANY: Hey!

PIRAGUA GUY, DANIELA, CARLA:	COMPANY:
¡Esa bonita bandera	Hey!
Contiene mi alma entera!	Hey!

USNAVI: In fact, can we sing so loud and raucous
They can hear us across the bridge in East Secaucus? ⑰

PIRAGUA GUY, SONNY, MEN, DANIELA, CARLA:	WOMEN, BENNY, GRAFFITI PETE, MEN:
¡Pa'rriba esa bandera!	Carnaval del
¡Álzala donde quiera!	barrio . . .

USNAVI: From Puerto Rico to Santo Domingo,
Wherever we go, we rep our people and the beat go . . .

PIRAGUA GUY, SONNY, MEN, DANIELA, CARLA:	WOMEN, BENNY, GRAFFITI PETE, MEN:
¡Esa bonita bandera	Carnaval del
Contiene mi alma entera!	barrio . . .

(USNAVI confronts VANESSA.)

USNAVI: Vanessa, forget about what coulda been.
Dance with me, one last night, in the hood again.

(A moment.)

DANIELA, CARLA: Wepa!

(The community explodes into a final chorus around VANESSA and USNAVI, as they slowly begin to dance.)

COMPANY: ¡Carnaval del barrio!
¡Carnaval del barrio!

COMPANY:	DANIELA:
¡Carnaval del barrio!	
	¡P'arriba esa bandera!
¡Carnaval del barrio!	¡Oye!
	¡Y cuando yo me muera,
	Entiérrame en mi tierra!
¡Del barrio!	¡Del barrio!

¡Alza la bandera
La bandera Dominicana!
¡Alza la bandera   ¡Alza la bandera!
La bandera Puertorriqueña!
¡Alza la bandera
La bandera
    Mexicana! ⑱   ¡Adiós!

COMPANY: Alza la bandera
La bandera
La bandera
La bandera
La bandera ⑲

DANIELA, PIRAGUA GUY:	COMPANY:
¡Del Barrio!	¡Alza la bandera!

(All cheer.)

17. I mean, if the GW Bridge is in the background, you may as well name-check New Jersey on the other side.

18. We did a lot of work between Off-Broadway and Broadway on bringing this number home: "button school," if you will. Daniela's riff on "Adiós" in this section is an inversion of the bridge in the Puerto Rican classic "En Mi Viejo San Juan."

19. And the final touch to bring it home was this harmonic repetition of "la bandera," which I believe was Lacamoire's idea. It's the button of all buttons.

WELCOME TO MY WORLD

BUT WILL IT TRANSLATE? The question has shadowed *In the Heights* since its days in the bookstore basement. Sure, the show exerts a powerful effect on the artists involved, such as members of the predominantly Latino cast, who have the chance to depict their community with loving specificity. But can it appeal to a broad audience?

A film that's intended for worldwide release is about as universal as a cultural phenomenon can get. (That's one reason some studio executives passed up the chance to turn the show into a movie back in 2011: They told Scott Sanders they didn't know how to find an audience for it.) When Jon Chu's movie version opens all around the world, it will supply the final answer to the question of how far this story about Usnavi and Vanessa and the GWB can go.

The *final* answer, but not the *only* answer—and maybe not the most interesting one.

The whole time that Lin and Quiara and Scott and Mara have been trying to get their movie made, the stage version has been circling the globe. Since 2011, it has been produced by dozens of theater companies scattered across six continents (but only six—penguins lack the steps). It amounts to a fascinating worldwide experiment.

We know what *In the Heights* means to a largely Latino company and to the city that sees itself reflected in the story. But when it's performed by and for people who are very far from Washington Heights, measured in miles and every other way, what does it mean for *them*?

SITTING IN THE RICHARD Rodgers Theatre, transfixed by what he was seeing onstage, Bobby Garcia thought: "This is how I grew up."

Like Nina, he had traveled a long way for college—all the way to New York. But he had spent his first seventeen years in the Philippines. That's where, in 2011, he would direct the first foreign production of *In the Heights*.

The particulars of life in northern Manhattan weren't familiar to most of the cast and crew he assembled in Manila, but plenty of other things were. The Philippines shares a history of Spanish rule with Puerto Rico, the Dominican Republic, and Cuba, so the show's mix of English and Spanish came naturally. Bobby also detected a common belief in the importance of family.

But the quality that seemed most familiar was its depiction of lives intertwined in communities, among neighbors who almost become kin. In the countryside of the Philippines, there's a long tradition of neighbors banding together to help one another move—literally, by

Manila

picking up a house and moving it to a new location. "*In the Heights* really felt like a celebration of that communal spirit," Bobby says. They call it "bayanihan."

The show evoked that spirit so faithfully, he says, that it changed the quality of their collaboration. "In our production, because it's a show about a community, the cast became a community." Which sounds a lot like what the New Yorkers said.

He detected one difference, though: The frozen treat he grew up eating wasn't piragua; it was something he used to call "dirty ice cream." (Really, it's called "sorbetes.")

IN PANAMA, THE LOCAL delicacy is neither piragua nor sorbetes—it's raspado. But the difference didn't bother Aaron Zebede when he saw *Heights* on Broadway.

Oh my God, I have to do this in Panama, he recalls thinking. *It's going to translate so well.*

In 2013, he directed the show at Teatro en Círculo, a 240-seat theater in Panama City that specializes in Broadway musicals. Aaron has played Tevye twice, which supplied a useful point of reference for talking about the show with his cast and production team. "This is like when we did *Fiddler* and they all have to leave Anatevka,"

"BECAUSE IT'S A SHOW ABOUT A COMMUNITY, THE CAST BECAME A COMMUNITY."

Manila ▶

he would say. "This show is moving that to the twenty-first century, where big corporations are doing the same thing to small owners." He was thinking of Casco Viejo, the oldest neighborhood in the city, a traditionally diverse place being squeezed by the wealthy, much as Washington Heights is.

Heights proved a major challenge for Aaron and his collaborators. They consider themselves a semiprofessional company, and the complexity of the show—the casting, the score, the dancing—tested the limits of what they could do. But they felt an acute desire to make it work. "I think it was a little more than a job for everybody," Aaron says. Through season after season of Broadway classics, they'd never had a chance to perform what they considered to be *their* music. "I remember the dancers saying, *Finally* we can dance salsa and merengue," he says.

This wave of pride carried them through rehearsals—they added a month to get the dances right—and bubbled over into the performances. While the cast was drawn from many countries, Piragua Guy, aka Raspado Guy, was Panama born and raised. In the middle of his big song, he pulled out a Panamanian flag. The crowd went wild.

Aaron is pleased to have helped that moment along: "It was my flag," he says. "The flag I use for soccer games."

IN A DIFFERENT PRODUCTION, in another of the great capitals of Latin America, flags were so abundant that Quiara couldn't even see the stage: Audience members waved them like crazy during "Carnaval del Barrio."

That city was San Juan. The show's run there wasn't an international production. (As the chorus sings in *West Side Story:* "Nobody knows in America/Puerto Rico's in America!") But Lin felt that the audience was responding in a way that was altogether different from what he'd heard in the continental United States. He was in a position to

Recuerdo

NÚMERO OCHO

EMIL NIELSEN

USNAVI IN THE 2018 PRODUCTION AT THE MUSICAL TALENT SCHOOL OF NYBORG, DENMARK

The hat I wore as Usnavi was my own sixpence, which I bought at the age of eighteen. I bought it in a small store in Jutland, Denmark, when I was there on vacation. The funny thing about the hat is that I spotted it in that store when I was about fifteen years old. I didn't buy it, because I was unsure if it was the right one for me. But the next year, I came back to the store, saw the hat again, and told my parents, "If this hat is here next year, I'll buy it!" And it was! And I've been wearing it ever since.

When my school was getting ready to do *In the Heights*, there were two of us guys left for the male roles. I went for Usnavi, and he went for Benny. I decided to wear my hat to the audition to cement my choice. Fortunately, the panel let me play the role. It was the greatest and most challenging role I've ever played, and I would gladly do it again.

FUN FACT: The hat I'm wearing in the musical is not the same hat I have today. It's the same kind of hat, from the same place, but it was bought at a later date, because the original hat got run over by a lawnmower when I dropped it at a party. Also, on the first day that I wore my new hat, I went for a walk, and it was shat on by a pigeon.

know, because he was hearing it from center stage: For the weeklong engagement, he had gone back into the show to play Usnavi.

There were cheers and laughs in the places he might have expected, like the references to Arecibo and "the hills of Vega Alta," but he was caught off guard by how vocally people reacted to little flickers of slang that had sailed right past the audience in New York. "I had forgotten how much Puerto Rico shit was in it," he says.

At the time, Lin called it the greatest week of his life. The kid who had always felt like an outsider, the New Yorker who showed up every summer with his weird accent, was becoming one of the island's most treasured voices.

The run in San Juan also garnered his all-time favorite review of *In the Heights*. A local critic called the show a love letter to the island from the family members who had left. Even now Lin tears up when he thinks about that description of the show "because that's *exactly* what the f--- it is."

NOT EVERYBODY HAD AN easy time with the Spanish.

Jesper Nielsen was a little surprised that he got the rights to do the show. He runs a musical theater training program for teenagers in Nyborg, a small town in Denmark. The show hadn't been done anywhere in Scandinavia: A condition of getting the rights was that he would have to translate the show to Danish himself.

He thought the students would love Lin's music and that the show would pose the right kind of challenge for teenagers hoping to make a career in the arts. Above all, he knew they would understand how Nina felt.

Young people have to leave Nyborg for college. The ninety-minute train ride to Copenhagen isn't exactly a flight to Stanford, but it still means saying goodbye to home. So his students would soon be facing Nina's dilemma. "Should I stay where I know everyone and everyone knows me, or go somewhere else, where I maybe fail?"

asks Jesper. "For us it was a story about having big dreams but maybe being afraid to follow them."

His young cast didn't know much about Washington Heights. Neither did he. On his next trip to New York, he rode the A train up to the neighborhood and took pictures. He made sure to bring home lots of candy—from an actual bodega—to stock the set.

During rehearsals, the students tried to absorb what they could of the language and the culture, but they faced a deeper conceptual challenge. Denmark doesn't have anything like the polyglot diversity of America, the cross-cutting ethnic and linguistic traditions. The students wondered how it must feel to have one identity based on where you live and another based on where your family comes from. "That was an aspect of the show that was more difficult for the actors to relate to," he says.

In Denmark, as in other places, the company grew unusually close. Jesper thinks this is partly because of how isolated they were from other productions of the show. They couldn't summon up memories of previous versions they'd seen. "It was really *our* show when it was done," he says. "We only had each other."

At the closing-night party, they ate all the candy.

FOR TAKESHI EGUCHI, it was the music. The energy and novelty of Lin's score inspired him to bring the show to Japan. He mounted a production that played in Tokyo and four other cities.

To do justice to the score, the director/choreographer Tetsuharu decided to reach beyond the ranks of Japan's musical theater artists. He cast newcomers in two key roles: Ayaka Umeda, who had been in a girl group, played Nina; Micro, who had a hip-hop career, was Usnavi.

Like the company that staged the show in Panama, the Japanese artists saw their society reflected in the show's depiction of old ways of life changing. But in this case, it was less about gentrification remaking a neighborhood and more about the shifting relationship between parents and children. The tension in the Rosario family can be felt throughout Japanese life, according to Eguchisan. Their society, like the show, is questioning "how a family should be."

In spite of early doubts about whether a Japanese production could work, the show turned out to be a hit—as one critic put it, "a reminder of the universal power of music and dance." A lot of the credit for that universality belongs to Kreva, the Japanese MC who translated Lin's lyrics. He said at the time that it seemed like a puzzle that couldn't be solved. He ultimately solved it so well that Benny's and Usnavi's flows have the same energy and dexterity in Japanese that they do in English and Spanish. Listening to them is like discovering a long-lost sonic twin.

Lin and Quiara certainly thought so. She remembers when they watched a clip of "96,000" on YouTube. "It was bonkers," she says. "Lin and I were screaming. It was so nuts—it sounds so musical in Japanese."

"LIN AND I WERE SCREAMING. IT WAS SO NUTS— IT SOUNDS SO MUSICAL IN JAPANESE."

A DIFFERENT PRODUCTION, on the other side of the planet, didn't need any translation—not of the language, nor of how the experience felt to the people involved. The London run of *In the Heights* is the closest cousin to the New York original.

For example: Both trace their roots to the Drama Book Shop. That's where the director Luke Sheppard picked up the published version of the script while visiting from London. He loved what he read. The Latino culture celebrated by the show was foreign to him, but he found something familiar all the same. Southwark Playhouse was in a rapidly transforming corner of London. As in Washington Heights and Casco Viejo, longtime residents and little businesses were being priced out. "It was starting to lose a big part of what had been integral to the city," he says.

Luke and his prospective collaborators knew the show would be a heavy lift. They didn't have many resources or a long track

▲ Tokyo

record. "We were nobodies, really," he says. But when they announced their production, they were "knocked sideways" by the response. They hadn't realized the show had so many British fans.

Much as the New Yorkers toiled in the bookstore basement, Luke and his collaborators rehearsed in an unorthodox (but affordable) spot: a church near the theater. The altar had a sign that said, "Please don't stand on here." People popped in during rehearsals to pray.

They made a commitment to getting the cultural details right. They brought in experts to help with the language, the customs. They also listened to knowledgeable voices in the room. David Bedella, who played Kevin, had spent years in New York. Ensemble member Gabriela Garcia, who was born and raised in Mexico, felt what she calls "a massive responsibility" to represent the world of Washington Heights faithfully, "for the Gabys who come see the show and want to change the world."

When participants describe the production at Southwark Playhouse, they sound like New Yorkers reminiscing about 37 Arts: the tight bonds formed while sharing a dressing room in an out-of-the-way theater; the delight in finally getting a chance to do something they

hadn't done before. A few years later, Luke would learn just how similar the experiences were. He collaborated on a project with Bill Sherman, who regaled him with stories about the show's early years.

That conversation convinced Luke that the affinity between the two productions wasn't because of the dressing rooms or the makeup of the company—it's the *show*.

"There's something woven into the material," he says. "Something in the script and music that's really joyful. That looks out on the world with a sense of optimism. And isn't overly worried about being too crafty or sophisticated or by-the-rulebook of musical theater. It just has a sense of hopefulness. I think all of us responded to that."

On the strength of word of mouth and great reviews, the show began selling out. So, like the New Yorkers before them, they got a chance to do it again. After an interval of nearly two years, they remounted the show in a bigger venue: King's Cross, a theater in a train station. They arranged the playing space between two banks of seats so it felt even more like a city street.

Some of the actors were so eager to do the show again that they extracted themselves from other projects. Gaby Garcia had always been the show's most ardent fan,

London ▶

▼ Gabriela Garcia

possibly anywhere, possibly ever. She related so deeply to Nina's story when she saw it on Broadway that it helped convince her that she could make a career in musical theater. She began the King's Cross run as an ensemble member and understudy. Eight months into the run, she took over the role of Nina. Her abuela happened to be visiting from Mexico at the time.

Like their fellow underdogs in New York, the London crew overachieved: They got four Olivier Award nominations—"We'd never even been *invited* before," Luke says—and David Bedella won. Also like the New Yorkers, they were sad when it had to end. "It's rare that you meet a bunch of people you love working with and make something you're inherently proud of," Gaby says.

One final parallel to the Broadway run: They ended on a high note. On closing night, Lin himself came to see them off.

"The company felt on fire," Gaby says. "The energy was incredible."

After all the clapping and the crying, she got to give Lin a hug.

"You know that Nina is my story, right?" he said.

And Gaby said, "It's my story, too!"

THESE GLOBE-SPANNING STORIES GO on and on. They echo again and again. None of these artists have met, but all of them have shared in the project of bringing Lin and Quiara's show to life in their societies.

Of all the creative challenges that this worldwide community faced, the one that reveals the most about how much we all share, and how much we differ, is the story of Abuela Claudia. What does it mean to look up to a beloved matriarch in a culture very different from the one depicted in the show—and to lose her? How do you stage "Alabanza," a song of communal grief and mourning, in different cultures and faith traditions?

The London company was so wrecked by the song that it took several rehearsals just to get through it. "That's

194

not just artistic folk being too connected to their work," Luke says. "Something about that story just connected to everybody's own relationship with grief."

In Denmark, telling Abuela Claudia's story required another leap of imagination from the students, Jesper says. Social services are so robust in their society that most young people go from school directly to organized programs, diminishing the role that neighborhood elders play. For the young Danish actors, the nearest point of reference they could summon was the retirees who help with amateur theater, the ones who have stories and are eager to share them. Their audience was moved by the song, though without "hordes of people crying," Jesper says, explaining: "On a general level, Americans are more emotional than Danish people are."

In the Philippines, Bobby Garcia grew up hearing the saying, "The spirit doesn't know it has passed." That's why he staged "Alabanza" so that when it started, Abuela Claudia was standing onstage, feeding pigeons. It was only when she heard everyone singing all around her, and discovered that they couldn't see her, that she realized what had happened. She moved upstage, turned back for one last look at her friends, then walked away.

When Luke Joslin staged "Alabanza" in Sydney, Australia, at the intimate Hayes Theatre, he broke the rules of stagecraft. Nina invited Usnavi and the rest of the community to form a circle; Sonny placed Abuela Claudia's scrapbook on the ground at its center. The circle, Luke felt, embodied the love and togetherness that meant so much to Abuela Claudia. It also had a spiritual meaning: It implied the infinite. The production moved people so strongly, and excited them so much, that it transferred to the gigantic stage of the Sydney Opera House—a place where patrons expect to see the actors' faces when they sing.

The producer, Joshua Robson, considered the possibility that the audience might be troubled by feeling that people were singing "Alabanza" only to one another. "But that's *exactly* what we want them to feel!" he says. "They're looking at a community grieving together, not one presenting its grief to somebody else. This lady brought her community together. We want to show how the connection continued." The circle stayed.

At Starcatcher Theater in Jerusalem, the production team never worried about the audience connecting to Abuela Claudia. On the contrary. According to directors Eli Kaplan-Wildmann and Yaeli Greenblatt, they worried that she was so much like the traditional figure of the Jewish bubbe that it might pull audiences out of the story. They thought that "Alabanza," in particular, didn't need anything extra from them. As written, it evokes grieving rituals that would be familiar to a Jewish audience: the candles, the eulogies, the coming together to mourn. (The only nod in the audience's direction came during "Paciencia y Fe." When Abuela Claudia sang about arriving in New York in the 1940s, a group of actors briefly huddled together behind her: That quick image of people seeking a home safer than the one they left behind was sure to resonate.)

The most telling sign of how the story connects across cultures comes from Jeff Rosenschein, one of Starcatcher's founders. Like most people in the company, he's not a theater professional: He teaches computer science. He also holds the distinction of being an immigrant who is both the son and the parent of an immigrant. (His mother and father, both Holocaust survivors, moved from Hungary to the United States. One of his own children was born before he moved to Israel.) And he was the music director of *In the Heights.*

▲ Jerusalem

Jerusalem

A few weeks before the first preview, he told the cast that he needed to leave for a little while. His mother, back in the States, had been in declining health for some time. Jeff had received word that he'd better come home. A few days after he arrived in Pennsylvania, she passed away.

During the painful period of mourning that followed, he received an email with a video attached. He opened it. Back in Jerusalem, the actors had gathered in the rehearsal studio to sing him an a cappella version of "Alabanza."

IF PEOPLE ACROSS THE PLANET find something familiar in Abuela Claudia's story, it's because Lin and Quiara wrote it with great honesty and big hearts. It's also because that's how Olga Merediz *wanted* people to feel when she gave the performance that's available for all time on the Broadway cast album.

"I kind of made her into the mother we all want to have: that quintessential supportive, nurturing, warm person that we all want in our lives," she says. To arrive at this universal figure, however, she tapped into the little details of her own life: "She's like me magnified, if I were

the matriarch of a community." Which is exactly what Olga became.

Late in 2018, nearly eight years after playing Abuela Claudia for the last time onstage, Olga auditioned to play the role in the movie. She wanted it so badly; it would be a dream to do it. Several excruciating weeks later, her phone rang.

It was Lin, as she'd expected. She launched into small talk, doing all she could to delay the news that somebody else had been cast. Finally he got a word in and told her the role was hers.

"I screamed," she says. "I screamed and started crying."

Olga is the only principal actor from the stage version to reprise her role onscreen. It gave her a special stature during production. Among other things, it made Mitchell Travers want her to be the first actor to come in for a costume fitting. For the first hour of the fitting, they didn't touch clothes, they just talked: about her life as a Cuban exile, about her experience with the show, about how it felt to be Abuela Claudia again. Mitchell recalls her saying, "I never thought it would be me—I thought I would have to watch someone else tell my story."

Olga Merediz ▶

196

He gave Olga some pieces to try on, clothes that would signal that Abuela Claudia thinks of the whole block, and not just her apartment, as her home. "There was so much power in the way that the character is literally in her bones," he says. "The moment we got her dressed, it changed the way she walked. She *is* Abuela. Period."

After all those years away, Olga found that playing the role demanded more effort in some ways, but came to her more naturally in others. "Just body-wise, it's easier to do the physicality," she says. As far back as 37 Arts, young castmates had looked up to her as a more experienced colleague. Now they came to her for guidance, for stories. They wanted to know about The Old Days, when *Heights* was still becoming what it became.

"Did you do it like *this*?" they would ask her. "Was it like *that*? Was it different in the show?"

On her last day on set, Jon, Alice, and members of the crew gathered around her to take a family picture. Today the photo makes her laugh: "It was like Saint Abuela Claudia," she says. But they were all sad when they took it. Nobody wanted to say goodbye to Abuela—not even Olga.

She and Jon shared a joke: One day he'll make a sequel, and she'll play the role yet again. But Olga does feel that, for the time being, she has "closed the book" on Abuela Claudia. Her last word on the experience—at least for now—could speak for Abuela Claudias everywhere.

"It really was heartwarming to play her and to have people feel good around her—around me—and to have that mutual love and understanding and respect," Olga says. "I personally don't have children, but I feel like everybody in that community, everybody on that day, I felt like these were all my children."

NOBODY WANTED TO SAY GOODBYE TO ABUELA—NOT EVEN OLGA.

1. I remember my inspiration for this tune was Juan Luis Guerra's ballads on *Ni Es Lo Mismo Ni Es Igual,* an album in heavy rotation when I was writing the first Wesleyan drafts of the show. The impulse came from the idea that the dispatch microphone would be the most efficient way to break the news to the neighborhood.

I wrote "Benny's Dispatch" after I wrote this song, so Benny's "Atención, yo, attention" in Act One would prepare the way for this song.

KEVIN: Atención. Atención.
Roll down your windows.
Turn up your radios.
Un momento, por favor.
Atención. Atención.
Please drive slow
Let everybody know
Abuela Claudia passed
     away at noon today.

Atención ①

Alabanza ①

USNAVI: She was found and
     pronounced . . . at the scene. ②
She was already lying in bed.
The paramedics said
That her heart gave out . . .
I mean, that's basically what they said,
     they said
A combination of the stress and the
     heat.
Why she never took her medicine I'll
     never understand.
I'd like to think she went out in peace
With pieces of bread crumbs in her
     hand.

Abuela Claudia had simple pleasures.
She sang the praises of things we
     ignore:
Glass Coke bottles, bread crumbs, a
     sky full of stars,
She cherished these things, she'd say
     "alabanza."
"Alabanza" means to raise this
Thing to God's face
And to sing, quite literally, "praise to
     this."
When she was here, the path was
     clear.
And she was just here, she was just
     here . . . ③

1. I wrote a killer of a song for this moment called "The Day Goes By." It's a beautiful meditation on life after losing a loved one. I want it played at *my* funeral. But it didn't work here. The suddenness of this loss requires an impromptu eulogy and for Usnavi to grapple with the loss in what feels like real time.

2. Just a character touch that Usnavi can't yet bring himself to say "dead." He manages, "She was found and pronounced . . ." and jumps over it. But the subsequent rhymes of bed/said underline what Usnavi can't yet say.

3. "And she was just here . . ." was when Olivo started crying during the first read-through, and she's tough as hell, so I knew this would work.

4. I'm sorry to every subsequent Nina in school productions who realizes they have to pick their starting note out of nowhere and stay on key until the band joins them on the second half of the chorus. It's just that Mandy Gonzalez can do anything, so I didn't realize how hard it was.

NINA: Alabanza
Alabanza a Doña Claudia, Señor ④
Alabanza, alabanza

Alabanza
Alabanza a Doña Claudia, Señor
Alabanza, alabanza

NINA, DANIELA, CARLA: Alabanza
Alabanza a Doña Claudia, Señor

+SONNY:
Alabanza, alabanza

+CAMILA, BENNY: Alabanza
Alabanza a Doña Claudia, Señor

+VANESSA, KEVIN: Alabanza, alabanza

CAMILA, VANESSA, PIRAGUA GUY, SONNY, KEVIN, BENNY, MAN:
Alabanza
Alabanza a Doña Claudia,
Señor

NINA, DANIELA, CARLA:
Alabanza

+WOMAN, GRAFFITI PETE:
Alabanza

Alabanza

+WOMAN:
Alabanza

ENSEMBLE, WOMAN, MEN:
Alabanza

+MAN:
Alabanza a Doña
Claudia, señor
Alabanza
Alabanza

COMPANY: Alabanza
Alabanza
Alabanza

USNAVI: Alabanza.

MEN:
Paciencia y fe ⑤

WOMEN:
Paciencia y fe

WOMEN, MEN:
Alabanza Doña
Claudia
Alabanza
Alabanza

NINA:
Alabanza

Paciencia y fe
Doña Claudia

Alabanza

Alabanza

5. And if you're not
crying at the top of
the song, we're going
to get you when we
bring back "Paciencia y
Fe." Seriously, though,
this is one of those
moments that just
brings casts together in
a deeper way. Mourning
together is a very
powerful and purifying
thing.

Eighteen

★ I MISS ★ YOUR FACE

JOSHUA HENRY JUMPED UP and down, giddy.

"Is it really Luis?" said Eliseo Román, right behind him.

It was. Luis Salgado stepped off the elevator, with eyes the size of spotlights, into a circle of hugs and shouted hellos. Javier Muñoz laughed in disbelief.

On a fall morning in 2019, a dozen actors gathered to record vocals for the *Heights* movie. All of them had history with the show and with one another: Some had done the national tour, most were part of the Broadway production. The reason for their bewilderment—why they were freaking out in their dozen separate ways—was not just the "who" but the "where." Somebody at Warner Bros. had booked a recording studio without realizing the significance of its address. Which is understandable: The actors didn't realize it, either.

"As I started walking, I said, 'This is familiar,' but I didn't put it together," recalls Eliseo. "Then I got to the corner and saw the sign and said, 'Oh my God—*we're going to 37 Arts.*'"

Standing in the lobby of the theater-turned-recording studio, Javi felt like he was reliving the whole journey—everything that happened during the Off-Broadway run in this building and everything in the twelve years that had passed since. The actors were laughing and shaking their heads about it all when Alex Lacamoire walked in. Another round of hugs, more shouted hellos. Then it was time to begin.

He told them they were going to record the ensemble vocals for the opening number. They would sing four bars at a time, doing as many takes as necessary. The goal wasn't just to get the correct sound but also the correct feeling. "We need the right storytelling; otherwise it's useless," he said.

Lac headed to the control room. A row of big monitors high on the wall gave him and the music supervisor, Steve Gizicki, a view of the studio, where singers were taking their seats in a curving row of booths. Some things had changed since they recorded the Broadway cast album together. The technology they used that morning was so new it mostly didn't exist in 2008 and was so sophisticated they couldn't have afforded it if it did. Derik Lee, the audio engineer, said he felt like Captain Kirk.

Lac had changed, too. When he'd worked on the cast album, the process had moved so fast that he'd barely had time to get clean takes from the singers. And even if he'd had more time, he might not have been able to sharpen their performances. "I didn't really have enough of a foundation—the right adjectives and life experience to draw from—to be able to do it," he says.

When he reunited with his old colleagues in 2019, he had time. And he had the benefit of a decade of experience on *Bring It On: The Musical, Dear Evan Hansen, The Greatest Showman,* and *Hamilton.* And all of them had the lively motivation of knowing that every syllable they recorded would be scrutinized by millions of listeners everywhere.

He slid a mic across the desk in front of him. It looked like the one Benny uses onstage in the car service. He pressed the button and addressed the singers: "Let's do a pass just to get comfortable, then we'll talk about vocal energy and intention."

Take after take, Lac coaxed the singers along with something that *hadn't* changed: his distinctive tone of warmhearted fanaticism, of meticulous cheer. Imagine you are having a wonderful lunch with a friend, so wonderful you never notice that the whole time you are chatting, he is using a magnifying glass to study every pore on your face.

"So the note was clean, but it wasn't *exciting,*" he said after one take.

"Think like a brass player," he said after another—meaning, have a sense of attack when singing the title of the movie.

After a third take, Lac offered a more expansive bit of direction: "Just make sure while you're singing notes and thinking about the cutoffs, you're still delivering a message. I want it to be about the things we always talk about when we do this show, right? The struggle that we go through, but the things that keep us moving, right? Whether it's the promise of a better tomorrow, whether providing for the family, whatever that honor is. Okay?"

It's hard to measure the benefit of any single adjustment, but as the morning progressed and the microscopic changes added up, you could hear life starting to flow through the speakers: twelve individual voices singing with passionate clarity about their hopes and struggles.

All the while, Lac made offhand comments that meant nothing to an outsider but got a big laugh from the singers.

"We have so many inside jokes it's stupid," Lac explained to Jon Chu, who had dropped by.

"I can tell," Jon replied.

Lac cued them to go again.

"WE HAVE SO MANY **INSIDE JOKES** IT'S STUPID," LAC EXPLAINED TO JON CHU.

I MISS YOUR FACE

AROUND NOON, LAC DEMONSTRATED how he'd like a particular lyric to be sung.

"You're in fine voice today," said Lin, who had turned up at the table next to him.

Lin was dressed up on this day, by Lin standards. (Still in jeans, but also a blazer.) He had spent the morning turning on the lights of the Empire State Building, which had chosen a song that he'd written with Broadway legend John Kander as its new theme music. In a few hours, he would step out of the booth to meet with Robert Lopez and Kristen Anderson-Lopez, the composer/lyricists of *Frozen*, to do a little work on a collaboration. Before bedtime, he would stop by Broadway's Booth Theatre to go onstage with his friends in *Freestyle Love Supreme* and cause another group of strangers to start screaming. So it was pretty much a typical day.

The big thrill of Lin's morning wasn't the skyscraper, it was a two-and-a-half-minute video on somebody's hard drive. The trailer for the movie had just been completed, and he was itching to share it. He invited the singers into the control room to watch it on one of the monitors. Jon pointed out that it was the largest group of people who would ever have seen it.

As the trailer began to roll, an already strange and emotional day for the singers became a lot stranger and more emotional. Here was proof, visual confirmation, that the story they had helped to launch in this very building a decade earlier was about to become a monumental global event.

Joshua, watching it, flashed back to the first table read for Off-Broadway, when Lac played all of the music and Lin sang all of the songs. By the time they reached the finale, Joshua had been sobbing in the arms of Eliseo and Michael Balderrama, unable to comprehend that somebody had put his world and its songs into a musical. "I don't need anything more than this," he had felt that day.

Luis had the opposite impulse while watching the trailer: His mind skipped ahead, thinking of the fresh memories they were making that day and imagining how they'll look back on them a decade from now.

Both of them, in their different ways, were thinking along the lines of "Everything I Know," a song that recognizes that memory is a form of navigation. Have you lost your place, like Nina? Are you unsure where you belong or where you're going? Try reckoning from where you have been and your remembrance of the people who were with you.

When the trailer ended, everybody clapped and cheered. Lin beamed. He hadn't looked at the screen—he had looked at his old castmates. "Oh, it was the highlight of my day watching y'all watch that shit," he said.

"WHAT ARE WE DOING in this building?!" exclaimed Janet Dacal. "This is bananas!"

A couple of hours later, a dozen women arrived to record their side of the ensemble vocals. They expressed the same stunned delight at being back at 37 Arts that the men had. Those who had been part of the show here a decade earlier—including Andréa Burns, Doreen Montalvo, and Nina Lafarga—started to reminisce.

Remember the dance parties on two-show days? Remember when Janet's mom—who is, like Abuela Claudia, a product of La Víbora—brought them a huge Cuban feast? Remember surviving on the coffee from the gas station on the corner?

In the studio, they got the same lovingly exact direction from Lac. ("Now, altos, at [measure] 178, I feel like you weren't singing the G-sharp with conviction.") And Lin screened the trailer for them. They were just as moved as the men.

When they said their goodbyes that day, the vibe was not the one that prevails at many other reunions—the see-you-in-five-years farewell. These people see one another *all the time*. Whatever strange adhesive power *Heights* has, it doesn't wear off quickly. It seems not to wear off at all.

When Doreen got married, Lin was her DJ; when Joshua got married, Luis and Eliseo were his groomsmen. Andréa went a step further for Kurt Crowley, the music director on the national tour and the conductor of this recording session. ("We are going for Washing-*tone*, not Washing-*tun*," he said at one point. He is a Lac protégé.) When he married Carlos Gonzalez, whom he'd met when they worked together on the show, Andréa officiated—she even sang a little of "Breathe" as a final a cappella blessing.

They have remained close enough to be involved with one another's children: Bill Sherman was at the hospital to meet both of Chris Jackson's kids; Janet is a de facto godmother to Andréa's son. They are even close enough to talk shit. "They all became my family. Any one of them can call me. Except Chris Jackson," says Karen Olivo.

They bonded in joy but also in heartache—all the perennial theatrical complaints: the disagreements over visibility, money, and credit; the showmances that went bust. "We had to live through that," Lin says. "But it all stayed family." That is why, in spite of the gigantic success of *Hamilton*

"THEY ALL BECAME MY FAMILY. ANY ONE OF THEM CAN CALL ME."

and how much he loves many members of that company, no show can rival the affection he feels for *Heights* or the people who made it.

"*Hamilton* is like, we were on this wave together and we survived it. But it's not family," he says. "I still call *Heights* people the way I call my family—my *for-real* family."

Chris Jackson feels the same way. In late 2019, after filming a brief featured role in the movie, he said, "People always ask me what my favorite show is. *Hamilton* is a different thing. We know very well what that experience represented to a lot of different people. But I always say this, and believe it to my bones: *Heights* is my favorite show, because it gave me my artistic life. If Doreen Montalvo called me up tomorrow and said, 'Chris, I need a kidney,' I'm going to the hospital. I'm going to do whatever I need to do to help my sister."

Nobody has needed a transplant, but since closing night on Broadway, they have seen one another through nearly every other affliction that life can throw in your path: career setbacks, the loss of loved ones, divorce—and, more recently, sickness.

A few weeks before this recording day, Mandy Gonzalez had arranged a get-together for the "Core 4 +1," the group of friends who had grown inseparable at 37 Arts: Mandy, Karen, Andréa, Janet, and Eliseo, who is the "+1." They had met at the restaurant that used to be Café Edison, their favorite place until it was pushed out by a fancier spot. She wanted to tell them in person, and all at once, that she had breast cancer.

They all cried. And then—"as the Core 4 +1 always do," she says—they got to work.

When Mandy went in for surgery, they visited. When she spoke out publicly about her diagnosis, to draw attention to the fight, they supported her—and the rest of the show's familia did, too. Two *Heights* friends who were working with her on *Hamilton,* where she was playing Angelica, promised to support her in every way they could. Tommy Kail and stage manager Amber White were as good as their word.

When it came time for chemotherapy, Priscilla Lopez—who inspired Mandy, then played her mother and became her friend—brought arroz con gandules.

I MISS YOUR FACE

Everything I Know [1]

1. I distinctly remember writing this song at the back of the theater at 37 Arts.

I remember thinking, *Okay, Lin, here's the moment where Nina reflects on everything that's happened to her and makes her big decision. You've been writing this show for seven years; time to use everything you know.* And then the record in my head scratched on "everything I know" as a perfect title, and I got to writing. The right title will get you most of the way there: specific, but pliable to the twists and turns the song needs to take as it will apply to a) Nina's schoolwork, b) Abuela's life in her homeland, c) Nina's relationship to her parents.

2. My Abuela Mundi, who helped raise me, managed to help me with my homework every night, despite having very little formal education. Her presence and her persistence carried me through.

3. As Nina reckons with Abuela's extraordinary journey, the first leg of which was entirely involuntary as a child, it forces her to contemplate her own.

4. In our basement, there are folders with, like, thousands of mementos. And this lyric is really for my mother, who has saved everything my sister and I have ever committed to paper.

NINA: In this album there's a picture
Of the ladies at Daniela's.
You can tell it's from the eighties
By the volume of their hair.
There you are, you're just a baby
Eighty-seven, Halloween!
If it happened on this block, Abuela
    was there.
Every afternoon I came
She'd make sure I did my homework.
She could barely write her name [2]
But even so . . .
She would stare at the paper and tell
    me,
"Bueno, let's review,
Why don't you tell me everything you
    know."

In this album there's a picture
Of Abuela in Havana.
She is holding a rag doll, unsmiling,
Black and white.
And I wonder what she's thinking
Does she know that she'll be leaving
For the city on a cold, dark night? [3]

And on the day they ran, did she
    dream of endless summer?
Did her mother have a plan?
Or did they just go?
Did somebody sit her down and say,
"Claudia, get ready to leave behind
    everything you know"?
Everything I know
What do I know?

In this folder there's a picture
From my high school graduation
With the program, mint condition,
And a star beside my name.
Here's a picture of my parents
As I left for California.
She saved everything we gave her
Every little scrap of paper.
And our lives are in these boxes [4]
While the woman who held us is gone.
But we go on, we grow, so . . .
Hold tight, Abuela, if you're up there
I'll make you proud of everything I
    know!
Thank you, for everything I know.

CHAPTER Nineteen

DON'T TUNE ★★ ME OUT

IT'S NOT ALWAYS CLEAR what people want. On a Friday night in October 2019, members of the Warner Bros. staff moved briskly to manage a crowd that had turned out in larger numbers than anybody anticipated. The 150-seat screening room that was being asked to accommodate somewhat more than 150 people was in the new Hudson Yards complex, twenty-two stories above what had been, relatively recently, a bunch of train tracks. (Developers had thought that what people wanted was another dozen blocks of the amenities that defined Manhattan real estate in the 2010s: first-class office space, high-end retail.)

When all the seats had filled, Jon Chu stepped to the front, mic in hand. He offered a quick welcome, then handed the mic to Lin, who couldn't stay. (He was due onstage at *Freestyle Love Supreme* and traffic was bad. He would end up running.)

"What do I want to say? What I want to say is that we have a rough draft of the movie, and you're the first people on earth to see it," Lin said. "It's been a long road to get here, one that I share with the amazing Quiara, our screenwriter."

Halfway up the bank of seats, Quiara smiled; everybody applauded.

Then Lin was gone and Jon was back. He offered a couple of disclaimers: They were only seven weeks into postproduction, which meant some of the visual effects and the music were still temporary; some sequences hadn't even been shot yet. Still, he hoped that everybody would have a good time. Then he leaned close to the mic and said, very dramatically, "*In the Heights,* ladies and gentlemen."

And then the first-ever screening of the movie began.

A FEW MINUTES AFTER leaving the theater, Lin returned. Now he was larger than life, bearded, and pushing a piragua cart across the screen.

It wasn't always the plan that Lin would play Piragua Guy—or be in the cast at all. By the time the movie had traveled far enough along its torturous path to assemble a cast, he thought he was too old to play Usnavi and too wounded by all the false starts to want to play anybody else. *I don't want to get heartbroken again if we don't get to a green light,* he remembers thinking.

Then he saw the work that Jon and his team had begun to do. He saw the sequences that were starting to emerge. And he started to change his mind.

"I went from feeling, 'Go forth with my blessing, I'm so proud of you,' to 'I'll kick myself forever if I'm not in this movie,'" he says.

Having a filmmaker appear briefly onscreen is a cinematic tradition, in the best Hollywood style. Lin had alluded to it before the screening began. While waiting for

208

everyone to get seated, he had circled the room, chatting up the folks. At one point, he had leaned across a row to greet a famous movie actor.

"Are you in it?" the actor had asked, shaking Lin's hand.

"For a minute," Lin had replied. "I'm Hitchcock."

WHEN THE MOVIE ENDED nearly two and a half hours later, everybody cheered. Then staffers streamed down the aisles, handing out surveys and pens. As people answered the questions, Jon did a brave thing.

He walked to the front of the theater, looked up at the 150-plus moviegoers looking down at him, and asked them what they thought of his movie. It was the opposite of fishing for a compliment: It was pointing to your chin and inviting people to punch it.

Jon wasn't worried that they would say mean stuff. If the audiences at screenings see a problem, he says later, "I'd much rather know. This is the point where we can actually change things." His only fear was that the attendees of this screening, which was reserved for friends and family, would be too *nice*. So Jon drew them out.

"Are there too many subtitles, or too few?" "How do you feel about the balance of the Nina and Vanessa stories?" "Do you want to see more about Sonny?" He pushed one question more than the rest: "Could you feel the reason for it to be onscreen?"

People gave long answers and short ones, thoughtful opinions and quick takes, many of which contradicted each other. But when everybody stood up to go home, Jon was pleased. He thought he had gotten what he needed.

So did Lin, who had been listening in the back. (He made a speedy return after he got offstage at *Freestyle*.) "The best feeling I came away with was, 'We have a good

"WE HAVE A GOOD MOVIE, FULL STOP.' BECAUSE WE DO."

movie, full stop.' Because we do," he recalls. "Now it's: 'How do we take this from good to great?'"

Lin has spent most of his life asking that question about *In the Heights,* ever since the show consisted of two songs for Benny and Lincoln and he was nineteen years old. This last phase of postproduction, trying to make the film the best possible version of itself in the time remaining, would mark a culmination. He's not finished with *Heights*—the show is sure to be back one day—but it will never again be a new story that he and his collaborators need to figure out how to tell.

The world premiere was eight months away, but a crucial date would arrive much sooner than that. In six weeks, they would screen the movie again. No friends and family this time: A carefully assembled audience would assign the movie numerical scores. And those scores would go a long way to determining how, and to what extent, the

209

movie would get marketed and what, if anything, they could do to make it better.

The kind words from friends and family were encouraging, but nobody was inclined to relax. The upcoming test audience might react in any number of ways, from rapture to the kind of response that didn't bear thinking about.

"You never know until you show it. You never really know," says Anthony Bregman.

ON MOST DAYS during the next six weeks, Jon worked a desk job. He showed up in the morning at Company 3, a postproduction facility near Union Square in Manhattan. Down a long hallway, then a shorter hallway, behind the last door on the left, he could often be found in the office of the film's editor, Myron Kerstein. It was nice, as editorial offices go. There were windows.

Jon and Myron spent days and nights poring over the first audience's responses: every comment in the Q&A, every answer on the survey, all the body language they observed. "They're like surgeons in terms of criticism," says Anthony. The prospect of making big changes didn't scare them. On the contrary. When they first worked together, on *Crazy Rich Asians,* Jon discovered that Myron could edit footage to deliver a scene exactly as scripted, but he also liked to try new things—which is the way that Jon approaches editing, too. "That's where we get to make the meal," he says.

Myron's approach to *Heights* was informed by a lifelong love of musicals. As a kid his taste ran to what he calls "maybe probably the dorky side of things," like *The Music*

Man. Later came *All That Jazz* and *Purple Rain.* But when he revisited those inspirations while piecing together *Heights,* he found that they didn't have much to teach him. "There aren't many musicals that are really grounded in reality the way our film is," he says. "I feel like oftentimes, they cue in the band, and a number begins, and you lose the story. In this film, they're one and the same. You have to take the story through the numbers."

Consider "Paciencia y Fe." In the stage version of *Heights,* the song played a clear role in the story: to reveal that Abuela Claudia won the lottery. But it didn't play that role onscreen, which is one reason why it hadn't entirely worked in the friends-and-family screening. "People loved it—and didn't know what it was doing in the movie," Quiara says. Armed with that response, Jon and Myron shifted the song to a different place in the movie. Now it once again played a role in the story, though not the same role it played onstage.

Would it work this way? They thought it would. But then, they'd thought it would work before.

In November, in offices all around the suite (the visual effects team to Myron's left, the sound editors to his right), the tempo quickened. To a theater person, the sensation was familiar. It felt like tech, the phase when the pursuit of greatness means long days in dark rooms, lavishing untold hours on microscopic details, a ticking clock warning you that the audience is on its way. There's a lesson here, maybe—another way that the mystique of show business departs from the lived reality. Be prepared to travel through the valley of the shadow, for weeks or months at a time, before your work gets to see the light.

▽ The first page of Jon Chu's script, signed by Lin

Jon had been making movies long enough to know how urgent this phase of postproduction could feel and how important it was to keep his perspective. "Experience is getting to the point where you trust the process," he says. Except that throughout *this* process, a question had been nagging at him—one that nothing in his experience could answer.

He had never made a movie as long as *In the Heights*. He had never crafted a film in which so much real estate is taken up by musical numbers. Could he hold the interest of an audience for nearly two and a half hours? He imagined a nightmare version of

how he and Myron might spend the next six months: suspecting that the movie was too long, but not being sure, so cutting things they loved in order to get the movie under some imagined maximum length. "We keep trimming, trimming, trimming, without taking out the heart."

With the test screening fast approaching, Jon got an idea—a way to know for sure whether time was a factor. He told Myron that they needed to make "a slash-and-burn cut," a second version of the movie that was only two hours and a couple of minutes long. It would focus on Usnavi and Vanessa's relationship and the tale Usnavi shares with their daughter, and it would omit everything that didn't directly serve that story.

Myron made the enormous cuts necessary to create that version, dropping huge sections of the score, devising new ways to tell the story even more concisely. They showed it to the producers. It worked—sort of. The general view, Jon says, was, "We can make this movie, we can release this movie, but it's not special." It would lack emotional punch, the details that make the characters vivid, specific, and true. In other words, the things that make *In the Heights* what it is.

Still, nobody was likely to say it was too long. So Jon proposed a new plan for the screening: They would test *both* versions. If the long version, the one that Jon preferred, turned out to be more movie than an audience cared to watch, they'd find out on the same day if the slash-and-burn version could work instead.

Myron Kerstein and Jon Chu

When Lin heard about Jon's plan, he was confused, as you would be. With "Sunrise," "Enough," "Inútil," and "Everything I Know" having already disappeared from his score, he now stood to lose "No Me Diga," "Benny's Dispatch," "Paciencia y Fe," and "Alabanza," too. He wondered why they were screening this version, especially if Jon himself wasn't all that enthusiastic.

"I need to know if time is an issue," Jon told him. "If it isn't an issue, it clears the pathway for us."

Lin agreed—and so did Quiara. She was the person whom Jon consulted the most about the details of this world. All through postproduction, she pushed for clear storytelling, honest emotion, moments that resonate. The night before the test screening, she managed only three

211

hours of sleep. She says it was a function of "a stew of happiness, giddiness, excitement, anxiety, nerves, terror, and art-love."

"I know we have a movie in there that is so exhilarating and so deep. And I really, really, really want us to make the movie that has both of those things—that's not just the exhilarating summer movie, you know? 'Cause we also could just do that."

She hoped the screening would go well. No matter what happened, she trusted the movie would be very good. But she also saw a new prospect coming into view. "There's a part of me that feels this could be once-in-a-lifetime—that it actually would be my dream come true. That's what I feel close to right now. And that's the part that makes me nervous. It's the feeling of making something that really matters and that speaks to something important."

What's that something?

"Oh, I can't summarize that. It's just the reason that I became a writer, you know?"

THE TEST SCREENING TOOK place in Pasadena, California, on Sunday, December 8, a day that Jon remembers being cool, damp, and extremely stressful. He arrived at the theater early in the morning so he could watch the movie all the way through, fine-tuning the sound. He even taped off seats that didn't offer the optimal view. Then he killed a few hours that stretched for years.

Just before one P.M., Jon, Quiara, Myron, the producers, and the studio executives convened. And right on time, there it was: the audience, a carefully curated bunch of strangers, unaware of how closely they were being scrutinized and how many silent pleas were being sent their way. "The fate of your movie is in the hands of these people who are standing in line," Jon says.

The long version went first.

There was applause when the title splashed onscreen and again when Lin and his beard appeared. Jon and Myron's changes paid off. There were more laughs, more gasps. "Paciencia y Fe," in its new location, packed a new emotional punch. To Anthony Bregman, it felt that people were responding to the movie the way they had made it: "with sympathy and love."

Awaiting scores after a test screening

Nelson Coates, our production designer, asked me what the numbers on the winning lottery ticket should be. I gave him numbers that had special meaning, like 7 and 26, because my wedding anniversary is July 26. Also, that was the date our baby was due to be born, right in the middle of our shoot. But when I got home and showed my wife, Kristin, a picture of the lottery ticket, she said, "You know our anniversary is July 27, right? That's the baby's due date, too.

So for weeks I had to live with this. Then, what do you know, the baby was born on July 26. Right on time.

When I got to set the next day, the production team gave me a call sheet commemorating his birth. It had his name, and his big sister's name, and the time he was born. For "Set," it said "Hospital Room," and under "Advance Schedule," it said "Sleep-deprived dad frantically buys diapers." So it was a really nice thought.

The decision of what to name him didn't come until way late. Kristin and I both wanted to call him Jonathan, but we kept going around and around in circles about his middle name. I don't remember why "Heights" suddenly came up. I just said, "'Heights' is such a beautiful word." And it is. It's looking up to the skies. It's being on top of the world. It's having aspiration. And it would capture the experience of making the movie, which meant so much to us both.

We looked up the name in a baby book, and saw that pretty much nobody was named that. But we loved it. I just felt like I needed to talk to Quiara and Lin first. I'm so glad they blessed the idea.

I still feel that "Heights" is the most beautiful word. I want our son to hear it all the time.

Recuerdo

NÚMERO NUEVE

JON M. CHU

DIRECTOR OF THE FILM VERSION

There was a Q&A afterward, but Jon didn't run this one. He and the rest of the team were in the lobby, not breathing. Eleven years after Broadway opening night and three thousand miles from the Richard Rodgers Theatre, the creators of *In the Heights* were once again waiting for somebody's gadget to ping and reveal their fate.

This time the gadget was a tablet, not a BlackBerry. And the verdict arrived in numbers, not in adjectives. But a rave is a rave. The score was high—*very* high. Higher than any movie Jon had ever made.

You could say they were relieved. Asked about his reaction later, Jon only says: "Thank God."

One screening hadn't turned their good movie into a great one. But the six weeks of revisions had moved them a long way toward that goal. They knew they wouldn't need to start cutting things they loved for the sake of a shorter movie. And when the slash-and-burn cut ended a few hours later, they got an unexpected bonus: Its score was practically the same as the longer version. Which meant that some of the new edits that Myron had dreamed up for that version could be incorporated into the final cut.

In other words: As on so many other occasions stretching back twenty years, *In the Heights* wouldn't be all of one thing or the other—it would combine the best of both.

DON'T TUNE ME OUT

Piragua (Reprise) [1]

1. Much of my connection to Puerto Rico begins with my connection to my Abuelo Guisin: best of men and best of grandfathers, he managed to make every summer trip to the island a dream come true. He took me all over the island. He borrowed a VHS camcorder from his employer, the town bank, when I showed an interest in making movies. He often starred in those movies or held the camera for me. He built a concrete aboveground pool when my sister and I were old enough to swim. I feel so lucky that he was able to see *In the Heights* in its first week of previews on Broadway: He died the weekend after opening night. So much of that year, exhilarating as it was, is shot through this prism of grief. When Jon cast me as Piragua Guy in the film, my only choice was to make the entire performance a love letter to my Abuelo Guisin. Hanging from my neck are his thick reading spectacles. Tucked away in my cart are the dime-store Estefanía cowboy novels he always had in his back pocket. The fanny pack, the cargo shorts: I'm playing Abuelo Guisin and bringing him around for an encore.

2. The fun of doing movies is learning skills that real life doesn't give you a chance to learn: In *Mary Poppins Returns*, I danced with animated penguins. In *His Dark Materials*, I got to brandish firearms for a righteous cause. As Piragua Guy? I got to have a full beard that the pores in my face simply cannot grow.

PIRAGUA GUY: It's hotter than the
islands are today.
And Mister Softee's truck has
broken down.
And here come all his customers
my way.
I told you, I run this town!

Piragua, piragua
One twenty-five, piragua!
Piragua, piragua
Two twenty-five, piragua!

New block of ice, hike up the price
Lai lo le lo lai, lai lo le lo lai
Blackouts are nice, blackouts are
nice
Lo le lo lai
Keep scraping by . . .
Piragua! [2]

SONNY

By
QUIARA ALEGRÍA HUDES

HAVING A SISTER born when I was thirteen set the tone and tempo of my adolescence. Kids are fun and keep you on your toes. They point out your bullcrap and straight-up laugh at your nostalgia. But at the end of the day, if you're loyal and loving and put in the hours, they adore and admire you. I put all of my baby sis into the character of Sonny. The humor, the pest, the cuteness, and the radical thinking. Kids see injustice more instantly and purely, even if they're goofballs half the time.

Sonny is the only lead character in *In the Heights* without a solo song. His character had to shine and come alive through the dialogue. I had very little real estate to make the audience love this kid. When Robin De Jesús came aboard at the O'Neill, the good collaborative juju was instant, like striking gold. His voice was so easy to write for. I'd toss him variations to try, and we'd sit on the grass or under the tree or at the picnic table and he'd make anything I wrote funny. He went all in, so totally over-the-top sincere, on calling himself "the Robin Hood of el barrio." Audience laugh, every night.

Sonny was my way to sneak politics into the story. He was the neighborhood's conscience. Because he's a teenage goofball, the audience wouldn't bristle or feel lectured. In a subtle way, I acknowledge the Chicano labor movement that advanced workers' rights in this country. I know it seems innocent and comic when Sonny says "Underage cousins of bodega workers unite!" But it's also a shout-out to César Chávez and Dolores Huerta, heroes of mine.

SONNY WAS MY WAY TO SNEAK POLITICS INTO THE STORY. HE WAS THE NEIGHBORHOOD'S CONSCIENCE.

In an annotation to "It Won't Be Long Now," Lin has described how we watched Chita Rivera's jaw drop when she heard Sonny say, "Like a drunk Chita Rivera." For me, a relatively unknown Latina playwright, it was a touchstone moment. The legend laughing at my joke, in which she was honored!

Later, in Act Two, Usnavi and Sonny have a goodbye scene. Abuela Claudia has won the lottery, and Usnavi tries to give Sonny his share. Sonny recoils, feeling abandoned by Usnavi's plan to leave for the Dominican Republic. Even in this poignant, sad moment, Robin De Jesús trusted that humor would raise the emotional stakes. Knowing that heartbreak

can be comic, he dove into Sonny's sadness. When Sonny ended the scene with "This is the end of an era!" it was the fourth consistent laugh in an eight-line scene. Playwright José Rivera says each line of dialogue should contain the entire play's DNA. *End of an era*. Bam. The block was changing, and lives were caught in those tectonic shifts.

For the movie, I doubled down on Sonny's interest in justice and his humor. Gregory Diaz was an actual kid: He said he never got to see *Heights* on Broadway because he was only three years old at the time. He is also a very different comic talent than Robin De Jesús. For instance, when Gregory drops into his lower vocal register, it's hilarious. Gregory's much drier than Robin—he says more with less.

Accordingly, I wrote entirely new jokes for Gregory's Sonny. With one exception: "Drunk Chita Rivera" stayed.

I see myself in Sonny, and I think I'm not alone. I am aspirational like him. I want the world to be a better place, and I see speaking truth as a pathway to effecting quantifiable change. Sonny is the character who was most updated for the contemporary moment. He takes Nina to a rally for immigrant rights. Though Sonny, like many kids, is far from the levers of change, he knows there is power in neighbors uniting— not just online but out on the streets. Thus, the rally. He's a kid who's world-building. We offered the protest leader role to Maria Hinojosa, an accomplished journalist in a very white, very male field, to show that our community's struggle for justice is,

historically and necessarily, intergenerational. Sonny as youth, Maria as heavy hitter. Both are essential.

In another scene, we go inside his home and glimpse Sonny's father, a man whose dreams slipped away long ago. Here again, we counterbalanced Sonny's youthfulness against the gravitas of Marc Anthony's portrayal of his father. Marc Anthony's acting in that scene still brings me to my knees, leaves me breathless. He is compassionate, bitter, loving, angry, and resigned all at once. We wish so much for Sonny—success, freedom, equality. The movie purposefully ends with a question— we know Sonny has the will to fight for his chapter in the American story, but we don't know if our country will rise to meet his needs or his truth.

I SEE **MYSELF** IN SONNY, AND I THINK I'M **NOT ALONE.**

CHAPTER *Twenty*

FIRE ESCAPE

FOUR DAYS AFTER the Pasadena screening, the *Heights* trailer lit up screens everywhere. Friends and fans sent congratulations to Jon, Lin, Quiara, the producers, and the cast. Few did so from a closer position than Bernie Telsey, the casting director. He had located many of the actors for the film, as he had for the stage version.

Sending congratulations to actors was not unusual for him—Telsey + Company has been assembling casts for more than thirty years—but the response he received was.

"Within two hours, every single actor wrote me back," he says. "And every one of them wrote, 'You don't know what it was like, Bernie. It was amazing.' They don't need to write me back—they already got the job! You can tell how moved they were being part of it. They wanted to talk about it."

Bernie had first encountered *Heights* at a staged reading before the show went to the O'Neill in 2005. *Okay—this is a new voice!* he remembers thinking. And also: *Oh, this is going to be hard to cast.*

They would need a company of young, fresh voices—always tricky to find, even without the diversity the show demanded. "It becomes a lot of detective work," he says. "You can't just think of fifty people to come in for Vanessa, fifty people for Sonny." (The sleuthing for those roles eventually turned up Karen Olivo and Robin De Jesús.)

The stodgy state of the Broadway musical in those years didn't help. "It's not like now, where every other show on Broadway has a pop score. This was still at a time when it seemed like a new kind of singing." And there was no place for a non-acting singer to hide: "Quiara and Lin, they wrote real acting parts. They're not *just* singing."

When Bernie came back to *Heights* after years away, the score continued to challenge actors, but everything else had changed. It's a little case study in how the world turns.

A show like *In the Heights* creates jobs for actors of color. That makes prospective young performers a little likelier to start a career and likelier to be able to sustain it if they do. Lin has heard from actors who are able to make a living by playing in *Heights* all over the country. When those actors give great performances and the show becomes a hit, producers find it more plausible to mount other shows like *Heights,* which opens up yet more opportunities. And so on.

Though *In the Heights* hired only a fraction of the actors who tried out for roles, the mere process of holding auditions gave up-and-coming performers a chance to shine. "It really became, for our office, a door opening for new talent," Bernie says. Some actors who didn't land a role in *Heights* did land one when Bernie's associates thought of them for a TV show, commercial, or play. Some of them will catch the eye of other directors and get cast in bigger roles and inspire more up-and-comers. And so on.

The best showcase for an actor, and the quickest way to advance, is still to book the gig. That's what happened to members of the original *Heights* cast. "Robin went on, and Karen went on, and Lin went on, because people in the industry saw how good they were. The movie will do that, too," Bernie predicts.

"All of Hollywood will go, 'Who the hell is Anthony, and Melissa, and Corey, and Leslie?'"

ANTHONY RAMOS, MELISSA BARRERA, Corey Hawkins, and Leslie Grace are the four young leads of *In the Heights*. They play Usnavi, Vanessa, Benny, and Nina, respectively.

Anthony didn't go through the casting process overseen by Bernie and his associates Bethany Knox and Tiffany Little Canfield: Lin, Quiara, and Jon knew they had their Usnavi. But his castmates had to win their roles through auditions—lots of them. Competition was fierce in every case.

Melissa had started auditioning for *In the Heights* almost as soon as there was an *In the Heights* to audition for. She saw the show while studying acting at NYU, thrilled by the sight of people who looked like her—and the flag of her native Mexico—on a Broadway stage. When the show announced a non-Equity open call, she went. A month later, she went again. She kept trying, on more occasions than she can count, without ever getting cast, or getting a callback, or fulfilling her goal of auditioning for Bernie himself. After a few years of doing theater and TV in Mexico, she had moved to Los Angeles and landed a starring role in the TV series *Vida* when the chance to act in her dream project came back around.

She went for it again—and went hard. This time, the casting agents noticed. When she arrived for one of her callbacks, the door was opened by the man himself: Bernie Telsey.

"It was like seeing Willy Wonka," she says. "Oh my God, I was so starstruck."

In December 2018, Melissa got her first chance to sing for Lin. That callback was also her first encounter with a couple of actors who happened to reach the front door of the building at the same time. In a scene familiar from a million rom-coms, the two even reached for the handle at the same instant. Neither of them knew where to go, which means that from the very beginning, Leslie and Corey found their way together.

Like Melissa, they satisfied Jon's request for fresh faces. Corey had gotten a big break a few years after leaving Juilliard, winning acclaim as Dr. Dre in *Straight Outta Compton,* but he had never sung in a movie. Leslie had built a career in music, releasing albums beginning at age sixteen, but she had never acted. So for all three of them, the jubilation of landing the role quickly gave way to a different emotion altogether.

▲ Corey Hawkins, Anthony Ramos, Leslie Grace, and Melissa Barrera on their first day of rehearsal

"QUIARA AND LIN, THEY WROTE REAL ACTING PARTS.
THEY'RE NOT *JUST* SINGING."

Leslie describes the extreme version of what they were feeling: "I was going to be *that* person: the one everybody finds out isn't supposed to be there, doesn't know what she's doing, misses her mark a million times, walks past the camera when she's supposed to be on, and doesn't even notice when she makes those mistakes," she says. "I was pretty much making myself feel like Nina felt at Stanford."

No chance to test the waters, either: It was deep end all the way. In March 2019, they began learning Chris Scott's choreography. Since none of them had danced in their auditions, there was a period of testing, and not just for Chris's benefit. Even *they* didn't know what they could do.

Melissa felt the most pressure. Vanessa is the heart of "The Club," the whirling salsa number at the heart of the movie. She had to learn a series of sophisticated steps—partnering, lifts, turns—and do it in the company of some of the best salsa dancers in the world. One day she excused herself from rehearsal, went to the bathroom, and cried. She credits Eddie Torres, Jr., an associate choreographer and the scion of New York's foremost salsa-dancing family, with helping her get where she needed to go.

Anthony, Melissa, Corey, and Leslie found the work difficult, sometimes demoralizing, occasionally painful. But the tougher things got, the closer the four of them grew. "We sweated all over each other," says Leslie. Their deepening bonds inspired them to work harder. Like their forebears a dozen years earlier, nobody wanted to let down la familia.

NO CHANCE TO TEST THE WATERS, EITHER: IT WAS DEEP END ALL THE WAY.

IN APRIL, WITH THE FIRST day of the shoot drawing nearer, it was time for the actors to learn Lin's songs, which was also challenging, though not as sweaty.

"Boot camp"—the phrase used by many of the participants to describe those weeks—was led by Kurt Crowley, who could draw on nearly a decade of experience with *Heights* and *Hamilton* to teach them. But sometimes they had a question that even he couldn't answer. Sometimes even *Lin* couldn't remember how a moment in a song ended up a certain way. It was lucky, then, that the film had the same musical brain trust as the show.

Like Lac, Bill Sherman feels that he brought new skills and experience with him when he returned to *Heights*. "As I get older and get more mature as a person, I get more mature musically," he says. "I'm just better at my job than I was then."

Lin noticed a shift in Bill's working relationship with Lac. "Candidly, Lac felt like the grown-up among us" in the bookstore basement days, Lin says. "He had worked on other Broadway shows. None of the rest of us had. He very lovingly fell in with us. I'll never be able to repay him for that.

"When Bill comes back to work on the movie, he's had ten years of experience as the music supervisor on *Sesame Street*. He has written musicals on his own. He has music-supervised other shows. So they come together again as equals."

Bill says that he and Lac drew on all they had learned and the vastly greater resources at their disposal to make sure they were doing the "2.0" version of all the music in the film. "Everything had to be recorded with adrenaline. It's louder, brighter, sweeter," he says. They tapped Adam Blackstone, Mike Elizondo, and Sergio George—some of the leading producers in pop, hip-hop, and Latin music—to contribute production to the tracks.

A small change that makes a huge difference: This time they got to have *strings*.

The young leading actors began working with Bill in May, when they would leave dance rehearsals to prerecord vocals at Reservoir, a studio in Midtown. "It got everybody in the mode of singing, of making a musical," Bill says. It also gave Bill a poignant reminder of how far they'd come.

One of his happiest memories is of the day he and Lin worked out the opening bars of "It Won't Be Long Now." They were still roommates back then, a couple of recent college grads wondering if or how they would make their way up the mountain. Batting around ideas in their living room, he had asked Lin, "What if it's something Oremus or Lacamoire would write?"

The intricate piano phrase that Bill suggested that day, long before they'd met the Broadway orchestrator Stephen Oremus or their future collaborator Alex Lacamoire, remains in the song today. When Melissa began to record the song for the movie, Bill turned around to look at his old friend.

Yup, Lin was crying, too.

BY THE TIME filming began, rehearsals had forged Anthony, Leslie, Corey, and Melissa into a tight group of friends. They found ways to spend time together even when they weren't on set in Washington Heights. It helped that all of them felt so at home there.

When Corey had arrived in New York City from his native Washington, D.C., for college, he had lived in Inwood and Washington Heights. Leslie might have been a newcomer to film sets, but she knew the world of *Heights* intimately enough to serve as an on-the-spot consultant for Jon: "I grew up in a salon," she says. Her Dominican-born mother had owned a series of salons, first in New York, where Leslie was born, then in Miami, where she was raised.

"The bodega?" says Anthony. "I lived that shit. I grew up in the hood. Getting a piragua, hanging out with the Vanessas and Ninas and Bennys—that was my life."

YUP, LIN WAS CRYING, TOO.

Melissa had always identified with Vanessa. By the time she saw Karen Olivo play the role on Broadway, she had left the small town outside Monterrey where she had grown up, certain that the things she wanted in life lay elsewhere. She was delighted with all the changes that Quiara made to Vanessa's story for the film version, including her new dream of becoming a fashion designer. It almost seemed to Melissa that she was playing a new character. Which did not in any way diminish the thrill she felt when Karen visited the set.

A meeting—a summit?—between the two Vanessas would have been strange enough. What's stranger still is that they had already met. During Karen's visit, Melissa pulled up a picture on her phone: a stage-door photo they'd taken a decade earlier. Melissa belatedly apologized for having stood *way, way too close* to Karen in the picture—a function of how starstruck she was. Karen didn't care about that. She couldn't believe what she was seeing: a photo of her with the woman she describes as "my younger self." It was surreal to think of all that the future held for both of them, smiling into a camera outside a stage door.

"We had hopes and big dreams, but perhaps Vanessas never really know their own potential," Karen says.

When pressed, the four young leads can't come up with a definite reason why they became as close as "brothers and sisters," in Corey's words. It helped that they shared a willingness to work their asses off. It also helped that Jon set such a loving vibe for the process and that they each felt a responsibility to the characters they were depicting—and the communities they were representing.

To Anthony, the deepest explanation is that *In the Heights* was doing what *In the Heights* does. He had been warned it would happen.

During his time at *Hamilton,* he grew friendly with Javier Muñoz. The role that Javi had adopted when *Heights* was at the O'Neill—Lin's alternate and eventual replacement—carried over to playing Alexander Hamilton.

"That show just brings out the love in you," Javi had told him.

SUMMER IN WASHINGTON HEIGHTS was drawing to a close. One by one, Melissa, Corey, and Anthony finished their work and said their goodbyes. So did the rest of the cast. By August 9, only Leslie was left.

She had one last line to deliver, a lyric in "Breathe." She would sing it on Nina's fire escape, looking to her left—the direction of the sunset, the George Washington Bridge, and her future. This moment wouldn't be filmed on location: The production had converted Brooklyn's cavernous Marcy Armory into a soundstage for things they couldn't shoot in Washington Heights.

"Just me and the GWB," Leslie would sing, "asking, 'Gee, Nina, what'll you be?'"

Because this was the last night of the shoot, dozens of people who had worked on the production had come back to watch. Jon, seeing them arrive, got an idea. He positioned people so that when Leslie sang, she would be looking toward her impromptu audience—three of its members in particular. Without telling her they were going to do it, Melissa, Corey, and Anthony had all come back to support her.

"We started this together, we're going to finish it together," Corey says.

Leslie, on her fire escape, spotted her friends. "It broke me down," she says. "I remember yelling from the wall, 'You guys did this to me! I can't do this right now!' I was crying so hard."

Quiara always sensed a lot of Nina's soul in Leslie, a young singer looking for new ways to express herself, wondering what she had the potential to be. On this night, the

"THE BODEGA?"
SAYS ANTHONY.
"I LIVED THAT SHIT.
I GREW UP
IN THE HOOD."

harmony between actor and role was unusually clear. Like the dancers who waved their flags during the filming of "Carnaval del Barrio," Leslie both was and wasn't acting. Two young women—one of them real, one conjured by Lin and Quiara—were facing an unknown future, but doing it in the company of loved ones, a circle of friendly faces.

Leslie remembers thinking, as she looked down at her friends, *I am coming back home.*

At his keyboard, Kurt Crowley started playing the song. Leslie sang her line. She did it again and again, a dozen times in all. In one take, her emotions got the best of her. She barely got the words out, emitting a little sob. "Sorry, guys," she said afterward.

She was ending the summer as she started it, trying her hardest to avoid letting everybody down. But there was no need to apologize: Jon and Myron chose that take for the movie.

BERNIE SAYS THAT THE stage version of *In the Heights* didn't change the culture the way that *Hamilton* did. "It couldn't have." But after watching the trailer, he thinks the film could be a different proposition. "Young Latino actors are going to see the movie. They're going to say, 'There I am.' I get chills thinking about it."

Around the time that Bernie offered this prediction, Anthony Ramos was walking down a New York street. He was stopped by a young man—a Dominican kid.

"Thank you, thank you," the kid kept saying.

"For what?" Anthony asked.

"I'm coming up, just like you," the kid said. "I'm doing this musical theater thing, just like you."

He had already seen the trailer. He was going to see the movie as soon as he could.

"He talked like me," says Anthony, marveling at the memory. "He looked like me."

Recuerdo

NÚMERO DIEZ

LESLIE GRACE

NINA IN THE FILM VERSION

I never got tired when we were making the movie. I didn't want to waste any time. That this is my first movie is crazy. That I made so many friends for life, people who went to their breaking points together, is amazing.

On the last night of filming, a friend left a bottle of champagne in my dressing room. I had no clue it was going to be there. But it was perfect—the perfect bow for our night. Anthony, Corey, and Melissa all joined me and had a little sip. We were all emotional wrecks. We invited everybody in, including one of our security guard friends.

When I look at the cork now, with the little gold shit, I think about Anthony's long-ass toast, which was super Bushwick, like, "Yo, fam, come on, man, we did it." I think about all the jokes we shared. And Melissa passing a bottle of tequila around the set. A lot of crying and tears of joy and hugging, hugging, hugging and just feeling overwhelmed with awe that we got to make this movie.

The cork brings me back to that moment: It's the end of the summer, and we did this, we all did this.

Champagne [1]

1. Off-Broadway, this was a song called "Goodbye." It was bittersweet and sad and centered on Usnavi attempting to give Vanessa some of his lottery winnings, ending with a plea for her to stay. She lets him down easy and leaves. But after writing "When the Sun Goes Down," we realized we couldn't have *both* couples singing bittersweet goodbye ballads, and so I started from scratch on this song. I wanted to accomplish the same thing but with a lighter touch. The idea came from an old Quiara line in the opening number: Vanessa saying, "First one out of the hood gets a bottle of champagne." I decided to center it on her bringing him a champagne bottle, and a bit of comic business: Usnavi's dreams are coming true, but he's so focused on opening the bottle and the task at hand that he's not seeing the larger gesture of her bringing the champagne in the first place: She loves you, you idiot. Most critically, it also puts the ball in Vanessa's court for the first time: She's just as invested in this relationship and willing to fight for it. After I wrote this song, we went back and I musicalized Quiara's "champagne" mention in the opening number so it would pay off here.

2. While I was trying to write this song, the cast got used to seeing me wander through rehearsals, mumbling to myself with an unopened $5 bottle of Korbel Brut in my hand. At one point, Karen Olivo asked, "Bruh. Are you okay?"

3. In the movie, Melissa Barrera and Anthony Ramos performed this whole song and scene live, in an uninterrupted take (I believe we used the ninth take). Infinite props to Mark Schmidt, our A-camera operator and Steadicam operator for this scene, for his virtuosic work in this apartment.

VANESSA: So I got you a present. I went downtown to get it. Doing anything tonight? [2]

USNAVI: Cleaning.

VANESSA: You're done for the day.

USNAVI: No way.

VANESSA: Cuz we got a date.

USNAVI: Okay— [3]

VANESSA: Before you board that plane I owe you a bottle of cold champagne.

4. Usnavi is the one who asks Daniela to cosign for Vanessa's apartment, an event that happens offstage in the show. I'm glad we actually see Usnavi doing it in the film, thanks to Quiara.

5. Here I *have* to shout out Shaun Taylor-Corbett, my understudy, who once took his work so seriously on Broadway that in this moment, the cork came flying out and CHAMPAGNE WENT EVERYWHERE. He niftily improvised, "See the twisty thing is broken, but now I've opened this damn champagne," then set to work cleaning as much of the stage as possible for the dancers while continuing the action of the scene, as a shocked Olivo looked on. The props department sealed the bottle permanently after that incident . . .

6. This turn is still so exciting after all this time. That the comic relief song kicks into a different emotional gear.

7. Again, Vanessa listing every reason except her feelings for him—the money, Sonny's future—and she gets hung up on the one that seems the most trivial but is actually their daily point of connection: the coffee he hands her for free every morning.

USNAVI: No . . .

VANESSA: Yeah, cold champagne.

USNAVI: Damn, the bottle's all sweaty and everything.
You went and got this—

VANESSA: Pop the champagne.

USNAVI: I don't know if we have coffee cups
Or plastic cups, I think Sonny has the cups—

VANESSA: Tonight we're drinking straight from the bottle.
Usnavi?

USNAVI: Yeah?

VANESSA: Daniela told me what you did for me ❹
And it's honestly the sweetest thing anyone ever did for me.
Now what can I say or do to possibly repay you for your kindness?

USNAVI: How do you get this gold shit off?

VANESSA: Usnavi!

USNAVI: Yeah!

VANESSA: Before we both leave town
Before the corner changes and the signs are taken down
Let's walk around the neighborhood and say our goodbyes.
Usnavi, are you all right?

USNAVI: I'm fine, I'm tryn'a open this champagne.
See the twisty thing is broken,
But I'm gonna open this damn champagne! ❺

VANESSA: Lemme see it.

USNAVI: No, I got it!

VANESSA: Yo, Usnavi, drop the champagne!

USNAVI: You went to all that trouble to get us a little bubbly—

VANESSA: And it's gonna be okay.

USNAVI: I'm sorry, it's been a long day.

VANESSA: You oughta stay. ❻

USNAVI: What?

VANESSA: You can use that money to fix this place.

USNAVI: Ha, ha, very funny.

VANESSA: And it's not like Sonny's got role models—

USNAVI: Role models?

VANESSA: Stepping up to the plate—

USNAVI: Yo, what are you talking about?

VANESSA: I'm just saying, I think your vacation can wait—

USNAVI: Vacation? Vanessa, you're leaving too—

VANESSA: I'm going down to West Fourth Street, you can take the A—

USNAVI: What are you trying to say?

VANESSA: You're leaving the country, and we're never gonna see you again—

USNAVI: What are you trying to say?

VANESSA: You get everyone addicted to your coffee and off you go. ❼

USNAVI: Vanessa, I don't know why you're mad at me.

VANESSA: I wish I was mad—

(She kisses him.)

I'm just too late.

CHAPTER Twenty-One

EN WASHINGTON HEIGHTS

"REMEMBER," NELSON COATES TOLD his team, "it's the hottest day of the year."

Everybody laughed and kept working.

Two months after the Pasadena screening, the staff and crew were back on the streets of Washington Heights. They said they were doing reshoots, but to be nitpicky about it, they weren't doing new takes of things they had already filmed. They were filling in blanks: filming people, mostly neighborhood residents, to round out the opening number and finish their movie.

There was a big difference from the last time they were all together, one that explains why Nelson's squad of set dressers found his remark at daybreak so amusing: It was early February and about seventy degrees shy of the hottest day of 2020.

At a bus stop on Amsterdam Avenue, in front of the shuttered and drained Highbridge Park pool, dozens of staff and crew members were positioning cameras, cables, and space heaters. Most of them wore wool hats and puffy coats; somebody circulated with a box of toe warmers. But inside the bus that was idling at the curb, it was balmy summer. Extras in T-shirts and shorts pretended to be commuting to work. Jon moved up and down the aisle, framing shots with his phone, talking over his shoulder to Alice Brooks.

A chimi truck was parked in front of the bus. Faded and weathered, it bore the marks of many years of serving customers who queue up for Dominican street food. In fact, until a couple of days earlier, this truck was a plain white box on wheels. Nelson's team transformed it, right down to the scuff marks and Dominican flag. In late morning, they applied some finishing touches so that as soon as Jon and Alice got the shot they needed on the bus, the truck would be ready for its close-up. It's as if fifty people were playing an elaborate, expensive game of leapfrog.

When Jon walked over, shooting was delayed not because of the truck but because of its make-believe proprietor. A couple of nights earlier, Jon had spotted a familiar face on a subway platform. It was Luis Salgado, the dancer and choreographer who had introduced him to *In the Heights* when he invited Jon to see it on Broadway. Jon had always wanted Luis to be in the movie, and that random encounter had given them a fresh chance to figure it out. Now here was Luis, in shorts and high-tops, getting ready to chop up chimi while mouthing the lyrics of a song he's been singing since 2007.

Jon and Luis talked about the shot with the choreographer, Chris Scott. The three of them were used to these exchanges, having worked together on Jon's first movie, *Step Up 2: The Streets*. Jon got a new idea: They should film Luis swinging open the panel on the side of the truck. Chris and Luis agreed. It's the kind of on-the-spot brain wave that could slow down production. Except that Nelson, having anticipated that Jon might want to try that, had already dressed everything that needed dressing to shoot it. Experiments on how Luis should hoist the panel began at once.

And that was good news for all of them, considering they had four or five days' worth of reshoots to do and only two days to do them.

The quality of a collaboration makes real, tangible differences to what people create—each of them separately or all of them together. Lin had the extreme good fortune to encounter Tommy, Lac, and Andy in the tadpole stage of his career and the extreme good sense to hang on to them. What they achieved together on *Hamilton* is unimaginable without the bonds they had forged on *Heights*. The same holds for Jon, who couldn't have made *Heights* without the history he shares with a handful of collaborators, all of whom were with him on set this day: Nelson, Chris, Myron Kerstein, Mitchell Travers, and especially Alice, his longest-standing creative partner, stretching all the way back to his student projects at USC.

"We practiced for ten years to do this," he told her.

If the film works, it'll be because of Lin's songs and Quiara's screenplay. It'll also be because of the collaboration among Jon and his team, a tight group of colleagues who are very different from the stage version's Voltron—and totally the same.

THE MISSION WASN'T TO turn Washington Heights into something new, Jon told them when their collaboration began: It was to capture the beauty that's already there.

Alice had no trouble seeing it. "I was constantly falling in love with the place," she says.

When they started visiting Washington Heights to scout locations, the sights, sounds, even the smells felt like home. She had grown up in Manhattan—her father had plays produced on Broadway—in a neighborhood with a strong Puerto Rican presence. She told Quiara that the second she saw the George Washington Bridge rise into view, "I felt like I could breathe."

Those early trips were a sort of quest: a search for what they called their *"Do the Right Thing* block." They wanted to find a single location where they could film most of the action of the movie, just as Spike Lee had filmed much of his masterpiece on a single street in Brooklyn.

Samson Jacobson, the location manager, says that his "Spidey sense" kept leading him back to one intersection in particular: 175th and Audubon. It had a bodega diagonally across from a car service and enough room for big dance numbers in the street. It even afforded a view of the GWB peeking over the rooftops to the west. *If this isn't it, then I'm on the wrong job,* he remembers thinking.

Everybody agreed: The movie had found a home. Now they had to figure out how to film it.

Capturing the authentic character of a neighborhood is more complicated than pointing a camera at it. What's distinctive about Washington Heights doesn't fit neatly in a frame: It has to be selected, composed, distilled. So the existing bodega would get a new awning; the daycare center across

Nelson Coates, Jon Chu, Alice Brooks, and Chris Scott

the street would get a new facade and become Daniela's salon. Nelson vowed that every element in his production design would be something he had seen in the neighborhood. Fortunately, he had seen everything: He had walked every street, visited every salon, every bodega.

He did not find this taxing. Like Alice, he calls *In the Heights* a dream job. He tracked the show from Broadway, where he saw it three times in a week, all along its convoluted path to the screen. When he met Jon to talk about working on *Crazy Rich Asians,* he nurtured the secret hope that if he landed the gig and everything went well, it would give him a shot at designing *Heights.*

Nelson did land the gig, and everything did go well. Jon admired the way that Nelson understood what characters needed—all of it informed by the voluminous knowledge he somehow amassed about every aspect of, well, everything.

"I love people who love what they do, the ones who'd be doing this whether they're getting paid or not," Jon says. "I get drawn to those people and like making things with those people. And Nelson is that. *Fully.*"

A few weeks into working on *Crazy Rich Asians,* Jon asked Nelson what he was doing next. Nelson said he wasn't sure.

"Would you be interested in doing a musical called *In the Heights?*" asked Jon.

Nelson, who used to be an actor, said, "That sounds okay."

Only months later did Nelson admit that he had been chasing the movie forever.

"Dork," Jon replied.

There's a parallel in the granular precision that Lac brings to the movie's music and Nelson brings to its design, except that for Nelson, "granular" isn't metaphorical. He wanted Usnavi to have a map of the Dominican Republic in his bodega, so his team made it using actual sand from the actual D.R.: A crew member brought it home from his honeymoon.

"My friends all joke, 'Tomorrow on *Oprah,* production designers who care too much,'" Nelson says. "Call it obsessive, I don't know. It's what I love to do, and I want to do right by the characters and the communities that are being represented."

His experience on *Crazy Rich Asians* bolstered his feeling that little details really matter. If they're done right, they make people feel seen and respected. And that representation affects how people are treated once the credits roll.

Mitchell Travers feels the same way, which is why he pushed as hard as he pushed to design the costumes of *Heights.* He admired what Lin and Jon had already created and felt sure that their collaboration would do some genuine good in the world. *I probably won't ever get a chance to do something like this again,* he remembers feeling about the chance to work with them.

THE MISSION WASN'T TO TURN WASHINGTON HEIGHTS INTO SOMETHING NEW: IT WAS TO CAPTURE THE BEAUTY THAT'S ALREADY THERE.

Leslie Grace ▶

THE TOP OF THE WORLD | PART TWO

A look inside the creative process of **NELSON COATES**, film production designer

▲ Mural based on artworks by Evaristo Angurria

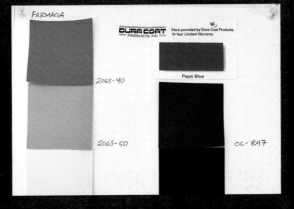

FARMACIA

2063-40

2063-50

Pepsi Blue

CC-247

POOL / **BEFORE**

POOL / **AFTER**

SALON / **BEFORE**

SALON / **AFTER**

FARMACIA / **BEFORE**

FARMACIA / **AFTER**

He tried to design the costumes without thinking too much like a costume designer. He got inspiration from sitting outside in Washington Heights, watching people pass by. He also told his team to spend time getting to know the actors before rolling out the clothing racks—especially the extras from the community. He wanted to reflect their lives, their energies, their stories. (Jon, applying a lesson from *Crazy Rich Asians,* took a similar approach to the actors' hair: He left more time to capture the beauty of curls. "Let's make sure we can see her eyes. Let's light it a little bit better instead of rushing through it or saying, 'Just change your hair because it's getting in our way.'")

The neighborhood turned out to be an eager collaborator. As the shoot was about to begin, a man approached Mitchell.

"M'ijo, m'ijo," he said. "I heard you need shoes."

Mitchell said he needed a million shoes—he had dozens of dancers on set every day.

"I'll take care of you," the man said.

By the time Mitchell got back to the wardrobe truck, the man had set up two full tables of sneakers. Mitchell bought the lot—and used them all. The process repeated with a woman selling jewelry and a woman selling scarves.

Mitchell loved it. "It was the best, because I would say, 'I need—' and the neighborhood would say, 'Here.'"

The traffic back and forth led to a certain porousness around the edges of the set. The actors and producers, having foregone many of the trailers where they would normally hole up, spent a lot of time on the sidewalks. Mara Jacobs, who was on set virtually every minute of every day, would go for walks when she needed to make a private phone call. She got used to seeing people from

THE NEIGHBORHOOD TURNED OUT TO BE AN EAGER COLLABORATOR.

the neighborhood bring the crew homemade food, especially when its favorite son was around.

"Washington Heights has two mayors: One is Lin-Manuel Miranda and the other is Luis Miranda," says Anthony Bregman, who was also on set nearly every minute of every day. So was David Nicksay, one of the film's executive producers. So was Quiara.

It could be dreamy on set, but that doesn't mean it was heaven: the rainouts, the heat, the push-pull over parking. Now and then, guys on motorcycles made a point of roaring by the set. All the same, Lin, Quiara, Jon, and most of his team say that Washington Heights in 2019 was the best summer of their lives.

So you can understand why it would be bittersweet to return on a cold February morning. Almost every trace of their summer had been erased. In real life, as in the movie, Daniela's salon was long gone. The most conspicuous sign that they had been here was a mural painted on the side of the bodega: a lonely sailor in a little boat under a Dominican flag. (See the photo at the top of page 237.)

It's been said that a true New Yorker walks the streets, looking at the buildings, remembering what they used to be.

ON THE SECOND DAY of reshoots, the action shifted to the lobby of an apartment building a few doors down from where Abuela Claudia used to live.

The super of the building was standing alone, holding his mop. A dozen people stared at him. He stared back. Down a hallway, a resident was singing in Spanish.

"Rolling!" somebody shouted. "Action!"

The opening number began to play. The super started mopping.

"Have more fun!" Jon told him. "Have more fun!"

They finished the take. Members of the film crew made some adjustments, then started again. "Instead of happy—sad," Jon said this time. "It's hard work."

On a later take, Jon said, "Now the *most* fun. Dance a little while you do it." And the super did. And now people cheered him on, and he seemed to be enjoying it.

"Say 'In the Heights,'" Jon said. *"Louder."*

In the midst of this, a young woman stepped out of her apartment, slalomed around a camera operator, the building's super, and the director of *Crazy Rich Asians*, pushed open the door, and went about her day, without having turned her head or broken her stride.

MOVIE EASTER EGGS

NELSON COATES
PRODUCTION DESIGNER

I love putting little Easter eggs around the set—details that will be meaningful to the people making the film. I think of them as blessings.

1. ROSARIO'S CAR SERVICE: The license number, LM&QHOB2008, means "Lin-Manuel Miranda & Quiara Hudes on Broadway 2008"

2. NADAL APARTMENTS: The last name of Lin's wife, Vanessa

3. HUDES HARDWARE: For Quiara

4. BOLERO RECORD: This record plays during the dinner scene. The name of the singer, Luisa Mundi, is inspired by Lin's abuela

5. LACAMOIRE MOTORS: For Alex

6. USNAVI'S MAP OF THE D.R.: Hanging behind the cash register, it incorporates actual sand from the island, plus items from the bodega such as MetroCards and keys

7. PIRAGUA CART: The subway train carved into the wood comes from a sketch of the show's logo that Lin made in a college notebook (see photo, page 5)

Jon decided they had what they needed. Everybody applauded. He high-fived the super, then posed for a selfie, both of them beaming.

As the crew streamed onto the sidewalk, headed for the next shot, the super, Juan Pichardo, resumed his day. He had worked in this building for fourteen years, he said, ever since he arrived from the Dominican Republic. He had shown the production team some apartments in the building, then got a call asking if he himself would like to be in the movie. He had said that sounded fine. He wasn't doing anything unusual for the cameras that morning—it's his motion picture debut, he says—just mopping the way he always mops.

Asked how he feels about the prospect of millions of moviegoers all over the planet watching him do his job as part of a montage honoring the too-frequently-overlooked day-to-day work that people do to provide for themselves, their families, and their neighbors, Juan smiles.

"That's nice," he says. "That's good."

He doesn't go to a lot of movies, he says. But his stepson was very happy to get a selfie with an actor when the movie was on the corner last summer.

Back to that corner, and a few doors down, reshoots were in full swing. It was warmer than the day before, so there was no more need for puffy coats—and anyway there wasn't room. To minimize the time they'd lose shifting the whole apparatus of filming from one location to another, they had taken over three apartments on the same floor of a single building. Hallways are narrow in the prewar buildings that still dominate this part of the city. Crew members got very nimble at crab-walking past their co-workers.

The atmosphere in those apartments, where Jon was filming vignettes of domestic life, was strange in some ways—movie people have more tape measures than you would expect—and deeply familiar in others. The air of quiet productivity, a lightness that conceals how intensely everybody is concentrating, felt like tech in one of Tommy Kail's collaborations with Lin. Artistically speaking, it's a kind of cold fusion: extraordinary things happen while remaining at room temperature.

What explains this vibe? Different people on Jon's team have different explanations.

"Here's the amazing thing about Jon," Mitchell says. "Jon gives you the widest arena to create in. But he's such a creative genius, I think, *Well, I have to keep up with Jon.* So then I really throw myself into it and push myself."

Alice says everybody worked as hard as they worked because of the material: Lin and Quiara wrote something that she would be proud to take her family to see. But Jon also fostered a cohesion unlike any film she has done. "Every single person was making the same movie," she says. "Usually it's, 'Oh, I know how to do this better.' It felt amazing to be part of a project where everyone felt their ideas were heard."

On the sidewalk outside, where they were able to extend both arms, Chris and Nelson theorized that the history they shared with Jon and each other was important. It would be either very difficult (Chris's view) or totally impossible (Nelson's) to make this movie without it. The collaboration Jon fostered on *Heights,* they were finding, wasn't a grudging arrival at decisions that everybody could live with. (His strict "No assholes" hiring policy surely helped.) Collaboration meant staying open to new ideas, to discovering what might be possible if they fully trusted one another. Chris says that Jon implicitly asked them: "What could we all do *together?*"

To illustrate the point, he takes out his phone and begins playing a video: a rehearsal of the number that probably captures more than anything else in the movie

"IT FELT AMAZING TO BE PART OF A PROJECT WHERE **EVERYONE FELT THEIR IDEAS WERE HEARD."**

how this group brought their taste and spirit to *Heights*. It is not a race-the-clock achievement like shooting "Carnaval del Barrio" in a day. It's a months-long test of their collaboration: how well they could conceive, design, and execute something that seemed worth doing precisely because it would require all of them to stretch in order to succeed.

"I never thought we would actually get there," Jon admits now when he thinks back to making "When the Sun Goes Down," the showstopping number that arrives late in the movie. "But we got there."

THEIR APPROACH TO THE song was sparked by Jon's insight into Nina and Benny's relationship—and, really, *every* relationship: "When you're in love, gravity doesn't mean anything."

He knew that other musicals had turned weightlessness into choreography: Think of Fred Astaire dancing across the ceiling in *Royal Wedding*. "How you do it *outside*— that's a whole other thing," Jon says. That would be something new and badass. It would also be a subtle way of underscoring one of the story's themes: that life isn't lived entirely in your living room. We exist in communities, in neighborhoods, on streets—and, sometimes, four stories above them, at a ninety-degree angle.

Jon's idea to have Benny and Nina dance up the side of a building might strike you as a little crazy, gravity being what it is. But Alice and Chris didn't think so. A decade earlier, the three of them had collaborated on the web series *The LXD: The Legion of Extraordinary Dancers*. Its thirty episodes offered them a laboratory to push the boundaries of how you can tell stories with dance. Those experiments are a big reason why Jon knew Alice was the ideal director of photography for *Heights:* Sure, she could shoot a number in any style with maximum flair, but she could also resist the temptation to turn the numbers into music videos, and focus on the human reality of the story.

Chris had never worked with perpendicular dancers before. Though he needed to choreograph fifteen songs

"WHEN YOU'RE **IN LOVE, GRAVITY** DOESN'T MEAN ANYTHING."

for the movie, each presenting its own challenge—from the watery spectacle of "96,000" to the single-take intimacy of "Champagne"—this one inspired him the most. He started working on it before he moved to New York, turning tables and chairs sideways on the floor of his L.A. studio to reorient his brain.

If they were going to put Benny and Nina on the side of a building, which building should it be? Nelson searched the neighborhood for the perfect spot. Near J. Hood Wright Park, on the south side of a street, he saw a building that seemed to offer the right arrangement of wall, sun, and bridge. The visual effects team used LiDAR technology to create a 3D version of that block. But the building that stood on the perfect spot didn't strike Nelson as the perfect building. So he took elements from three different buildings around the neighborhood—all designed by the same architect, a very Nelson touch—and combined them to get what he needed.

Next came a motion-capture phase, a long Saturday on which Jon and Alice watched dancers in special suits perform Chris's choreography. Jon used a sophisticated rig—like a camera without a lens—to record their movement, feeding the images to a computer that placed them in the 3D landscape already populated with the scanned block and Nelson's composite building. As Emilio Dosal and Melanie Moore moved, Jon trailed them with the rig, a third dancer in their duet. (As part of Jon's training to be an all-American kid, he took twelve years of tap dance.)

The test got the production team excited about the idea: "It was thrilling," says Quiara. "Just when you think there's no more tricks to pull out in the movie." Myron loved it, too. He decided he wouldn't do much cutting in this song. The more restraint he used, the more astonishing it would be. It also taught Jon a more immediate lesson: "We were finding out how much we could get away with without needing to tilt the building."

But they would still need to tilt the building.

This is where the song gets more complicated, more expensive, and more dangerous. At Marcy Armory, the crew built a real-world version of one wall of Nelson's building. Half of it was flat on the ground; the other half—twenty-four feet high by twenty feet wide—stood straight up in the air. It was like any other wall, except there was no building behind it and it was bolted to a row of enormously powerful hydraulic hinges that could tilt it all the way to the ground in five seconds. The only way to sell the number, they had found, was for the wall to move under the actors while they danced.

Ah yes, the actors.

During rehearsals, Leslie got a text from someone on Jon's staff asking if she was afraid of heights. She said she wasn't. A couple of minutes later, Jon called—he wanted to be sure. "Yeah, bro, whatever you need," she told him.

This is how Leslie and Corey ended up spending weeks of rehearsal figuring out how to dance a duet while surfing a twenty-four-foot metal wall with no harness. It was difficult to figure out the choreography in the studio and difficult all over again in the few days they got to spend on the wall itself. Each of them needed strength and balance, and both of them needed trust—in Chris, in Jon, and in each other. They didn't need anybody to spell out why this song was the last dancing they were scheduled to do: If they got hurt, it wouldn't hamper the rest of the shoot. Corey says it's the most challenging thing he's done in his film career. Leslie says it is the most challenging thing she has done, period.

The song's late placement in the production calendar created an opening for one final flourish. Shortly before they filmed it, Jon shared a rough assembly of "When You're Home" with Chris. He realized too late that they had missed their best chance in the whole movie to have Benny and Nina kiss.

Chris suggested they try it in "When the Sun Goes Down." He hadn't choreographed a kiss, but he could try to work it in.

Jon said go ahead.

Leslie and Corey spent parts of three days on the wall. That's how long it took to synchronize the actors, the building, the camera (mounted at the end of a robotic arm, rotating in sync with the building), the sun (really an arc light on a crane with a two-foot-diameter lens), and Lin's song. Even the costumes required precision engineering. Mitchell had to make sure that no piece of clothing or jewelry would sway in the wrong direction and spoil the effect. So Leslie wore her hair in braids, and ear cuffs instead of earrings; Corey's shirt looks loose, but it was stitched to a tank top so it wouldn't move. Their *shoelaces* were sewn tight.

When the music started, the wall would tilt part of the way to the floor. Corey would shift his feet from the fire escape to the wall, then he would help Leslie to join him—the cue for the wall to drop the rest of the way. Then they could dance, expressing what Benny and Nina were feeling—something that Jon and the rest of them were feeling, too. As Corey puts it, "Let's imagine what it was like when New York was their playground, what it was like at the beginning of that summer, and always let it live in our imaginations."

As the number drew to a close, the wall tilted up to about forty-five degrees, then stopped. Leslie lay down on it, and Corey lay down next to her. They kissed. According to the plan, the wall would tilt all the way vertical, and they would slide down to the fire escape. But how to get there? Leslie found that if she used her foot as a brake, they got stuck. So they just let go, putting their faith in gravity and each other. As ever, Leslie and Corey were finding their way together.

"I think it's the best shot in the movie," says Alice.

JON AND HIS TEAM feel they are stewards of the artists who came before them. (And of audiences—Mitchell gave Usnavi a Kangol cap as a way of honoring the Broadway fans.) They admire Tommy Kail and his colleagues, who first brought Lin and Quiara's story to life onstage. After all, most of the key filmmakers—including Jon—fell in love with *Heights* while watching the original Broadway production.

So it means a lot to Jon and his team to hear that Andy Blankenbuehler, seeing a glimpse of "When the Sun Goes Down" in the trailer, has said: "Dancing on the side of a building? That's f---ing money." It means something, too, when Lin credits Jon with "seeing things we can't." A decade ago, they never could have come up with his approach, "but it's the purest expression of that song."

As for the rest of us, who will be watching with our popcorn, they'd prefer that we don't think about them or their web of relationships or the mechanics of the collaboration, at least not on first viewing. If they really did the job, we'll think: *What a kiss.*

"I THINK IT'S THE BEST SHOT IN THE MOVIE."

When the Sun Goes Down

1. I *know* that calling cards are not as omnipresent as they once were, but as long as bodegas still sell 'em, I'm keeping this calling card/falling hard lyric.

2. This song has never quite fit in the time line the way we needed it to: In the stage version, it's been an awfully long day if the sun is just setting now. In the film version, the blackout references only make sense with Quiara's setup dialogue: "Let's pretend we're still in the blackout." BUT THE SONG WILL NOT BE DENIED.

3. When we did student matinees, they couldn't help but snap along with the snap in this tune. But the 2/4 bar pause before Benny begins the second verse throws 'em off every time.

4. This song, truly one of the last I wrote for the show, brought my journey with *In the Heights* full circle. Remember way back to Chapter One: The initial impulse and *time* I had to write this show came from my first girlfriend and first real love leaving to study abroad. We both knew it was time to part ways. We didn't know how. This song has all the words I didn't have when I was nineteen.

5. This song is a bit of a Rorschach test: For Quiara, who married her high school sweetheart, Benny and Nina survive as a couple. For me (see earlier note), it's a breakup song. We wrote the thing, and we see it differently. It allows space for all of it.

6. Me, a romantic: This notion of thinking of each other at a certain time of day was inspired by Philip Pullman's incredible *His Dark Materials* series, concerning two characters who pledge to share a moment on the same park bench in two parallel universes.
   You, a scold: But, Lin, the sun would set at different times on the East and West Coast—
   Me: Shhhhhhhhhhhh . . .

BENNY: When the sun goes down
You're gonna need a flashlight
You're gonna need a candle—

NINA: I think I can handle that.

BENNY: When you leave town
I'm gonna buy you a calling card. ①

BENNY, NINA: Cuz I am falling hard for you. ②

NINA: I go back on Labor Day.

BENNY: And I will try to make my way

BENNY, NINA: Out west to California.

BENNY: So we've got this summer.

NINA: And we've got each other
Perhaps even longer. ③

BENNY: When you're on your own
And suddenly without me,
Will you forget about me?

NINA: I couldn't if I tried.

BENNY: When I'm all alone
And I close my eyes

BENNY, NINA: That's when I'll see your face again. ④

BENNY: And when you're gone,
You know that I'll be waiting when you're gone.

NINA: But you're here with me right now . . .

BENNY: We'll be working hard, but
If we should drift apart

NINA: Benny—

BENNY: Lemme take this moment just to say—

NINA: No, no—

BENNY: You are gonna change the world someday—

NINA: I'll be thinking of home— ⑤

BENNY, NINA: And I'll think of you every night
At the same time—

BENNY: When the sun goes down.

NINA: When the sun goes down.

BENNY: When the sun goes down. ⑥

CHAPTER Twenty-Two

★ FINALE ★

WHEN RESHOOTS ENDED, QUIARA skipped town. It was time for a much-needed getaway with her family. But even in Puerto Rico, her work on *Heights* continued.

The world premiere was set for June 26—just four months away. The festivities would take place at the United Palace, the massive gilded movie theater at the heart of the neighborhood. It promised to be the *Heights* party to end all *Heights* parties. With the deadline approaching, Jon had begun summoning actors to rerecord dialogue, which sometimes required tweaks to the script: a different word here, an extra syllable there. So Quiara would hike or sightsee with her family during the day, then stay up late to write what Jon needed. "It reminded me of the O'Neill a little bit, except not stressful," she says. "It was really fun."

Refreshed and recharged, she flew home to New York in late February. That's when her husband, Ray, got sick. *Very* sick.

In any other year, the illness would have been easy to diagnose. Ray seemed to have a bad case of the flu. But since the start of 2020, the world had watched with growing alarm as a mysterious coronavirus had begun to spread. The first reports had come from China. Then from Italy. Then Seattle. Then everywhere.

Could Ray have contracted COVID-19? Nobody knew then; nobody knows now. Whatever the illness might have been, he sequestered himself for two weeks, then got better—a huge relief to family and friends.

Still a sense of dread was spreading, particularly in New York. By early March, the city's hospitals were overflowing; ambulances screamed day and night. History doesn't often divide neatly into "before" and "after." Sweeping changes take time. Except when they don't.

Consider how members of the *Heights* community experienced one of the pandemic's decisive days.

On Thursday, March 12, Andy Blankenbuehler started his morning at the gym, the same one where watching the video for "Thriller" had unlocked "96,000" for him a dozen years earlier. While processing the startling COVID news from the night before—the NBA had canceled its entire season; Tom Hanks and Rita Wilson were sick—Andy noticed that the exercise bike next to him was occupied by a woman wearing a mask and surgical gloves. "I was of course freaked out," he says.

He crossed the room for some hand sanitizer. The dispenser was empty. It seemed like time to go.

On his way out, he bumped into another *Heights* alum, Joshua Henry, who had begun stocking up on essential supplies for the widespread shortage that many believed was imminent.

"It felt like the world was ending," Andy says.

Soon his phone rang: It was Jeffrey Seller calling to discuss *Hamilton*. (Andy had won his second Tony Award for choreographing the show.) They considered a question that would have seemed preposterous a few weeks earlier: Was it safe to perform that night? Jeffrey didn't think so. He was headed to an emergency meeting at The Broadway League, the organization of leading commercial producers. Crowded into a conference room— "That in and of itself could have been a superspreader event," Jeffrey would say later—they tried to coordinate a response with New York's elected officials.

As Jeffrey, Kevin McCollum, and other producers strategized, Andréa Burns arrived at her voice doctor for a checkup. She was glad to hear that everything looked good, since she was due in San Diego in two weeks to work on a new musical. "That's not going to happen," her doctor told her—not with this virus looming. On her way home, she got a call from her son, Hudson, who was no longer the young mascot of the *Heights* company, but a sixteen-year-old high school junior thinking about colleges. He broke the news that Broadway—*all* of Broadway—had just shut down.

It was afternoon now; events moved faster. At the Richard Rodgers Theatre, wardrobe assistants for *Hamilton* waited for the washers and dryers to finish their cycles, lest Paul Tazewell's costumes rot away before Mandy Gonzalez, Daniel Yearwood, and other *Heights* alumni in the cast could resume performing. A few blocks away, at the Stephen Sondheim Theatre, Kevin told the company of *Mrs. Doubtfire,* including Doreen Montalvo, that the show was suspended. They should gather their things and go home. He gave the company of *Six* the same message, but it was even more painful to deliver. When he arrived at the Brooks Atkinson Theatre, he had to edge past a mountain of presents, flowers, champagne: It was supposed to be opening night.

On opposite coasts, the two Vanessas, Melissa Barrera and Karen Olivo, reacted that afternoon much as their character might have. Melissa, in Los Angeles, felt a Vanessa-like determination to get to work, virus be damned. She planned to fly to New York for a busy weekend of rerecording dialogue, taking part in a photo shoot,

and—a particular thrill for a Vanessa—attending the Met Gala, the highlight of the fashion year. She had no intention of letting a pandemic stop her. ("I was in complete denial," she says now.) She texted her team for updates: *When could she fly?*

Three thousand miles away, Karen demonstrated a Vanessa-like instinct for survival. "I was out of my apartment within thirty minutes of them shutting down Broadway," she says. She believed—rightly—that if Broadway had closed, the whole city was soon to follow. She gathered her husband and their dog and headed for LaGuardia. They didn't even clean out their fridge.

Karen made it home to Wisconsin; Melissa, blocked in her attempt to reach New York, joined her husband in Sonora. Before long, both of the Vanessas would be sick, likely with COVID-19.

Jon had spent the morning on a mixing stage in Manhattan, finessing the sound of the movie. By afternoon, he was watching colleagues scramble. Parents

"IT FELT LIKE THE WORLD WAS ENDING."

faced the sudden prospect of schools closing: *What would they do with the kids?* His own wife and children had flown home to Los Angeles a few weeks earlier. In a flash, he realized that he might get stuck in New York, a continent away from them.

Warner Bros. told him it was too risky to fly. "That's when I knew I had to leave," he says.

On the cab ride to the hotel—rushing in for his things, rushing out for his flight—he passed by a movie set. The piles of fake snow gave him a hunch about which movie it might be. A text exchange with Alice Brooks, the director of photography, proved him right. Unlikely as it sounds, the set was for *Tick, Tick . . . Boom!,* Netflix's adaptation of Jonathan Larson's musical. Its director was Lin.

The virus had gotten Lin's filmmaking career off to a peculiar start: everybody on set staying six feet apart, the city eerily still around them. ("It was beginning to look like *Vanilla Sky,*" he says.) But he had been dreaming of directing movies even longer than he'd been writing *In the Heights,* so he was determined to make the most of the chance. He and Alice shot as much as they could before they got the order to stop. It arrived late on Friday the thirteenth. He called "Cut" one last time, then the cast and crew scattered for safety.

Back home in Washington Heights, Lin felt whiplash. How had it happened so fast? One day, frenetic activity; the next, enforced stillness. He worried about his wife and sons and parents and friends. As New York's lockdown grew more complete, and the ambulances screamed louder, he tried to imagine what might happen next.

One sure sign that a strange new reality had dawned: "I didn't make anything for a month," Lin says.

IT WASN'T JUST NEW Yorkers—or even Americans. Spin the globe: Wherever it stops, you'll find members of the *Heights* community whose lives were disrupted that day and in the days that followed.

At the same moment that Kevin was canceling the opening night of *Six,* Jeff Rosenschein was leading a band through the curtain call music of *Chicago,* in the same Jerusalem theater where he had conducted *In the Heights.* Because of newly imposed restrictions on public

gatherings, the actors no sooner finished their bows than they began to strike the set, carting it away amid what Jeff calls "tremendous chaos and confusion." A few hours later, Bobby Garcia arrived at the Manila theater where he'd staged the international premiere of *Heights,* preparing to celebrate the same milestone for *The Band's Visit.* Instead, a nurse recorded the actors' temperatures as their set was torn down.

A still more painful disruption occurred in Egypt, where students at the Modern English School Cairo had been rehearsing *In the Heights.* Jonathan Todd, the director, had noticed that they were connecting to the show's themes—the importance of family, the promise and danger of leaving home—more fully than they had connected to any other show they'd done. In particular, the characters' mourning for Abuela Claudia resonated in an Islamic context. "To hold something up to God for blessing is an act that's very familiar to the students," he says. The pandemic closed their school—and their show—before opening night.

With a killer virus circling the globe, the fate of a movie wasn't anybody's chief worry. But it was still a worry. Once the basic safety of their families was assured, Warner Bros. executives and the *Heights* creative team reckoned with how COVID-19 would affect their plans. It was hard to imagine that audiences would brave a pandemic to go to the movies, and even less likely that the crisis would be under control in three months' time. Should they stick to

▲ Cairo

"WE HAVE TO BE READY. AND WE HAVE TO HOPE THE WORLD IS READY."

the original release date but stream the movie on HBO Max? Or should they preserve the theatrical release, but push back the date? Since Toby Emmerich, chairman of the Warner Bros. Pictures Group, felt that *Heights* was a summer movie, a delay would last a full year.

At first, Lin didn't want to wait. "My heart sank," he says. He felt like he was back at the O'Neill, when he and the rest of Voltron thought they were Broadway bound, only to have the producers say the show still didn't work. He wanted people to see the movie as soon as it was ready, no matter where or how they saw it.

Quiara was inclined to delay. More people would feel comfortable venturing out to see the movie if they waited. And though it brought her no joy to say it, she felt sure that the themes of *Heights*—particularly its concern with immigrants and the fate of the undocumented—would remain just as relevant in 2021. Above all, she believed in the work they had done: "I've been making this shit for so long, I was like, *I'll wait a year.*"

Jon favored waiting, too. His experience with *Crazy Rich Asians* taught him that beyond raising the profile of the movie itself, a theatrical release would activate a global marketing machine that could turn the actors into stars. "If the movie becomes a big hit, they go off and carry other movies. I've seen it happen," he says. "A whole new lane gets created. And that has even more longevity than the movie."

That argument persuaded Lin, even if it didn't cheer him up. "I get that it's better to wait, but I don't want that to be the right answer," he says. "My heart, which just wants to share the movie with the world, doesn't want that to be the case."

After the delay became official, the actors would be haunted by the ghost of their original plan. Calendar apps would ping, reminding them it was time for some interview or screening or photo shoot, long since canceled. On June 26, Leslie Grace used the cast's group text to point out that they were supposed to be at the United Palace that night. "We would have been dancing in the aisles," she says. "Anthony, Melissa, Corey, and I would have been crying the whole night in disbelief."

The heartache of pushing back the movie did yield one slender benefit: more time to get it right. Before lockdown, Lin had felt that they were rushing to complete the soundtrack. Now they had a chance to finish it properly. In particular, they could include more Latin superstars. (Yes, that *is* Rubén Blades you're hearing at the top of "Breathe.")

It also meant more time to fine-tune the movie itself. Jon persuaded Warner Bros. to install an Avid editing system in Myron Kerstein's living room. This is not, to say the least, standard studio protocol. But it was the only option, since the virus kept Myron from going to a proper editing suite. Working remotely, he and Jon explored ways to speed up a section late in the film the film by intercutting scenes. They also fielded a proposal from Lin to remove a crucial few lines in Usnavi and Vanessa's final conversation. Myron was initially against the idea: Vanessa's lines about becoming an artist seemed vital to drive home one of the movie's themes. But Lin compared the spare new version to the ending of *Hamilton,* when the music drops away and Alexander delivers his final soliloquy a cappella.

Myron laughs as he recalls what he told Jon: "If it's good enough for *Hamilton,* it's good enough for us." He made the cut. He's certain it never would have happened if the movie had stuck to the original release plan.

As for the revised plan, it would change one more time before it was done. In December, Warner Bros. announced that it would release *Heights* and the rest of its 2021 movies simultaneously on the big screen *and* HBO Max. As this book goes to press, the film's release is scheduled for June 11, and the prevailing vibe of the whole enterprise (guarded optimism amid wild uncertainty) is best stated by Toby Emmerich: "We have to be ready. And we have to hope the world is ready."

BY THE TIME THE WORLD is ready, it will have endured a wrenching year. There are ways to tabulate the economic damage and lost lives, but not the toll of isolation on a global scale. Millions of people feared that spending time with their friends, neighbors, or relatives might prove deadly. Social bonds frayed; expressions of community waned.

Throughout the summer of 2020, late in the day, Quiara and her husband would walk around Washington Heights. Less than a year had passed since the movie had filmed there, but the differences were profound. Highbridge Pool, where dozens of actors had danced and swum through "96,000," never opened. Its dry expanse was home to enormous tents: a COVID testing site. Across the neighborhood, which prided itself on its countless small businesses, restaurants shut down and storefronts went dark, victims of mandatory closures and economic distress. Quiara could feel the desperation in the air—"a sense of loss in the center," she calls it—even as the streets flared more vividly to life. The music seemed louder, the lights brighter.

Members of the *Heights* community lent their time, talent, and prominence to organizations that were trying to stave off the worst of the year's effects. Lin went on *The Tonight Show* to raise money for Broadway Cares/Equity Fights AIDS. Mandy Gonzalez reunited with Chris Jackson to sing "When You're Home"—a way of reminding people not to go out and risk spreading the virus if they could help it. (A ray of light in a dark year: Mandy finished her chemotherapy treatment. Her *Heights* friends weren't allowed to be with her in person. They joined by video.) Javier Muñoz co-created the Broadway Relief Project, which marshaled the skills of Broadway costume designers to make desperately needed protective equipment for healthcare workers.

He did it all without leaving home, since his HIV status made it too risky to go outside. One afternoon, when the coast finally seemed clear, he walked to a park near his apartment, the spot where Leslie Grace and Corey Hawkins sing the movie version of "When You're Home." He wept to feel the sun on his face.

While the country fought what often felt like a losing battle with the coronavirus, a second reckoning arrived. The killing of George Floyd on May 25 sparked nationwide protests against racial injustice. Tens of millions of Americans rallied to the cry that Black Lives Matter. Institutions of every kind faced a demand to confront the systems that visit harm on Black and Latino communities.

Shedding light on those systems has long been the mission of Maria Hinojosa, a leading journalist and the founder of Futuro Media. In 2019, her friendship with Lin and Quiara had led to an invitation to appear in the movie. She'd expected a cameo, which would have satisfied her lifelong dream of being an actor. Instead she played a more consequential role: the leader of a protest on behalf of undocumented immigrants. She didn't find it hard to get into character—"I had *been* an angry protest leader in college," she says—though she found that Lin, Quiara, and Jon had something other than anger in mind. They wanted her to lead with an affirmative demand: a forthright chant to "Tell our stories."

The movie doesn't just issue that call, it also *answers* that call, as the stage version did. As Jimmy Smits says, "We're putting something out there that's positive, that shows us in all of our beauty, and the diversity within our culture." Maria thinks that *Heights* will land with more force after the protests of 2020, because when the movie insists that attention be paid to Latino lives and Latino stories, the claiming of space isn't just a metaphor: "The film takes over the streets—*literally*. It takes over the pool—*literally*. That's going to resonate."

At this point, nobody should need more evidence about the life-and-death stakes of the inequities that millions of Americans protested in 2020, but the virus provided it anyway. On almost any metric related to COVID-19, Black and Latino communities suffered a disproportionately heavy toll. (Maria herself contracted the virus, losing a month

"HEIGHTS'S JOURNEY IS INDISTINGUISHABLE FROM MY JOURNEY."

to a slow and painful recovery.) Here is where the *Heights* community's experience of 2020 takes a tragic turn.

Blanca Camacho, who joined the *Heights* cast shortly before its move to Broadway, has played many roles in the show over the years, including Abuela Claudia, Daniela, and Camila. Her longtime partner, Felipe Gorostiza, was with her every step of the way—"my plus-one to all our *Heights* events," she says. In the pandemic's early days, when the disease was a terrifying unknown, he began to feel ill. A month later, Felipe—a Cuban immigrant, a person whom Blanca calls "a warm, charming, gregarious, generous soul"—was gone.

For the *Heights* community, another blow was yet to fall. As Lin points out in a note on page 258, Doreen Montalvo was the first actor to audition for *In the Heights* in New York. She made her Broadway debut in the show, then played different roles in different productions in later years. She's also featured in the movie. If any actor is at the heart of the *Heights* community, it's her. In September 2020, she fell ill—not COVID-19, but severe all the same. She died a few weeks later, just fifty-six years old.

Her castmates, bewildered and grieving, took to social media to offer tributes. You should know that if you've been in a school or regional production of *In the Heights,* there's a chance that she has been *your* castmate, too. Producers who license the show have the option to use a prerecorded bolero: the scratched record whose lyrics run "No te vayas / Si me dejas." The voice you hear in that bolero is Doreen's. If you count those recordings and add them to her involvement in the original Broadway run, plus the subsequent productions in which she starred, she holds the distinction, now and probably forever, of appearing in more performances of *In the Heights* than any other actor.

Doreen loved it when friends realized it was her voice flowing out of their speakers. "They would say, 'Hey, you're here with us!'" she recalled in an interview in early 2020, laughing at the memory. "I feel like I'm the musical ghost that lives through all the *In the Heights*es."

AFTER THE ORDEALS OF 2020, the old saying about tomorrow not being guaranteed feels more banal than usual—and more true. These days, nobody can feel sure about what the future will bring.

One small thing is certain: By the time of the movie's world premiere, at least twenty-one years will have passed since Lin's parents gathered a few friends in their living room to hear what their son had written. That's more than half a lifetime. Looking back over this long story, Lin sees that the musical he started making when he was nineteen has grown up alongside him, and vice versa. "*Heights*'s journey is indistinguishable from my journey," he says.

In those twenty-one years (and counting), he has experienced a lot of what he wrote about in college. The son pining for his high school girlfriend is now a husband and father of two; the upstart who wrote about young people chasing their dreams now gets to write movies and to direct them. (He resumed shooting *Tick, Tick . . . Boom!* in late 2020. With luck it'll be out in a year.) He started writing the Wesleyan version of *In the Heights* while wrestling with a question: *How do I get a seat at the table?* He'll watch the world premiere of its film adaptation while pondering a different one, no less vexing: *What do you do with that seat once you get it?*

One answer is: Save the bookstore.

▲ Planning the new Drama Book Shop

We've seen how crucial the Drama Book Shop was in the early days of *Heights*—and in Lin's life more generally. That's where he bonded with Tommy Kail, Alex Lacamoire, Chris Jackson, and other people he still counts among his closest friends and collaborators. (No bookstore, no *Heights*, no *Hamilton*.) So when he heard that the place was shutting down, he joined forces with Tommy, Jeffrey Seller, and James L. Nederlander to buy it. The closure it announced in 2019 has turned out to be more of an intermission. Or at least it will be, once the virus allows its new location on West 39th Street to welcome its first customer.

One part of the bookstore won't open as quickly as the rest. Down a flight of stairs lies a tantalizingly empty space, not so different from the subterranean black box that meant so much to *In the Heights*. "It was such a seminal incubator and essential safe space for us, and such a foundational part of our community," says Tommy. "We want this to be a place for people to develop and think and dream—as we did for so many years."

The reopening of the bookshop is an outward sign of the most remarkable way that *Heights* has changed Lin's life. In the early days of the show, he identified most closely with Nina: a young striver stuck between worlds, never feeling entirely at home. He aspired to be more like Usnavi, the storyteller at the center of the action. Today, isn't that who Lin has become?

Owning a small business is only the beginning of the resemblance. The young composer who said he never felt

cool with everybody in Washington Heights has become its unelected mayor. (Once *Hamilton* landed him on magazine covers and TV shows, he started wearing a hoodie and hat to walk around incognito. Now people recognize the hoodie and the hat.) In the finale, Usnavi declares himself the chronicler of the neighborhood, rapping, "I illuminate the stories of the people in the street." When the movie finally gets its premiere, the whole world will see the stories about Washington Heights that Lin and his colleagues have drawn into the light.

The last and most significant resemblance isn't confined to the neighborhood. Lin wrote a musical while dreaming of a community where he could feel that all the parts of his life belonged. He succeeded so well that his dream came true. A new community really *did* emerge. It comprises the people who have been part of *In the Heights*, or have been affected by it, or who feel connected to one another because of it. Usually that community is far-flung and a little abstract. But one day during the filming of the movie, it came vibrantly alive. "A culmination," Lin calls it.

In the final scene of the film, Noah Catala, the movie's Graffiti Pete, spray-paints a wall of the bodega. Usnavi looks at the mural, looks at Vanessa, and understands that his place is here, in Washington Heights. What happens next is suggested by a single line in Quiara's screenplay: They step out of the bodega and see "neighbors full of life around them." That's when everybody sings the part of the finale that even now affects Lin so much: "The hydrants are open / Cool breezes blow."

Before filming began, Jon hit on an idea for how he wanted to shoot that scene. "I realized how emotional it could be to have people from the original cast there in the crowd to sing 'The hydrants are open,'" he says. "They're the ones who opened the hydrants in their production. They led the way for the rest of us."

The producers sent invitations far and wide. On July 9, 2019, people from all corners of the *In the Heights* community assembled in the actual Heights: Lin's wife and her family were there, as were Quiara, her sister, her mother, and her stepfather. Members of the Broadway company, people who had worked on the movie, residents of the neighborhood itself—they all came together at 175th and Audubon.

"It was like, *Holy s---! We're here! It's so beautiful!*" recalls Javier Muñoz. Some members of the Broadway cast hadn't seen one another in years; others had accepted the invitation to bring their parents or children or partners. So there were introductions as well as reunions in the cast holding room, and when a spontaneous rendition of the finale broke out, enthusiastic novices sang along with polished veterans. "It's family—it's home. That's what the day felt like," Javi continues. "The day felt like home."

At the center of all of these concentric circles stood the man who had dreamed of such a community, then written it into existence. You do not often find Lin-Manuel Miranda at a loss for words, but when he is asked how that day felt, he says only "It's just all of the things at once."

Jon was happy to see that his plan was working, but he was too busy to revel in it. The finishing touches of the scene were supplied by fire hydrants—five of them, spraying actual New York City water high into the air. Jon, Alice, and Nelson Coates tried to calibrate them for maximum visual impact, only to find that the city water supply is not so easily tamed. Every time a nearby resident flushed a toilet, the pressure dropped, spraying water everywhere. With time running short—"the sun was dropping, dropping, dropping," Jon recalls—he gave up fine-tuning and rolled camera.

"That's the spirit of *In the Heights*," he says. "Whatever happens, you just do it. You *go*."

Watching the scene now, with the pandemic dragging on, you see a poignant reminder of the shared public life that the virus has taken from us—the easy association that we've been denied for so long. The scene also lets us see, more clearly than before, what *In the Heights* adds to the tradition of New York musicals. *West Side Story* remains the supreme fantasy of escape, of young lovers looking for a way out. *Company* offers fleeting encounters amid the crowds that come and go. But *In the Heights* celebrates the people who choose to stay. It rejoices in the ties that endure among neighbors in the face of gentrification and other, more powerful erasers.

Already the intersection doesn't look how it did on that day in July. Already Felipe and Doreen are gone. But they were there that afternoon, adding their voices to the song. Lin and Quiara weave a vital message through *In the Heights*. In "96,000" it arrives with hope, in "Alabanza" with sorrow, in "Carnaval del Barrio" with pride and defiance, and in "Finale," supremely, with gratitude and joy. The message is: True community is possible, and it's precious, which means it's worth saving—and this is how it sounds.

Home is the people who sing with you.

Finale

1. The bolero singer on Broadway is the bolero singer you hear in the film, the first person who auditioned for *In the Heights* in the basement of the Drama Book Shop: the great Doreen Montalvo. She sang La Lupe's "Qué Te Pedí" and embedded herself in my heart in an instant. Her voice had that tear in it—that *lágrima*. Inimitable and hers. She played Benny's mom, Alma, that first year. We cut the role. So she played Camila, then Daniela, then Abuela Claudia, and by 2007 she was so invaluable to us that she covered all those roles both off and on Broadway, in addition to her ensemble role, whom Quiara nicknamed Cuca. The name stuck, and became the name of the charater Dascha Polanco would create for the film.

In 2010, she happily became Doreen Montalvo Mann— I DJed the wedding. She and Michael held it around the corner from the theater, and every incarnation of our cast was there. Everyone who met Doreen became her new friend. She held friends so dearly and easily. You'd go to her cabaret show and see people *you* hadn't seen in years. But Doreen had stayed in touch. Everyone stayed in touch with Doreen.

She passed away suddenly in the fall of 2020, the first of our alumni family to do so. I am so grateful that her voice lives on in the film, singing her moments in "Breathe" and "Siempre." To quote Camila, "The scratch in the record is my favorite part."

2. And here are the movie lyrics, updated to reflect Sonny's new journey:

Lights up on Washington Heights, and now the crack of dawn.
I pack, as life goes on and on and on . . .
Time to go, but I'm doing the math
On this cash money to have Sonny stay on his path.

RECORDED BOLERO SINGER: ❶

No te vayas . . .
Si me dejas . . .
Si te alejas de mi . . .
Seguirás en mis recuerdos para
    siempre . . .
Para siempre . . . para
    siempre . . .
Para siempre . . .
("Para siempre" skip continues
    under Usnavi's rap)

(USNAVI has entered and sees the boarded-up businesses: the salon and Rosario's car service. He sits on his stoop.) ❷

USNAVI: Lights out on
    Washington Heights, and
    now the crack of dawn.
The blackout goes on and on
    and on . . .
Sonny's out back, sortin' the
    trash

As I think about the past, with a sack full of cash.
Abuela really wanted me up on a beach
With margaritas in my reach, and
Soon that's how it's gonna be . . .
Imagine me, leaving today

On a seven-forty-seven boardin' JFK . . .

CARLA: The hydrants are open
Cool breezes blow.

CARLA, DANIELA: The hydrants are open
Cool breezes blow. ❸

3. The finale of this show came to me in exactly the same way as the finale of *Hamilton:* waking up at four A.M. on the final morning of a workshop full of actors who are waiting for the last song, which they are to perform for an audience *that day.* (Forever doing my homework on the bus to school. It doesn't go away, kids.) The impulse began with wanting to hear a solo from Janet Dacal, who at this point in 2004 had played Nina, Vanessa, and everyone in between throughout our basement workshops and readings before finally landing on Carla when that character was created. She was foundational in the development of our show, and I know her voice as well as Chris Jackson's or my own. It's also so lovely for Carla to anchor this canon in such a beautiful, simple observation: The hydrants are open, cool breezes blow. Anyway, I cried a lot writing this, lol.

DANIELA, CARLA:
The hydrants are
    open
Cool breezes blow.

KEVIN:
Good morning.

PIRAGUA GUY:
Piragua, piragua
New block of ice,
    piragua
So sweet and nice,
    piragua
Piragua, piragua [4]

4. The power of the right reprise at the right time really unfolds during this canon.

The hydrants are
    open
Cool breezes blow.

Good morning.

Piragua, piragua
New block of ice,
    piragua
So sweet and nice,
    piragua
Piragua, piragua

CAMILA:
Siempre . . .
Seguirás en mis
    recuerdos para
    siempre . . .

The hydrants are
    open
Cool breezes blow.

Good morning.

Piragua, piragua
New block of ice,
    piragua
So sweet and nice,
    piragua
Piragua, piragua

Siempre . . .
Seguirás en mis
    recuerdos para
    siempre . . .

VANESSA:
I'll be downtown . . .

It won't be long
    now . . .

(USNAVI is out on the sidewalk.)

USNAVI: There's a breeze off the Hudson ❺
And just when
You think you're sick of living here the memory floods in.
The morning light off the fire escapes,
The nights in Bennett Park blasting Big Pun tapes.
I'mma miss this place, to tell you the truth
Kevin dispensin' wisdom from his dispatch booth
And at dawn, Vanessa at the salon, we gotta move on,
But who's gonna notice we're gone?
When our job's done, as the evening winds
Down to a crawl, son, can I ease my mind
When we're all done, when we've resigned
In the long run, what do we leave behind?
Most of all, I'll miss Abuela's whispers,
Doin' the Lotto Pick Six every Christmas.
In five years, when this whole city's rich folks and hipsters,
Who's gonna miss this raggedy little business? ❻

(USNAVI arrives at the bodega. SONNY and GRAFFITI PETE are there.)

GRAFFITI PETE: *What it do? Great sunlight this morning.*

SONNY: *Yo cuz! We fixed the grate!*

USNAVI (TO SONNY): *What did I tell you about this punk?*

SONNY: *You have to commission an artist while his rate is still good.*

GRAFFITI PETE: *The first work in my new series.*

(GRAFFITI PETE rolls down the gate. There is a huge graffiti mural of ABUELA CLAUDIA that says "Paciencia y fe." Silence.) ❼

GRAFFITI PETE: *He hates it.*

SONNY: *Shh. He's forming an artistic opinion.*

(The beat crescendos back in.)

USNAVI: You did this last night?

GRAFFITI PETE: Yeah.

USNAVI: There goes my flight.

SONNY: What?

USNAVI: Graffiti Pete, you're gonna need some new cans!
Here's some money, finish up, there's been a slight change of plans!

GRAFFITI PETE: Nice!

USNAVI: Listen up guys, you got a job, I'm not playin'.
You gotta go now, tell the whole block I'm stayin'!
Y'all go ahead, tell everyone we know!

(GRAFFITI PETE runs off.)

Sonny . . .

(USNAVI starts to say something but gets choked up, motions to his own heart.)

All right, go!

(SONNY runs off.)

Yeah, I'm a streetlight!
Chillin' in the heat!
I illuminate the stories of the people in the street.
Some have happy endings,
Some are bittersweet,
But I know them all and that's what makes my life complete.

(NINA enters, sees the mural.)

NINA: We're home—

USNAVI: And if not me, who keeps our legacies? ❽
Who's gonna keep the coffee sweet with secret recipes?
Abuela, rest in peace, you live in my memories
But Sonny's gotta eat, and this corner is my destiny.

SONNY, NINA, CARLA, DANIELA: We're home—

5. I'm writing this note on August 29, 2020, twenty years after my first draft. I'm staring out the window on the same view of the George Washington Bridge that Anna Louizos hung on our Broadway set. In the other room, my wife, Vanessa, is with our two boys. We live on the same block where she grew up, just a few blocks south of where I grew up, in this neighborhood. So believe me when I tell you that there has been a catch in my throat every time I've sung this lyric, and maybe there always will be.

6. I hope New York City, and Washington Heights in particular, never loses the economic and cultural diversity that makes Usnavi's bodega possible. On some blocks, it's already happened; other blocks are unchanged from when I was a child. Surely the pandemic happening at the time of this writing changes everything. I do know this: The East Village of Jonathan Larson's *Rent* is all but gone; the Upper West Side of *West Side Story* was razed to create Lincoln Center. But they live on in their shows.

7. This is an interesting place where the show and movie diverge. In the stage show, the mural reveals that everything Usnavi assumed about Graffiti Pete is wrong; he's a great artist and he's used his gifts to cement Abuela's legacy in the neighborhood. It shifts the tectonic plates in Usnavi's heart and lets him see his own corner anew. The same is true in the film, but Quiara multiplies it by adding Vanessa's artistic vision and light. Usnavi is not just seeing his past conjured in Graffiti Pete's mural: In Vanessa's eyes, he's seeing his future.

8. Legacy popping up in my tunes again . . .

USNAVI: Brings out the best in me, we pass a test and we
Keep pressin' and yes indeed, you know I'll never leave.
If you close your eyes that hydrant is a beach,
That siren is a breeze, that fire escape's a leaf on a palm tree.

CARLA, DANIELA, NINA, CAMILA, VANESSA, SONNY, PIRAGUA GUY, KEVIN: We're home—

USNAVI: Abuela, I'm sorry,
But I ain't goin' back because I'm telling your story!
And I can say goodbye to you smilin', I found my island,
I've been on it this whole time. **9**
I'm home!

GROUP 1 **(NINA, CAMILA, DANIELA, CARLA, SONNY, BENNY, KEVIN, PIRAGUA GUY, MAN):**	**GROUP 2** **(VANESSA, WOMEN, MEN GRAFFITI PETE):**
We're home—	The hydrants are open Cool breezes blow—

USNAVI: This is a wonderful life that I've known—
Merry Christmas, you ol' building and loan!
I'm home! **10**

GROUP 1:	**GROUP 2:**
We're home—	The hydrants are open Cool breezes blow—

USNAVI: Abuela, that ain't a stoop, that's your throne—
Long after ya birds have all flown,

USNAVI:
I'm home!
Where the coffee's nonstop
And I drop this hip-hop in my
Mom-and-pop shop, I'm home!
Where people come
People go
Let me show all of these
People what I know, there's
No place like home!
And let me set the record
Straight!
I'm steppin' to Vanessa,
I'm gettin' a second date!
I'm home!
Where it's a hundred in the
Shade,
But with patience and faith,
We remain unafraid,
I'm home!
You hear that music in the
Air?
Take the train to the top of
The world, and I'm there,
I'm home!

GROUP 1:
We're home!

COMPANY:
We're home! **11**

We're home!

We're home!

Home!

Home!

Home!

Home!

9. I find it amazing that Quiara took these lyrics and elevated them to the narrative structure of the film. HE'S BEEN ON IT THIS WHOLE TIME!

10. A little love note to Tommy Kail, for whom *It's a Wonderful Life* is a foundational film (his production company is named after George Bailey's address).

11. The rush of this final Usnavi section stays with me always, and my prevailing memory of performing it is the faces in the front row of the Rodgers Theatre: our $20 section, often filled with young people seeing their first musical on Broadway. I lock eyes with them, night after night, and as their eyes fill with tears, so do mine. I'm delivering these words, but I'm also trying to tell them: I'm home, and Usnavi's home, and in this time you've chosen to spend with us, so are you. Welcome home.

Home All Summer[1]

1. Listen, I miss the 1990s trend of closing-credit rap songs that summarize the entire plot of the movie (*Teenage Mutant Ninja Turtles*, *The Addams Family*, *Bulworth* . . . it's a whole thing), but that didn't make sense here. So I decided to write a song pairing that never existed: Nina and Usnavi, both of whom love the neighborhood—one from afar, one from the corner. Friends celebrating the summer together.

2. Imagine you are me: You've written this song in November of 2019, and then a pandemic forces the world to literally stay *home all summer*. But no one can hear it, because the movie's been pushed a year because everyone's *home all summer*.

3. This is on her fire escape in my head.

NINA, USNAVI: I'll be home all summer [2]
I'll be home all summer
If you're gonna be around
You can find me uptown.

COMPANY: Uptown uptown uptown up!

NINA, USNAVI: I'll be home all summer
I'll be home all summer
If you're gonna be around
You can find me uptown.

COMPANY: Uptown uptown uptown up!

NINA: I'm, I'm missing the view from
My old hometown, so I
Climb, way up to the Heights
And I won't come down now. [3]

NINA, USNAVI: You, you always remind me
Where I belong, come
Through, yeah, find me and
Play me my favorite song, so

USNAVI: Saca los dominós
Let all the homies know
Tell everyone we know
Yo, she's coming home.

Yeah, sube el volumen
Until the bass is boomin' [4]
Until the place is movin'
Until the faces in the room are me and
    you
What it do when we're—

NINA, USNAVI: I'll be home all summer
I'll be home all summer
If you're gonna be around
You can find me uptown.

COMPANY: Uptown uptown uptown up!

NINA, USNAVI: I'll be home all summer
I'll be home all summer
If you're gonna be around
You can find me uptown.

COMPANY: Uptown uptown uptown up!

USNAVI: I, I know the view from the corner store so
I, I wake up longing for so much more, then ❺

NINA, USNAVI: You, you're back in town, you hold me down,
You are my wandering star
Come through, I'm not alone, thank you for showin' me home is
Where you are, so

USNAVI: Saca los dominós
Let all the homies know
Tell everyone we know
Yo, she's coming home.

Yeah, sube el volumen
Until the bass is boomin'
Until the place is movin'
Until the faces in the room are me and you.
What it do when we're—

NINA, USNAVI: Home all summer
I'll be home all summer
If you're gonna be around
You can find me uptown.

MARC: ❻ Hey yeah
You can always come back home
Hey yeah
You can always come back home
Whoa, welcome home.

USNAVI: When the power goes down
When the rent goes up
We'll survive uptown
We will raise our cup.

NINA, USNAVI: When the sun goes down
Turn the music up
I will hold you down
I will lift you up.

MARC: ❼ Hey yeah
You can always come back home
Hey yeah
You can always come back home
Whoa, welcome home!

(Chorus and out.)

4. Volumen/boomin': When you write bilingually, you have access to rhymes the monolinguists don't!

5. Let's just pause and adore Anthony Ramos's voice here.

6. So is Marc Anthony Marc Anthony in this song, or is he *in character* as Sonny's dad? You decide! (But my bucket list dream to write for Marc Anthony is *checked*.)

7. To go from seeing Marc Anthony in *The Capeman* on Broadway at age eighteen to having him acting and singing in the *Heights* movie is actually still too much for my brain to process.

ACKNOWLEDGMENTS

THE AUTHORS WOULD LIKE TO THANK:

BARBARA BACHMAN

JOHN BUZZETTI

ANDY CHAN

TED CHAPIN

JON CHU

OLIVIA DEL CAMPO

DREW DOCKSER

RICHARD ELMAN

SEAN FLAHAVEN

ANDREW FRIED

BEN GREENBERG

SCOTT HEDLEY

MORGAN HOLT

VERONICA JACKSON

JENNIFER JOEL

TOMMY KAIL

LONDON KING

STEPHANIE KLEMONS

DAVID KORINS

ALEX LACAMOIRE

JANE LEE

JOSH LEHRER

KATHRYN MAUGHAN

ANDY MCNICOL

MOMOKO MIKI

SARA ELISA MILLER

LUIS MIRANDA

LOREN NOVECK

LAURA PALESE

OWEN PANETTIERI

ANDY PANG

STEPHANIE PHILLIPS

ROBIN POMATTO

JEFFREY SELLER

ERIC SIMONOFF

KAELI SUBBERWAL

ELLIOTT TRAEGER

YVONNE FORCE VILLAREAL

PHOTO CREDITS

ABOUT THE AUTHORS

LIN-MANUEL MIRANDA is a Pulitzer Prize, Grammy, Emmy, and Tony Award–winning songwriter, actor, and director, as well as a *New York Times* bestselling author (*Hamilton: The Revolution; Gmorning, Gnight!: Little Pep Talks for Me & You*). He is the creator and original star of Broadway's Tony-winning *Hamilton* and *In the Heights*. Additional Broadway credits include: *Freestyle Love Supreme* (co-founder, guest star), *Bring It On: The Musical* (co-composer/co-lyricist), and *West Side Story* (2009 revival, Spanish translations). He is a recipient of a 2015 MacArthur Foundation Award, a 2018 Kennedy Center Honor, and a 2019 Portrait of a Nation Prize. Miranda and the Miranda family actively support initiatives that increase BIPOC representation in the arts and government, ensure access to women's reproductive health, and foster resilience in Puerto Rico. He lives with his family in New York.

linmanuel.com

QUIARA ALEGRÍA HUDES is the Pulitzer Prize–winning playwright of *Water by the Spoonful* and the author of a memoir, *My Broken Language*. She wrote the book for the Tony-winning Broadway musical *In the Heights* and later adapted it for the screen. Her notable essays include "High Tide of Heartbreak" in *American Theatre* magazine and "Corey Couldn't Take It Anymore" in *The Cut*. As a prison reform activist, Hudes and her cousin founded Emancipated Stories, a platform where people behind bars can share one page of their life story with the world. She lives with her family in New York but frequently returns to her native Philly.

quiara.com   TWITTER: @quiarahudes

JEREMY McCARTER is the author of *Young Radicals* and co-author, with Lin-Manuel Miranda, of the #1 *New York Times* bestseller *Hamilton: The Revolution*. He is the founder and executive producer of Make-Believe Association, a Chicago-based production company. He spent five years on the artistic staff of the Public Theater and has served on the jury of the Pulitzer Prize for Drama. He has written about culture and politics for *New York* magazine, *The New York Times*, *The Wall Street Journal*, and other publications. He lives in Chicago with his family.

jeremymccarter.com

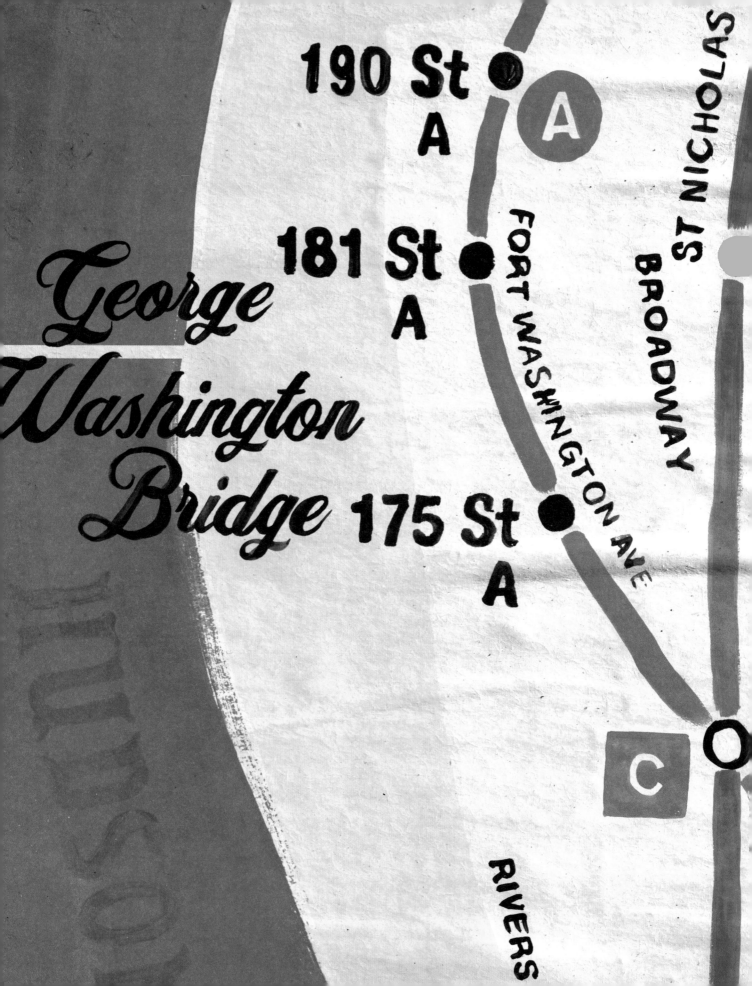